Antifeminism and Family Terrorism

A Critical Feminist Perspective

Rhonda Hammer

ROWMAN & LITTLEFIELD PUBLISHERS, INC.
Lanham • Boulder • New York • Oxford

ROWMAN & LITTLEFIELD PUBLISHERS, INC.

Published in the United States of America
by Rowman & Littlefield Publishers, Inc.
4720 Boston Way, Lanham, Maryland 20706
www.rowmanlittlefield.com

12 Hid's Copse Road, Cumnor Hill, Oxford OX2 9JJ, England

British Library Cataloguing in Publication Information Available

Library of Congress Cataloging-in-Publication Data

Hammer, Rhonda.
    Antifeminism and family terrorism : a critical feminist perspective / Rhonda
Hammer.
        p.   cm.—(Culture and politics series)
    Includes bibliographical references and index.
    ISBN 0-7425-1049-2 (cloth : alk. paper)—ISBN 0-7425-1050-6 (pbk. : alk. paper) ✓
    1. Feminist theory.   2. Feminist criticism.   3. Anti-feminism.   4. Family violence.
5. Women—Crimes against.   6. Poor women—Social conditions.   7. Battered
women syndrome.   I. Title.   II. Series.
HQ1190 .H35   2002
305.42'01—dc21   2001019088

Printed in the United States of America

♾ ™ The paper used in this publication meets the minimum requirements of American
National Standard for Information Sciences—Permanence of Paper for Printed Library
Materials, ANSI/NISO Z39.48-1992.

For D.M.K. who gives good theory!

Contents

Acknowledgments

This project has been evolving over a number of years and owes much to the discussions and ideas of many, many people. My mother, Miriam ("Mim") Hammer has been a constant source of sustenance throughout my life and a full-time champion of my work and often "eccentric" lifestyle (although she would be happier with it if I phoned and visited more often). My extended family of long-time friends has also provided me with the kind of encouragement and counsel that inspired me to persevere. Shifra ("Bobbi") Zisman, my "best girlfriend," since our junior high school days, in the year "dot," and my "honorary daughters," Laine and Bailey Zisman-Newman have been an essential part of my life, especially in helping to shape many of my beliefs and ideas about children's rights and contemporary girl culture.

Carmen and Alan Luke and I have shared so many ideas, and life-shifting experiences over the years, that I often take for granted the import of their contributions. Carmen's critical feminist wisdom on theory and practice has proven especially invaluable to this book. Dale Hall has taught me much about human rights and feminist praxis throughout our long friendship. Discussions with Kevin Bishop, whose celebration of difference and involvement in the movement to end sexual abuse of children has clarified and helped me to expand on many of the positions raised in this book. Shahrzad Mojab and Amir Hassanpour are two of the most dedicated and committed scholars and political activists I have ever known. Their generosity toward me, during a particularly difficult period in my life (and theirs), helped me to endure and transcend what we referred to as the "Windsor Experience." I'd also like to thank Jenny McLaren for sharing her literacy of the codes of life and survival in Los Angeles, as well as her expert editorial advice and, of course, friendship over the years.

I have had the privilege of having been taught by a number of great teachers and brilliant scholars. I would like to thank Ray Morris's gift of long-term guidance that has been integral to my education, pedagogical beliefs, and understandings of social justice. Ray and Ruth Morris's dedication to activist causes, including prison reform and urban shelters for the disenfranchised, has always been a source of inspiration. The recent death of my mentor and friend, Ioan

Davies, has been a bitter loss. He managed to teach me much about classical critical theory, revolutionary thought and the philosophical nature and epistemological realities of contradiction and paradox. It is perhaps his immense passion for learning and teaching that was his greatest gift. I'd also like to thank Ato Sekyi-Otu for the many hours of discussion we've shared, especially in relation to his dialectical re-reading and translation of the works of Frantz Fanon.

This book is indebted to members of the UCLA Center for the Study of Women, women's studies, as well as the Communications Program at UCLA. Sandra Harding and Chris Littleton, in particular, have been a constant source of inspiration, and have also provided me with a numerous resources and references, which were integral to this writing. I'd like to thank them for their scholarly and professional counsel, as well as their support for and interest in my work. Vivian Sobchack also encouraged me in this venture. The assistance and advice of administrative staff members Rex King, at the UCLA Center for the Study of Women and Mary Margaret Smith, of women's studies, have been essential in regard to both my research and teaching. I'd also like to thank them for their patience in listening, to my habitual "kvetching" throughout the writing of this book. The many eclectic and diverse research scholars at the UCLA Center for the Study of Women, including Director Miriam Silverberg, have contributed greatly to my literacy in feminist theory, practice and activism, and provided me with significant feedback and suggestions for many of the ideas and examples within this book. It is an honor and a privilege to be associated with this remarkable group of women. The opportunity to attend and participate in a cornucopia of lectures, roundtables, and discussions of feminist scholars, sponsored by these programs, has expanded my vision and provided for an exciting haven from an often "chilly" and selfish world. As well, I would like to thank Kathy Higgins, University of Texas at Austin, for sharing her feminist philosophical expertise with me, especially in regards to the writings of Camille Paglia. All of these women undermine a myth of popular culture and anti-feminism which demonizes feminists as "femi-nazis."

I'd also like to extend my gratitude to Neil Malamuth for providing me with the opportunities to be involved in the UCLA's Communications Program. My students at UCLA have provided me with a wealth of contemporary information, including documentation, stats and websites eminently relevant to this book, while also demonstrating a keen interest in many of the areas I have written about—assuring me that the book, or parts of it, are germane to a diversity of audiences and disciplines. Leslie Henrickson, Fred Flores, and Sandeep Parmar, in particular, assisted me in many of my quests (for no renumeration or credit, I must add) through their expertise in cyberspace and access to specialized and activist resources. Thanks also to Cindi S. Moskovic, Director of the Iris Cantor–UCLA Women's Health Education and Resource Center, for her invaluable assistance in the area of violence against women, children and the elderly, as well as Camille Davtyan, of the Iris Cantor–UCLA Women's Health Care, for her insights and references regarding contemporary training of medical students in issues of "family terrorism." LeAnna Gutierrez, the Nina C. Liebman Fellow at the California Women's Law Center, provided me with important information and feedback in relation to violence against women and the legal and judiciary system.

I am also indebted to my editor at Rowman & Littlefield, Dean Birkenkamp, to Christine Gatliffe, and to other members of the editorial staff, for support and understanding during the production of this book. I would especially like to thank Renee Jardine for her help at the stage of editing the manuscript and page proofs and her timely and helpful e-mail and telephone communications. I'd also like to thank Henry Giroux for choosing my study to be part of his Culture and Politics series. Finally, I'd like to thank Doug Kellner for his critial commentary on seemingly endless drafts of this text and his continuing encouragement and support over the past decade.

The human population of earth exceeds 6 billion. It grows by 10,000 every hour. Time and again, the nations of the world have convened to declare that all people are born free, equal in dignity, endowed with the same human rights. Despite these declarations there exist profound cultural and economic inequities that effectively marginalize half the world's population.

This half does most of the world's work, yet earns a fraction of its income. This same half is often the target of violence, is deprived of education and health care and denied a role in civic life. This half is comprised of women and girls. The discrimination they endure, solely as a consequence of their gender, is universal. It occurs in virtually every country in the home and workplace at worship and play in classrooms and courtrooms.

—United Nations Population Fund (UNFPA) 2000

Introduction

The 1995 annual American Medical Association guidelines reported that "family violence—domestic violence, child physical abuse and neglect, child sexual abuse and mistreatment of the elderly—was widespread. Each year in the United States . . . two million women are battered, 1,500 women are killed by intimate partners, 1.8 million elderly people are mistreated and 1.7 million reports of child abuse are filed" (*New York Times*, Nov. 7, 1995). A 1998 National Violence against Women Survey sponsored by the U.S. Department of Justice reports that

> using a definition of physical assault that includes a range of behaviors, from slapping and hitting to using a gun, the survey found that physical assault is widespread among American women: 52 percent of surveyed women said they were physically assaulted as a child by an adult caretaker and/or as an adult by any type of perpetrator; 1.9 percent of surveyed women said they were physically assaulted in the previous 12 months. Based on these estimates, approximately 1.9 million women are physically assaulted annually in the United States.[1]

Such brutal statistics are hardly particular to the United States. These often unnoticed and proliferating instances of what I am calling "family terrorism" are a global phenomenon. Moreover, the targets of so-called domestic violence are typically women and children. Usually, but not always, violence is perpetuated by collective or individual men—especially in the case of intimate partner violence, rape, child sexual abuse, abuse of the elderly, torture, and instances of political terrorism, such as the events of September 11, 2001, and their devastating aftermath.[2]

The expansion of poverty and abuse, especially in regard to women and children, has been escalating on a global scale. The degradation of poverty is not exclusive to developing nations as the U.S. Census Bureau reveals that "46 million Americans, or 17 percent of the population, would be recognized as officially below the [poverty] line" (*New York Times*, Oct. 18, 1999). And the majority of America's poor, like the global poor, tend to be primarily women and children. The reality of the effects of globalization for the new millennium, for the majority of people in both the overdeveloped and developing nations, is that the rich are getting richer and the poor, poorer (Bales 1999). As Kevin Bales explains it:

1

In many developing countries modernization brought immense wealth to the elite and continued or increased the impoverishment of the poor majority. Throughout Africa and Asia the last fifty years have been scarred by civil war and the wholesale looting of resources by home-town dictators, often supported by one of the super-powers. To hold on to power, ruling kleptocrats have been paid enormous sums for weaponry, money raised by mortgaging their countries. Meanwhile traditional ways of life and subsistence have been sacrificed to the cash crop and quick profit. . . . The forced shift from subsistence to cash-crop agriculture, the loss of common land, and government policies that suppress farm income in favor of cheap food for the cities have all helped bankrupt millions of peasants and driven them from their land. (1999, 12–13)

While hardly comparable, there are also glaring divergences between the rich and the poor in the overdeveloped United States that would appear to substantiate criticisms concerning globalization's economic benefits. For example, according to the Center on Budget and Policy Priorities, a nonprofit organization in Washington:

The gap between rich and poor has grown into an economic chasm so wide that this year the richest 2.7 million Americans, the top 1 percent, had as much as the bottom 100 million. . . . Though the economic pie has grown over the past 22 years, the congressional Budget Office data show that the poorest one-fifth of households have not shared in the bounty. The average after-tax household income of the poor, adjusted for inflation, has fallen 12 percent since 1977. . . . The poorest one-fifth of households will average $8,800 of income this year, down from $10,000 in 1977. (*New York Times*, Sept. 5, 1999, 14)

This poverty provides the soil from which much of contemporary abuse and violence grows. In addition, the dramatic increase in world population following World War II has played a key role in intensifying poverty and violence, especially within the developing nations: "since 1945 the world population has almost tripled, increasing from about 2 billion people to more than 5.7 billion" (Bales 1999, 12). The greatest growth has occurred in Southeast Asia, the Indian sub-continent, Africa, and the Arab countries "where populations have more than tripled and countries are flooded with children" (Bales 1999, 12). In fact:

Over half the population in some countries is under the age of fifteen. In countries that were already poor, the sheer weight of numbers overwhelms the resources at hand. Without work and with increasing fear as resources diminish, people become desperate and life becomes cheap. (Bales 1999, 12)

Despite the ubiquity of brutality and abuse of women and children, there has been a startling de-emphasis and disregard for the centrality of the issues of violence against women and children and attendant relations of poverty and oppression within certain schools of feminism. In addition, there is a growing cadre of antifeminist pseudofeminists such as Camille Paglia, Christina Hoff Sommers, and Katie Roiphe (see chapters 1 and 2). These feminist impersonators not only deny the virulence of violence against women and children but also attack those feminists and activists who address it. Against such one-dimensional, dismissive, and derogatory approaches to issues of violence against women and children, I align my studies with a loose network of feminist scholars and activists. These sources include activist groups and critical feminist theorists who work with and do research on abused women, children, and the elderly, and struggle for global human rights. Joy James, for instance, provides us with an example of such feminist, critical, multiethnic, and activist research:

> Countering state violence requires political language and coalition work that go beyond difference and multiculturalism. Such efforts are embodied in the activism of racially and politically marginalized women who are engaged in transnational organizing. (James 1996, 235)

James advocates "political formations and organizing that emphasize human-rights activism and covenants" and argue for "multiracial, international coalitions based on human-rights conventions as indispensable for strategic, progressive interventions against repression and violence" (James 1996, x). In turn, Angela Davis points out that James's analyses emphasizes how "complex transformative struggles become if we take seriously the challenge to consider how deeply our personal and political lives are shaped by myriad forms of racialist, gendered and class-infected violence" (Davis 1996, viii).

Some of this transformative feminist work takes place within the domain of organizations loosely described as "NGOs" (nongovernmental organizations).[3] Indeed, evidence of the consistency and dedication of opposition to violence against women and children on a global scale is especially apparent within the report from the Fourth World United Nations Conference on Women in 1995. Important discussions and reports from its "sister" conference, carried out by NGOs, which was held 30 miles away from the Beijing forum, have also documented activist responses to global and local violence. These conferences confronted human rights for women and "freedom from violence" as central and fundamental issues that international women's groups and individuals must seriously address (Bunch and Fried 1996, 200).

Moreover, within the United States for a brief period in 1994 and 1995, during the O. J. Simpson murder trial, "spousal abuse" had become the flavor of the month, soon to be discarded in favor of the next. Earlier, issues of sexual harassment attained public attention with Anita Hill and Clarence Thomas,[4] date rape with Patricia Bowman and William Kennedy-Smith;[5] and family violence associated with Hedda Nussbaum and Joel Steinberg.[6] These key feminist issues, after a brief moment of media attention, were soon relegated to the duplicitous twilight zone of hypocrisy and silence that is often afforded crimes against women and children. But this is hardly surprising in light of the following shocking realities.

- Approximately 1.5 million women are raped or physically assaulted by an intimate partner annually in the United States. Because many victims are victimized more than once, the number of intimate partner victimizations exceeds the number of intimate partner victims annually. Thus, approximately 4.8 million intimate partner rapes and physical assaults are perpetrated against American women annually (Tjaden and Thoennes 2000).
- "In 1996, females were the victims of 75 percent of intimate murders and about 85 percent of the victims of nonlethal intimate violence" (Bureau of Justice Statistics, 1997 in Violence Against Women Fact Sheet, www.acog .org).
- "Estimates of the prevalence of violence during pregnancy" have indicated "that of the 3.9 million U.S. women who delivered live-born infants in 1995 . . . 152,000 to 324,000 women experienced violence during their pregnancies" (National Center for Chronic Disease Prevention and Health Promotion, Mar. 28, 2000; www.cdc.gov).
- "Using a definition of stalking that requires the victim to feel a high level of fear, the survey found that stalking is more prevalent than previously thought. . . . According to survey estimates, approximately 1 million women are stalked annually in the United States" (Tjaden and Thoennes 1998, 2).
- "An estimated 1.01 million elders became victims of various types of domestic elder abuse in 1996, excluding self-neglect" (National Center on Elder Abuse, 1994, www.acog.org).
- "Women make up 68.3 of elder abuse victims" (National Center on Elder Abuse, 1994, www.acog.org).
- "Child protective services agencies determined that almost 1 million children were identified as victims of substantiated or indicated abuse or neglect in 1996, an approximate 18% increase since 1990" (U.S. Department of Health and Human Services, 1998, www.acog.org).
- "[Child] victims of physical and sexual abuse, compared to victims of neglect and medical neglect, were more likely to be maltreated by a male parent. Acting alone. In cases of sexual abuse, more than half (55.9%) of victims were abused by male parents, male relative, or others" (*Child Maltreatment*, U.S. Department of Health and Human Services, 2000).
- "Victims of rape are disproportionately children and adolescent girls—60% of forcible rapes occur before the victim is 18 years old; 29% of victims are younger than 11 years old when raped" (Bureau of Justice Statistics, 1997, www.acog.org).

- "Violence in the home is truly universal. According to World Bank figures at least 20% of women have been sexually assaulted. Official reports in the U.S. say a woman is battered every 15 seconds and 700,000 are raped each year" ("Broken Bodies, Shattered Minds—The Torture of Women Worldwide," Amnesty International News Release, Mar. 6, 2001, www.amnesty .org).
- "The trafficking of people, especially women and children, for prostitution and forced labor is one of the fastest growing areas of international criminal activity, and one that is of increasing concern to the United States and the international community. Although men are also victimized, the over- whelming majority of those trafficked are women and children. According to official estimates, over 1 million people are trafficked each year worldwide for forced labor, domestic servitude, or sexual exploitation. An estimated 50,000 persons are trafficked each year to the United States. Trafficking is now considered the third largest source of profit for organized crime, behind only drugs and arms, generating billions of dollars annually" (RL30545: "Trafficking in Women and Children: The U.S. and International Response," Congressional Research Service, 2001).
- "Trafficked women are particularly vulnerable to physical violence, including rape, unlawful confinement, confiscation of identity papers and enslavement" ("Broken Bodies, Shattered Minds—The Torture of Women Worldwide," Amnesty International News Release, Mar. 6, 2001, www.amnesty.org).

What is even more appalling is that these represent only a tiny fraction of the statistics concerning violence against women, children, and the elderly extracted from a far more expansive ledger of atrocities. It was such issues that provoked the concerns of this text. Drawing on the writings of feminist theorists, research in the areas of colonization in both theory and praxis, Hegelian and Marxian dialectics, subaltern studies, and critical social theory, I attempt to investigate the relationships between violence against women and children and notions of family terrorism, colonization, and patriarchy. I argue that there is a serious failure in certain strands of postfeminist and academic feminist theory and practice to ade- quately address and redress male violence against women and abuse of children. Moreover, the conservative backlash against feminism helps to veil the extent and brutality of this problem and to block efforts to deal with it.

Indeed, this backlash has plagued the feminist movement since its inception, but as of late it has taken on a particularly dangerous guise, within the seductively poisonous ideological form of an antifeminist "feminism" propagated by Camille Paglia and others. This agenda is being advanced by a growing assortment of collaborators, who are misrepresenting themselves—largely through the efforts of the mainstream media—as feminists or feminist proponents (see chapters 1 and 2).

In this study, I will accordingly polemicize against media-promoted versions of anti-, post- and pseudofeminism, which I will argue cover over and mystify the issue of violence against women and children. Much fashionable pseudo-feminist theory overlooks the practical social relations constraining women and children—and especially the concrete economic, social, and political relations of violence, abuse, and poverty. Antifeminists explicitly deny the ubiquity of violence against women or trivialize it. Yet other approaches naturalize male violence as if it were an inherent biological given of the male species (i.e. Paglia).

Against this biological determinism, I will argue that instances of violence against women and children cannot be oversimplified and essentialized with uni-versalizations about inherent biological tendencies. Moreover, at another level, male abuse of women and male and female violence against children cannot be placed in one-dimensional, simplistic, often individualistic, psychosocial cause-and-effect relations. Such modes attribute one primary societal cause to what is, in reality, a complex system of pathologies of violence. Reductive approaches decontextualize and divorce relations and constituents of violence from their multiple individual and general circumstances. Instead, it is necessary to contex-tualize relations of violence within a critical, multidimensional, dialectical per-spective that is responsive to both theory and practice and that begins to provide an adequate response to the problem.

My project is accordingly to develop broad theoretical and critical perspectives to address problems of violence against women and children and to contest those who would deny, ignore, or decontextualize it. Historian Linda Gordon has writ-ten that there are "two camps" that have researched questions of "family vio-lence": "A psychological interpretation explains the problem in terms of personality disorder and childhood experience. A sociological explanatory model attributes the problem primarily to social stress factors such as poverty, unem-ployment, drinking, and isolation. . . . But both sides have often ignored the gen-der politics of family-violence issues, and the gender implications of policy recommendations" (1988, 5).

Attempting to overcome such dichotomous and apolitical models, I combine in my studies a diversity of historical, sociological, psychological, and cultural material in a multiperspective dialectical framework aimed at progressive political practice as part of what Joy James calls "transformative feminism" (1996). To doc-ument the problem of violence against women and children and to explicate the intensity and complexity of the problem, I draw heavily on a diversity of sources. I feel that the eloquence, passion, and verisimilitude of specific positions are best presented in the writers' own words, and I believe that identifying specific cases of family terrorism concretizes, contextualizes, and dramatizes what in statistical studies might seem abstract. Accordingly, in chapter 3, I include a case study of Hedda Nussbaum/Joel Steinberg, one of the most publicized cases of family violence (see also note 6 at the end of this introduction), as a vivid example of wife battering and murderous family terror against children.

But I believe that concrete case studies and empirical research require a broad historical and theoretical framework for contextualization. Thus, a major thrust of my studies is to provide theoretical and practical categories and perspectives to address violence against women and children and to promote a transformative politics that engages the multiple constituents of the problem. I endorse earlier feminist theories that stressed that patriarchies share common attributes or qualities, and I believe that the role of patriarchies is often de-emphasized or ignored in too many schools of feminist thought. I agree, however, with Linda Gordon's rejection of ahistorical notions of "patriarchy" as a "universal, unchanging, deterministic social structure which denies agency to women" (1988, vi). Gordon writes, "I prefer to use the term . . . in a narrower sense, referring to a form of male dominance in which fathers control families and families are the unit of social and economic power" (1988, vi). It is this historically specific sense in which I use the term *patriarchy* in the following studies.

Briefly put, one of my central arguments is that the nature of women's plight is not simply a consequence of the system of capitalism or patriarchy, or of the fact of gender alone. Rather, the oppression and domination of women is part of a far more complex and debilitating process that can be described as colonization (see chapter 5). Contrary to the dominant ideology, people are not born with a "colonized mentality." Colonial characteristics are not inherent, they are learned. Ideological histories, role models, and values, together with societally imposed constraints that perpetuate these oppressive belief systems, keep the colonized in their place. For the oppressed are colonized historically, socially, politically, and economically within both the physical and psychological domains. Moreover, the colonizer, through the use of "tokens" and the aid of "collaborators," ensures that the colonized remain in a state of "false" or "imaginary" consciousness. In other words, the colonized are taught to believe the dominant ideological myths about their collective being and behave accordingly.

An appropriate understanding of the multileveled process of the colonization of women, which takes into account race, class, ethnicity, and sexual difference as well as various levels of oppression, requires the development of transdisciplinary dialectical perspectives that reject Cartesian logic and reductive, mechanistic explanations. This involves the development of a critical feminist epistemology that includes an explication of key categories of the dialectical method, critique of binary logic, and the advancement of theoretical perspectives on domination and subordination. Moreover, these theoretical positions will inform the practical analyses of colonization and the potential for decolonization of women developed throughout this text.

In the quest to explore and interrogate colonization and the integral part played by collaborators within this process (and how it applies to a range of situations of women), I argue against ahistorical and noncontextual feminisms and antifeminism that reify theoretical abstractions and deny acute contemporary problems. Instead, I am arguing for an emergent critical feminist epistemology that embraces a subject/object dialectic that views all forms of behavior in contextual and materialist terms. In this regard, feminisms that embrace a dialectical epistemology and that stress a transformative politics, inclusiveness, and activism in a passionate concern for addressing concrete contemporary issues in a theoretical and practical fashion are identified as contributing to the development of a critical feminist perspective.

The significance of this approach will, it is hoped, be demonstrated through the unfolding of the complexity of relevant current debates within contemporary feminism concerning violence against women and children. Chapter 1 provides a critical analysis of the backlash against feminism in the last decade, while chapter 2 engages the research and writings of a number of faux feminist writers, who either deny the prevalence of violence against women or explain it away. These studies identify the common assumptions and "the pattern which connects" (Bateson 1979) in the writings of some prominent writers of contemporary feminism, who, however, claim feminist affiliation, including Camille Paglia, Christina Hoff Sommers, Naomi Wolf, and Katie Roiphe. Their conception of "victim feminism" or "victimization" emerges as a common thread. Moreover, the investigation of some of the writings of these revisionary pseudofeminist thinkers exposes the incendiary role of collaborators in the complex and sophisticated system of colonization, thus providing insight into both this process and the contemporary backlash against feminism. In fact, the extensive critique of both the form and substance of some of their ideas and conceptualizations shows the relevancy of the contextual dimensions of a critical feminist approach.

Because many of the feminists these false feminists choose to attack are related to antiviolence feminisms, it seems appropriate to critique the antifeminists' work within the framework of a contextualized, highly detailed examination of some of the realities of the conditions and investigations of what is often described as family violence. Hence, in chapter 3, I examine the Hedda Nussbaum/Joel Steinberg case as a way of talking about how pseudofeminists have exploited the issue of so-called domestic abuse to advance a pernicious blame-the-victim approach. Incorporating a wide variety of related research and empirical findings, a number of central arguments of various pseudofeminist pronouncements are disputed or attacked. Because the Nussbaum/Steinberg case became an allegory for battered women and victimization, the responses of various feminists to these kinds of family violence is revelatory.

In chapter 4, I address the complex issue of "why battered women don't leave" and critique prevailing myths concerning battered women and children. I develop a concept of "family terrorism" to provide replacements for the discourse of "domestic abuse" and to discuss the multiple sources of violence in the family. Often, the complex and multileveled relations that produce family violence are reduced to quantitative "statistics." One of the most disastrous consequences of this process, as Dianne Chisholm points out, has been "an apolitical discourse on violence against women which has found . . . impressive popularity" (1993, 52).

Chapter 4 also contains discussion of the ways that poverty and material conditions help produce family terrorism, a topic that has become unfashionable in much of both popular antifeminsm and academic feminisms. It also engages the issue of scapegoating and "blaming the victim" and the failure of public institutions to redress the problems of violence against women and children.

Chapter 5 applies colonization theory and borderland feminism to develop theoretical and political perspectives to better illuminate the complex nature of violence against women and children. It also identifies transformative attempts to overcome this pathological set of relations and to work toward the decolonization of violence against women and children at individual and global levels. Colonization theory reveals how divisions in various feminist domains produce the kinds of splits that all too often occur within colonized groups. This is a result of one of the most effective tactics of the strategy of colonization—the technique of "divide and rule." So prevalent are these divisions that the very core of feminism, in all its various incarnations, is seriously threatened: the dialectical recognition, respect and embrace of difference within a sociopolitical economic, cultural context of global sisterhood and solidarity (e.g., what Maria Lugones has called "solidarity in multiplicity" [cited in Donaldson 1992, 157]). And, as a result, the key ingredients of successful colonization—violence and domination—are being erroneously disregarded or misrepresented and counterproductively attacked by various members and schools within the feminist movement.

Moreover, in chapter 5, family terrorism is recontextualized within the framework of colonization and globalization as I discuss violence against women and children on a global scale. This discussion requires analysis of poverty and globalization, slavery, and prostitution within developing countries. I conclude with some analyses of the ways that dialectical conceptions of contradiction and struggle, the translation of theory into practice, and the dynamics of a transformative politics can develop notions of agency and analyses of the ways in which women can organize to form alliances to address issues such as violence against women and children.

NOTES

1. See www.ncjrs.org/txtfiles/172837.txt. Another recent survey sponsored by the Department of Justice, "National Crime Victimization Survey," reports a decline in "intimate violence" during the past few years, noting that "in 1998 women experienced an estimated 876,340 violent offenses at the hands of an intimate" (www.ojp.usdoj.gov/bjs/abstract/ipv.htm). It is difficult to explain why there would be such a divergence in statistics, and in chapter 3 I will discuss problems with abstract, decontextualized, and problem-

atic statistics concerning violence against women and children. Thus, although throughout my study I will draw on various quantitative and empirical studies to provide documentary material to illustrate issues of violence against women and children, I attempt to provide theoretical contextualization to interpret this material. While there are a tremendous amount of Internet and other resources that contain a wealth of data and material that address the topic, some surveys and statistics are problematic. Many empirical studies depend on the bias or interest of researchers, funding agencies, survey protocols, methodologies, and other dimensions. Critics of feminist research often attack specific figures and statistical sources. Indeed, as I argue in chapter 3, there are significant problems in many studies of violence against women and children. My argument will be that sound statistics require proper research methodology, theoretical interpretation, contextualization, and critique. Further, I will argue for a combination of empirical research and theoretical perspectives on violence against women and children. Although I draw upon quantitative and empirical material that are an important component of feminist research, I am also concerned to develop broad critical feminist perspectives to interpret this material and help contextualize and explain violence against women and children.

2. On violence against women and children, I will draw upon Linda Gordon's history (1988) and studies like Dobash and Dobash 1979, Jones 1994a and 1996, Sidel 1996, and a wide range of additional historical and sociological research.

3. Activist groups and charities are usually called NGOs (nongovernmental organizations) in the developing world (Bales 1999, 230).

4. Clarence Thomas was nominated by George Bush as a Supreme Court justice in 1991 and was accused by Anita Hill of sexual harassment. Although Thomas's appointment was confirmed, widespread media discussion of the issue of sexual harassment surrounded the confirmation; see James 1996 and Phelps and Winternitz 1992.

5. William Kennedy-Smith was acquitted of raping Patricia Bowman, even though there were three other women who alleged that Smith had sexually assaulted them in the past. Judge Mary Lupo decided not to admit this testimony (Devitt 1992, 9).

6. The case of Hedda Nussbaum and Joel Steinberg is dealt with in greater detail in chapter 3. Hedda Nussbaum became a public figure when she accepted immunity and testified against her partner, Joel Steinberg, identifying him as the murderer of their six-year-old, illegally adopted daughter, Lisa, in the first televised trial in New York in December 1988. The case is highly significant and continues to be a source of contention for a number of reasons related to issues associated with wife battery, child abuse, "victimization," and the so-called battered wife syndrome. Nussbaum was tortured by Joel Steinberg for numerous years. Due to the widespread publicity of her case, she represents, for many, the first real living battered woman to speak about the horrors of abuse she experienced. Thus, Nussbaum became the "poster child" for battered women. Devitt and Downey (1992) provide a useful description of the misrepresentation of the "battered wife syndrome" by the mass media: "Using Hedda Nussbaum as the model, the media have taken battered woman's syndrome—originally a description of the powerlessness and apathy that set in *after* repeated trauma—and turned it into a kind of female masochism that makes women seek out violent men." The *Chicago Tribune* (Dec. 20, 1991, 15) reported that eight women serving time for killing their abusers were the " 'victims of battered-wife-syndrome,' rather than of battering men."

Indeed, the case provoked highly contentious arguments, battles, and divisions within contemporary feminisms, as well as a diversity of other sociological, psychological, and humanistic arenas of thought and action, regarding numerous issues related to family terrorism and violence against women. In particular, however, the Nussbaum case raised serious questions and debates regarding "victimization," which is a central problematic addressed in this study.

1

Antifeminism, Postfeminism, and the Backlash

In the 1970s, while Joe Frazier and Muhammad Ali were pounding the crap out of each other around the globe, we had our own feminist Thrilla in Manila right here in America. This was what the debates about feminism got reduced to in the mass media: a catfight. . . . The catfight—which in the 1960s we only got to see in B movies like Russ Meyer's *Faster Pussycat! Kill! Kill!*—made it into the mainstream in the 1970s and '80s. We tend to think of the catfight as a staple of the nighttime soaps, and the daytime soaps as well. So it's worth reminding ourselves that the catfight was first revived not in prime time but through a more respectable venue, the news media. (Douglas 1994, 221–22)

Susan Douglas's analysis of the media's role in misrepresenting and diminishing the underlying philosophy and goals of the feminist movement of the 1970s is not just a tactical relic of the past. As Douglas explains it, the ideals of early second-wave feminists of universal sisterhood were threatening, especially in light of the potential for passage of the ERA (Equal Rights Amendment) in the United States. The ERA could have produced a series of important social-political and economic changes, including extensions of Social Security benefits to housewives, government funding for day care, and national health plans for all Americans, to name a few. Although at first blush these proposals appear to be hardly radical, that there continues to be a lack of these basic rights and services suggests that such demands (both then and now) are of an incendiary nature.

Indeed, as Douglas points out, the most effective way to both paralyze and prevent widespread support for the feminist movement was not so much to disseminate those voices who represent the hardcore conservative and patriarchal opponents to feminism. Rather, publicizing and exploiting critiques by women was a more effective antifeminist tactic, employing members of the very disenfranchised groups the feminist platform resolved to empower. Hence:

13

women with no economic or political power were used as stand ins for men who opposed feminism. Through this tactic, male journalists could ask why men should support changes even most women didn't want, and they could smirk over one of their favorite events, the catfight, while smiling knowingly and maintaining that women *were* different from men, and weren't the differences cute and delightful. (Douglas 1994, 186)

The effectiveness of this type of tactic has once again been confirmed in its current media incarnation. Indeed, in collusion with a group of opportunistic antifeminist women, media culture has resurrected the spectacle of the catfight in an attempt to trash and discredit the contemporary women's movement. Unlike the women who attacked the movement in the 1970s, however, in this age of makeovers and special effects, the new breed of collaborators has been spuriously presented as "new" or "postfeminists." And this masquerade enhances the ideological view that the concept of sisterhood, in practice, is not feasible given the inherent competitive and catty nature of the female species. Hardly exclusive to the mainstream media, even more specialized "intellectual" or "scholarly" forums exploit and advance this pernicious myth (Ginsberg and Lennox 1996, 185). In fact, the promotion and escalation of this antifeminist phantasmagoria is evident within the academic domain as well as the mainstream media, as Elaine Ginsberg and Sara Lennox document. They argue that "debates within the ranks of feminists, more than disagreements in other disciplines, seem to draw attention-getting headlines such as 'Feminist Scholars Ask Whether Their Sparring Marks Healthy Debate or a Splintering "Catfight"'" (*The Chronicle of Higher Education*)" (Ginsberg and Lennox 1996, 185).

This divide-and-conquer strategy tends to neutralize, trivialize, and reduce the real multidimensional and urgent issues associated with the feminist terrain that need to be addressed in a public forum. But, as Douglas reminds us that

the news media will opt for the simplistic yet coercive metaphor of woman-on-woman violence whenever possible. The reason Camille Paglia has become such a media darling, despite an ego the size of Australia and two books that don't make a lick of sense, is that she loves to trash feminists—or, at least, her particular caricature of feminists. Ditto for Katie Roiphe, whose attacks on women twice her age who work in rape crisis centers or battered women's shelters have helped make her famous. The mainstream media's love of the catfight has made it hard for feminists who value debate and dislike orthodoxy to welcome such debate. (1994, 244)

Moreover, due to the media's tendency to one-dimensionalize and reduce the quality of argument of feminist or antifeminist debate, many critical feminists defer from participating "because disagreements among some feminists [and especially those in regards to antifeminists] are simply used to cast all women as face-clawing, eye-scratching hysterics" (Douglas 1994). Yet this has not stopped 1990s antifeminists and their hordes of pseudofeminist imitators from actively engaging, generating, and inciting these "catfight" forums in often successful and highly profitable attempts to publicize their own texts and increase their celebrity status.

Indeed, rather than identifying representative feminists of the variety of schools of thought or feminist practices they trash, they instead tend to misrepresent others of similar ilk (or high profile mainstream feminists) as leading feminist proponents, and attack those they presume will respond in kind. Given the wide variety of multiplying cyber and print media forums that depend upon and often thrive on these kinds of so-called debates, the "catfight" has become an integral component of the "marketed popularized" dominant version of media postfeminism, which confuses "feminism with successful women" (Eisenstein 1996, 112). These postfeminist women appear to display no guilt or sense of responsibility at being the butt of a codified sexist joke nor exploiting sexual stereotyping for their own selfish gain, even through their enlistment in the war against feminist women. Christina Hoff Sommers, for example, seems to actively invite and relish these encounters, which she often incites through her books. Indeed, even her longstanding attacks on Carol Gilligan (who Pollitt, 1994, describes as a "difference feminist") are recycled from her first book and a series of published attacks and debates. They form part of the basis for her 2000 text, *The War against Boys*. Gilligan has repeatedly countered her attacks, which focus on Gilligan's alleged lack of "scientific rigor." Yet, the widely accessible media public forums and publicity afforded celebrity anti- or "dissident" feminists is hardly available to critical feminists, especially when popularized media and pseudofeminists prefer to "debate" each other within the sensationalized catfight framework.

In another example, Wendy Shalit garnered enormous publicity and media attention for her 1999 antifeminist treatise *A Return to Modesty: Discovering the Lost Virtue* through what could be described as a cunning orchestration and transmutation of the "catfight" scenario into a self-serving art form. Katha Pollitt provides an apt synopsis of the text:

> In "A Return to Modesty," a 23-year-old conservative journalist, Wendy Shalit, cites her experience in fourth grade sex ed to argue that feminism and liberal sexual mores have encouraged men to degrade women. The solution: women could stay virgins, and arm themselves, as Shalit implies she did, with blushes and long skirts to inspire chivalry in men. (*New York Times*, Apr. 18, 1999)

Shalit's book attacks the value of what she erroneously presents as an essentialized women's movement's responsibilities for propagating a "sexual revolution" that "crossed into territory that has been unhealthy for women." She "suggests that a correlation between the sexes could be made through a reemphasis on sexual modesty" that celebrates religious values and moralities of the past (Shari Roan, *LA Times*, Mar. 22, 1999, S2). In other words: "Shalit believes feminism sold women down the river by encouraging them to be sexually available" and claims that she wants "to invite feminists to consider whether the cause of all this unhappiness might be something other than the patriarchy." However, what really sensationalized and abetted the selling of both the book and Shalit were her claims to being a twenty-three-year-old virgin at the time of the book's publication. Moreover, who is it she chooses to attack from her pulpit? Rather than second-wave feminists of the 1960s and 1970s, whom she obviously deems responsible for the so-called immodest plight of women, she lines up "Naomi Wolf, Paglia, Roiphe and [Gloria] Steinem among others like ducks in a shooting gallery [and] takes aim at them all." Shalit has obviously groomed herself as a "catfight" contender, for as Sharon Krum explains it: "When the attacks grew more ferocious in print and across the airwaves, it only served to strengthen Shalit's confidence and resolve. 'I knew they would attack me and I see it as a compliment,' she says, explaining that the heat generated by the debate simply allows her to spread her gospel" (*The Guardian*, Apr. 1, 1999).

Indeed, Wendy Shalit's celebrity was so established that it appears that many other self-serving antifeminists like journalist Cathy Moore (the author of the 1999 *Ceasefire: Why Men and Women Must Join Forces to Achieve True Equality* who was "vice chairwoman of the [conservative] Women's Freedom Network") attacked her writings in order to publicize their own texts (Ginsberg and Lennox 1996, 189). In a highly bizarre "dialogue," obviously designed to sell more books and further publicize and legitimate these two opportunist antifeminists, Moore and Shalit were afforded eight pages in *Slate*, in which they trashed each other's writings by primarily advertising their own texts and employing public relations interviews and extensive citations from each other's works (www.slate.com, Feb. 8, 1999, 59–68).

Yet many critical and activist feminists have been wading into the fray in an attempt to recontextualize the concrete, pragmatic realities and theoretical debates that the media-staged catfights suppress and conceal. For as bell hooks notes: "As with any other 'hot' marketable topic, feminism has become an issue that can be pimped opportunistically by feminists and non-feminists alike" (1994a, 92). In this context, it is important to criticize nonfeminist pseudofeminism so that feminists can better organize to "intervene strategically and alter the public understanding of feminism that audiences receive from the messages of [Camille] Paglia" (and her peers and descendants) (hooks 1994a, 87). And the demand to heed hooks's admonitions are even more urgent, given the current continuing escalation of what she astutely identified as a popular trend to exploit and commodify feminist issues.

It is these kinds of responses to the constant and refurbished attacks on feminism by antifeminist pundits that have provoked my criticism of this tendency. And although much of my critique is directed at particular antifeminists who were prominent in the 1990s, it is by no means inclusive. In fact, ever more frequently, new women critics of feminism are appearing and are being supported by antifeminist forces and popularized in the media.[1] Indeed, this antifeminist media characterization was epitomized in an outlandish *Time* magazine cover that purported to pictorially depict the history of U.S. feminism, underlined with a written query that asked (again) "Is Feminism Dead?" (June 29, 1998). The faces on *Time*'s cover depict the historical progression from Susan B. Anthony to Betty Friedan to Gloria Steinem—to Ally McBeal (a fictional television character created by a man, David E. Kelley, an ex-lawyer turned TV mogul and producer, who is hardly a feminist sympathizer). The *Time* cover story presents a completely invented reality of the so-called contemporary feminist terrain that is devoid of any references to the real multidimensional state of current feminist theory or practice. Instead, it presents an imaginary pseudofeminist domain, inhabited by a plethora of "chic young feminist thinkers" (such as Lisa Palac[2] and Courtney Love), whose primary concerns are "Their bodies! [and] Themselves!" and who are "wed to the culture of celebrity and self-obsession" (Bellafante 1998, 54, 57).[3] Paradoxically, Bellafante also includes in her obituary of feminism that feminism's death is not only due to "terminal silliness," but also to its intellectual elitism (Pollitt 2001, xviii). Hence, this now notorious cover story epitomizes how backlash media, often in collaboration with feminist impersonators, attacks and employs its own Frankensteinian creations to condemn a caricature of feminism that is depicted as both vacuous and so exclusive that it is incomprehensible and completely out of touch with reality. Hence, feminism is irrelevant. This ploy is so successful that every few years this same tired oxymoronic theme is recycled, often under the facade of yet another new set of postfeminist celebrity pundits.

Although hardly as well publicized, many feminists do respond to these periodic antifeminist proselytizers. For example, a number of feminists from a variety of disciplines have provided astute and diverse commentary on historical and contemporary episodes of pseudofeminist backlash as well as critical interpretations of many of the antifeminists addressed in this text (see, for example, such edited volumes as Maglin and Perry 1996; Stan 1995; Clark, Garner, Higonnet, and Katrak 1996). In this chapter, I am attempting to contribute to this critique by providing a contextual reading of the 1990s wave of pseudofeminist antifeminism that continues through the present. Within a framework of a developing critical dialectical feminist approach, I endeavor to summarize and assess the underlying ideological nature of the dominant themes and ideas of many of these antifeminist writers and demonstrate the similarities and replications of many of their arguments.

A textual reading and critique of media-supported antifeminist discourse is necessary in order to identify and make apparent the "pattern which connects" so many of these interventions. It is precisely because they are so cleverly devised, well publicized, and influential that they cannot be ignored by the feminist community. This notion of recognizing patterns in both similar and seemingly disparate theory and praxis are important dimensions of the kinds of critical feminist dialectical epistemology being advocated in this text. As visionary communications philosopher Gregory Bateson described it: *"Break the pattern which connects the items of learning and you necessarily destroy all quality"* (Bateson 1979, 8). Gloria Anzaldua's revolutionary contributions to transformational feminisms also advance this contextual pattern-oriented perspective as part of a larger dialectical approach. As she explains it, "The connections are there, but you need to be in a certain frame of mind in order to recognize them" (Keating 2000, 286).

THE FEMINIST BACKLASH:
A CONTEXTUAL EXAMINATION

The catfight metaphor is only one in the arsenal of ideologically persuasive weapons employed by the media to discredit feminist movements. More often than not, the catfight scenario provides the subtext for the recurrent media proclamations announcing the demise of feminism. Canadian feminist journalist Michelle Landsberg provides an astute analysis and documented overview of this repetitive pattern.

> What a faithful old warhorse it is, what a reliable subject to peddle an editor! Ah yes, the oft-reported death of the women's movement. Every couple of years, for a least as long as I've been able to read, the popular media have staged a funeral for feminism. Entire flotillas of lugubrious prose are launched on a sea of crocodile tears. (Landsberg 1998)

This ploy, as Susan Faludi points out, is hardly particular to the contemporary media backlash against feminism. In fact:

> Ever since the media discovered feminism in the mid-nineteenth century, they have been more inclined to denounce it than study it. In the last round of feminism's revival, in the late sixties and early seventies, the "grand press blitz" lasted all of three months. By 1971, the press was calling the women's movement a "fad," or a "bore," and "dead"—and taking a rather active role in hastening the movement's last rites. (Faludi 1995, 33)

In this sense, it is imperative that we contextualize each attack on feminisms as part of a recurrent historical pattern. Feminist historians and critics Moira Ferguson, Kety Katrak, and Valerie Miner (1996) situate the particular 1980s backlash against feminisms within the rise and popularity of the religious right in the late 1970s and Reaganite conservatism in the 1980s.[4] Hardly particular to the 1970s and 1980s however, Eisenstein demonstrates the long-term endurance of this republican ideological backlash that is so deeply entrenched that it has transcended U.S. boundaries.

This republican backlash, which also crosses party lines, defines the enemy as illegal immigrants, women and children on welfare, and an overly committed government that must be privatized. Feminism and civil rights are the enemies of this nation. (Eisenstein 1996, 122)

Ferguson et al. go on to attribute the success of 1980s and 1990s antifeminism, in part, to "the media, including computerized information superhighways, electronic international mail networks, and other access into virtual realties that can ignore, negate, or render invisible the real conditions governing people's ordinary lives" (1996, 51). Moreover:

Hollywood movies, popular psychology, conservative talk radio shows have found ways to turn on their head such goals as autonomy and independence that feminism struggled for, as if these gains in women's self-reliance are responsible now for all of women's ills, whether depression, unemployment, or teenage pregnancy. Publications, as different as the *New York Times, Vanity Fair, The Nation* have issued indictments against the women's movement with such headlines as "When Feminism Failed or The Awful Truth About Women's Lib"; "Professional women are suffering 'burnout' and succumbing to an 'infertility epidemic' "; "Single women are grieving from a 'man shortage.' " (Ferguson, Katrak, and Miner 1996, 51)

Indeed, as a key component of the ongoing incendiary "culture wars," feminism continues to serve as a prominent target in the new right's witch-hunt of an imaginary conspiracy of an almighty leftist and feminist cabala. This supposed conspiracy is allegedly dedicated to the entrenchment of an elitist and undemocratic ideology, bearing the nebulous and rather ambiguous label of "political correctness." Ferguson, Katrak, and Miner document how the "culture wars of the 1980s and 1990s" have glorified new right nuclear family values, "laissez-faire economics," and traditional notions of femininity and motherhood in a campaign that converged biases against feminism with antagonism to diverse "ethnic and multicultural studies" (1996, 48). They note "such antiprogressive stances take refuge in the popular slogan of 'political correctness,' which is evoked in order to undercut modest progress in the educational and cultural life of the U.S." (1996, 48). Moreover, Ferguson et al. point out that these culture wars have expanded—in large part due to an assortment of media-friendly, "celebrity," conservative academics—far beyond the perimeters of the university. The culture wars encompass "a rhetoric against poor people, gays and lesbians, immigrants, and against safe abortions and other reproductive rights, as well as, increasingly, in opposition to affirmative action" (1996, 48).

This "reactionary backlash," Johanna Brenner stresses, has been so effective that mainstream feminism has in response developed a defensive position that has had serious implications for more progressive agendas, especially antiviolence mandates (Brenner 1993, 144). "Accused of encouraging 'family breakdown', 'divorce, drugs and delinquency', feminists have attempted to reappropriate the family from the Right by putting 'family' at the centre of their own politics, with unfortunately conservatizing consequences" (1993, 144).

Unlike her collaborationist sisters, who were mainly silent subordinates to male domination in previous decades, this new species of antifeminist claims affiliations with and often identifies herself as "feminist," usually of a particular kind (the adjective is typically a term she herself has coined, for example, "power feminist"). Previous antifeminists demonized and assaulted any position or issue deemed to be even remotely associated with a taint of progressive feminism, while advocating conservative values of the dominant white, Christian, often fundamentalist, organizations to which they were aligned. The newer breed of antifeminist (pseudo)feminists, by contrast, often couch their reactionary edicts within the guise of liberal individualism and, in fact, bear more resemblance to their male counterparts, in that they are most habitually presented as being independent members or associates of the intellectual elite. Ferguson, Katrak, and Miner provide an apt commentary on these most recent collaborationist converts to the antifeminist fold.

> [J]oining this bandwagon of attacks on feminisms are some women who nonetheless consider themselves "feminist," and who are welcomed particularly by the mainstream publishing industry. Who better than one of our own to condemn our goals, such as a successful career woman who bemoans the shortcomings of feminism (similar to non-white Dinesh D'Souza, who does the dirty work against minorities even better than a William Bennet or an Allan Bloom)? Let us call them gender insiders, these antifeminist feminists who are given increasing attention by mainstream media. (1996, 49)

It is within the environment of these ever-expanding culture wars on the so-called politically or "sexually correct" (a later more revisionary take on the original appropriated slogan) that their victimology discourse takes on multiple dimensions. Indeed, it is so effective and seductive a ploy that it promises to be the underlying tenet of antifeminist feminists for a long time. In fact, a wave of antifeminism by conservative women from the late 1990s into the present continues to indict feminists by claiming that they celebrate victimhood and condemn motherhood (Tanehaus 1999, 148).

Hence, this chapter and the following one constitute a type of ideological-critical intervention against a wave of antifeminism that has emerged from the 1980s and continues to escalate. I demonstrate that an analysis of the research and writings of major 1990s antifeminists (many of whom masquerade as feminists) introduces a variety of issues, discussions, and concepts that are crucial to understanding the backlash against feminism and the ways that the serious issue of violence against women is trivialized or distorted by the mainstream media. My analysis shows how antifeminist women are collaborators in this enterprise and identifies a need for a theory of colonization that explains how women can betray other women and work against our common interests. Indeed, because the antifeminists frequently employ ideological simulacra of real feminist concerns within inappropriate, restricted, one-dimensional frameworks, a critique of their arguments allows for an examination into both the reductive and dualistic nature of antifeminist discourse. It also provides identification of mythical characteristics and attributes that the antifeminists apply to contemporary feminist critique and practice.

It is through investigation and appraisal of certain backlash antifeminist positions that key conceptualizations, notions, and theoretical perspectives that are pivotal to the central concerns of this text will be developed. My approach also allows and encourages us to acknowledge the wide medley of voices that personify the diverse nature of contemporary feminist thought, which, counter to antifeminist claims, embraces debate and difference and eschews any kind of rigid party line.

Moreover, an analysis of key antifeminists and their positions assists in an understanding of how women—within the frames and levels of hierarchies of difference they inhabit in the real world—share many characteristics of what has been defined as the process of colonization. Furthermore, this analogy helps elucidate the insidiousness of a range of processes of domination and violence. For as Frantz Fanon, who is recognized as one of the most literate and prolific scholar/activists in the area of colonization, explains it, collaboration is an integral part of the colonization process. Indeed, his analysis explicating collaboration within the particular realm of the French colonization of Algeria constitutes an apt description of the 1990s so-called new feminists and their followers. As Fanon explains it:

> The people who at the beginning of the struggle had adopted the primitive Manicheism of the settler—Blacks and Whites, Arabs and Christians—realize as they go along that it sometimes happens that you get Blacks who are whiter than the Whites and that the fact of having a national flag and the hope of an independent nation does not always tempt certain strata of the population to give up their interests or privileges. The people come to realize that natives like themselves do not lose sight of the main chance, but quite on the contrary seem to make use of the war in order to strengthen their material situation and their growing power. Certain natives continue to profiteer and exploit the war, making their gains at the expense of the people. (Fanon 1968, 144–45)

This chapter's emphasis on the antifeminist attack on contemporary feminism is intended to disclose the collaborationist nature of antifeminist women who use the gains of earlier feminisms to promote their own literary ambitions. My analysis is multiperspectival in that it criticizes dualistic and reductive antifeminist positions and argues for a multiplicity of critical feminist theories to address issues like violence against women. I am concerned primarily with a "pattern which connects" in the treatises of these so-called new feminists in relation to an underlying dichotomous approach that I fear often neutralizes the productive elements for feminist change and growth, purportedly expressed by these writers.

"POD FEMINISTS": INVASION OF THE
FEMINIST IMPERSONATORS

Susan Faludi, in her now classic 1995 article "I'm Not a Feminist But I Play One
on TV," has identified those who have been popularly misclassified as third-wave
feminists as media-made "pod feminists" planted by the right. The "pod" metaphor is one that Faludi cleverly borrowed and translated from the classic 1956
science fiction film *Invasion of the Body Snatchers*. The film presents a frightening
and prophetic parable about the residents of a small town who are being mysteri-
ously replaced by identical replicas of themselves, hatched by plant-like alien
pods. Faludi uses the metaphor to describe the implanting of the feminist label
on a variety of women who are really antifeminists.

> What is being celebrated is no natural birth of a movement—and the press that orig-
> inated the celebration is no benign midwife. It would be more accurate to describe
> this drama as a media-assisted invasion of the body of the women's movement: the
> Invasion of the Feminist Snatchers, intent on repopulating the ranks with Pod Femi-
> nists. (Faludi 1995, 32)

Indeed, the invasion of these "pod feminists" is part of an alarmingly escalating
movement of transparently self-serving women, who are inventing a generic
"straw-dog" type of feminism (composed of euphemistically "dogmatic" women,
I might add) that they criticize, under an allegedly "feminist" guise. Although
their attacks center on a diversity of feminist dimensions (ranging from issues of
date rape to university women's studies programs), they dismiss widely shared
and important feminist positions as hostile to the interests of women. I attempt
to demonstrate in this text that pod feminist shares deep-structural discourse
based on a one-dimensional, reductionist, and binary mode of thought that
reduces complex feminist positions to either-or imaginary dilemmas through
which they dismiss their feminist opponents and promote their own positions.

Faux-feminist Christina Hoff Sommers provides us with a graphic example of
this type of ideological viewpoint in her identification of a monolithic and mighty
feminist party (composed of mostly loud, unattractive, fat women, with decidedly
lesbian proclivities). She and others like her often prefer to employ a diversity of
euphemisms to denote this mythical stereotypical feminist. Moreover, the shared
reductionism of what "next generation feminist"[5] Veronica Chambers (1995) has
labeled "betrayal feminism" is to depict feminism as if it was a Manichaean mind-
set that divides feminism into good and evil, with the betrayal feminists firmly
entrenched in the leadership positions of the "good" feminist camp. It only follows, then, that the adoption of this inappropriate simplistic dualistic position
allows these "captains" to choose up sides, because "it is their bat and thus their
baseball game."

Hoff Sommers has chosen to call the "bad guys" "gender feminists" or "gender warriors." She situates herself, by contrast, within the "equity-feminist" team—which she associates with an overgeneralized fleeting description of "that older 'First Wave' kind of feminism whose main goal is equity, especially in politics and education" (Hoff Sommers 1994, 22). Katie Roiphe identifies the "evil" side as "rape-crisis" or "campus" feminists (Roiphe 1993). Like Naomi Wolf, whom she ironically demonizes as one of the "feminist prophets of rape crisis," Roiphe identifies herself as a new-age spunky feminist "bad girl" or "sexual rebel" in righteous battle with those brainwashed by the old "fuddy-duddy" Victorian prude side of the imaginary equation. Although it is difficult to discern any real distinction between them in this regard, Wolf claims that Roiphe's version of "bad girl" feminism, unlike her own, "is a call for women to yield their self-respect in the name of bogus liberation" (Wolf 1993, 192). In fact, their arguments over the ownership of this "bad girls" terminology (which has become particularly fashionable among some of the self-defined postfeminists within the realms of the arts and popular forms of cultural criticism and performance arts) appears to be typical of the kinds of competition that inscribe the pseudofeminist domain. It is, however, difficult to judge if these expressed differences with one another are sincere or are catfight-style exhibitions, played out for the media to ensure publicity and to further their own personal celebrity ambitions.

These "media-constructed cartoon characters" (Rapping 1996, 265), however, advance this imaginary oppositional duality within what is often described within the popular culture as the "gender wars." And these so-called gender wars, when used in this context, are in fact a euphemism for this reconfigured 1990s form of feminist backlash. Katha Pollitt reveals how these kinds of fabrications create a distracting, demented—but seductive—oxymoronic rationale. "In the old Backlash, feminism was bad; now feminism is good—it's just the women's movement that's bad" (1996, 8).

Elayne Rapping expands upon the inaccuracies and dangers in the invention of an "either-or," "good girl/bad girl," "victim/power feminist" dichotomy that reduces and distorts the real multidimensionalities and differences that characterize contemporary feminism. It perpetuates a "paradigm which is wrong and self-defeating in this current, media-fueled debate about what kind of 'feminism' we should be practicing or endorsing" (Rapping 1996, 267).

It is within this context that I introduce the term *impersonator feminism* to characterize the pseudofeminists who employ these kinds of deceptive techniques under the mask of feminism and who use the pretense of feminism to attack a wide range of feminist theory and practice. I argue that these feminist impersonators are assuming the guise of feminism in order to attack its most emancipatory tenets and politics and are thus part of the backlash against feminism itself. Although some young feminists (who call themselves third-wave feminists) have labeled these antifeminists *postfeminists* (Heywood and Drake 1997),[6] the term is often confusing because of the wide variety of feminisms in the areas of deconstruction, poststructuralism, postmodernism and postcolonialism that are also described as postfeminist (Brooks 1997).[7] "Third wave" has also proved problem-atic because it, too, has been appropriated by the media. Therefore, I inter-changeably use the terms *betrayal feminism, pseudofeminism, antifeminist feminism*, and *impersonator feminism* in this text.

POSTFEMINISM IN THE CONTEMPORARY ERA

As we enter a new millennium, the backlash against feminism that erupted in the 1980s, and that became more firmly established in the 1990s, continues to esca-late and proliferate. Indeed, in light of a rapidly multiplying number of women writers who call themselves "feminist" and then systematically present antifemi-nist arguments, the very word *feminist* is losing its meaning. This is due, in part, to a number of virulent antifeminist pundits who attained celebrity status in the 1990s and opened the floodgates for an industry that is loosely described by the media as "postfeminist." Indeed, the expansion of pseudofeminist antifeminism (as well as what Zillah Eisenstein describes as "popularized media feminism") owes much to women like Camille Paglia, Katie Roiphe, Christina Hoff Som-mers, and others whose work is examined in detail in this text. According to Elaine Ginsberg and Sara Lennox, their 1990s texts were "the opening shot in a much larger campaign against feminism, directed this time by antifeminist women" (1996, 189).

Best-selling author Laura Doyle epitomizes the extreme of this flourishing phenomena. In early 2001, Doyle's book *The Surrendered Wife* found itself on the Amazon.com Top 10 List. "Its thesis is that the secret of a happy marriage is a submissive wife, who never says no, never nags her husband, and if she disagrees with him, says [so] through gritted teeth if she must" (Sharon Krum, *The Inde-pendent*, Feb. 22, 2001). Astonishingly, Doyle describes herself and her antifemi-nist advice manual as "feminist," leading a critic to note:

> There have been feminist back-lashes, and revisions of sexual politics, but none quite as silly or as regressive as Laura Doyle's "new phase of feminism." Maybe it's a joke, or an odd blip in the publishing world, or maybe it's a sign that times they are a'chan-ging. . . . Laura Doyle was and is, apparently, a feminist—though the narrow-minded, shallow variety kind, who thought that feminism was all about keeping your own surname and making your man do what you say. (Vicky Allan, *The Scotsman Publications Ltd*, Jan. 21, 2001)

Indeed, Doyle does not even resort to the popular euphemism of "dissident feminist," employed by so many pseudo- and antifeminist writers. Incredibly, Doyle told *Ms.* "that since she wants to help women stay married and thus be emotionally and financially better off—she figures that she is a feminist" (Laurel Rayburn, *Ms.*, Apr./May 2001, 13). Her text, like other successful books of its ilk (such as Wendy Shalit's 1999 *A Return to Modesty: Discovering the Lost Virtue*), advocates "a return to the morality and gender roles of former days." It indicts feminism as the cause of women's plights, as it unwittingly demonstrates the lucrative nature of the commoditization and "naturalization" of feminism as a marketing device (Mary Jo Kochakian, *The Washington Post*, Feb. 28, 2001).

Doyle's best-seller perhaps best personifies what Zillah Eisenstein (1996) identifies as the media commercialization and depoliticization of feminism. It was, in fact, media hype, astute marketing sense, and self-promotion that transformed Doyle's book from a self-published title to a "controversial" best-seller and afforded her celebrity status. Doyle, an advertising copywriter from Los Angeles, made parts of her text available on the Internet, developed a *Surrendered Wife* Web site that includes a "bulletin board of discussion and advice," and links to numerous newspaper and magazine articles. She set up self-help groups called "Surrendered Circles" in several countries; she also conducted seminars and become a fixture on the lecture and media circuit. Kate Clinton notes that Doyle's "Surrendered Circles" "have sprung up faster than Promise Keeper stadium rallies" (*The Progressive*, May 2001; www.progressive.org). Doyle's publishers doubled the initial print run of her book to one hundred thousand copies, thanks to "media and academic interest," and arranged for an extensive series of television and radio interviews. Kate Clinton argues that this subordinate attitude is being adapted by contemporary conservative women and even celebrated, especially by the power elite, since George W. Bush came to power.[8]

Devoid of conscience and morality, and bursting with ambition and overwhelming individualism, Laura Doyle seems to be representative of her antifeminist peers and 1990s forebears, like Camille Paglia, who exploit feminism for personal gain. Escalating numbers of feminist impersonators, like Doyle, seem to be emerging as heirs apparent to their overtly antifeminist predecessors of the 1990s. Doyle's goals and mode of operation, like so many of her "postfeminist" contemporaries, epitomizes a "new breed" of pseudofeminist, described by Ong Soh Chin as "Fem Lites," whose commitments to their positions seem to be mediated by money, fame, and power (*The Straits Times*, May 17, 2000). The proliferation and endorsement of these kinds of "postfeminist" texts appear to typify what hooks has identified as "a culture of narcissism" (2000a, 64). Moreover, shifts in the nature of successful and acknowledged anti- and pseudofeminist writings reflect changes in an emerging dominant ideology that adapts in accordance with historical, sociopolitical, economic, globalized relations and transmutations. As hooks explains it:

> While the sixties and seventies can be characterized as a time in the nation when there was a widespread sense of bounty that could be shared precisely because excess was frowned upon, the eighties and nineties are the years where fear of scarcity increased even as a culture of hedonistic excess began to fully emerge. Widespread communal concern for justice and social welfare was swiftly replaced by conservative notions of individual accountability and self-centered materialism. (2000a, 64)

One of the unfortunate consequences of this appalling cultural shift has been to neutralize the complexities and multiplicities of meanings and ideas that characterize feminisms. Indeed, it would seem that even the basic underlying tenet of feminisms, which bell hooks simply delineates as "feminism is a movement to end sexism, sexist exploitation, and oppression" (2000b, 1), is absent from many contemporary "postfeminist" writings.[9]

Many of these relatively new "prefixed" and descriptive feminist labels are confusing, due to shifting meanings and appropriation of expressions that describe specific feminist schools of thought and ideas. The "postfeminism" label appears particularly problematic because within feminist theorizing, especially within the academy, postfeminism sometimes "refers to the challenges of current feminist theory and practices as informed by poststructuralist, postmodernist, and multiculturalist modes of analysis" (Siegel 1997a, 82n43). Yet the mainstream media's appropriation, exploitation, and manipulation of the postfeminist label, as denoting the end of feminism, seems to predominate and has become a euphemism for much of the 1990s and expanding antifeminist and pseudofeminist "New Blather," as Katha Pollitt describes it (1996, 6). Deborah Siegel describes the current typical perception as well as the concurrent alarming "ideological implication" of the "popular connotation" of "postfeminism" within media culture:

> When invoked in the popular press, "postfeminist" most often describes a moment when women's movements are, for whatever reasons, no longer moving, no longer vital, no longer relevant; the term suggests that the gains forged by previous generations of women have so completely pervaded all tiers of our social existence that those still "harping" about women's victim status are embarrassingly out of touch. (Siegel 1997a, 75)

Siegel traces one of the earliest evocations of "postfeminism" in popular culture to a series of resurrected media backlash enquiries into the "death of feminism." In 1994, *Newsweek* published a review of five recently published books assessing and critiquing women's movements in the United States. Later the same year, PBS aired the conservative "William F. Buckley Jr. hosting an edition of *Firing Line* wishfully entitled 'Resolved: The Women's Movement Has Been Disastrous.'" The demise of feminism continues to be a hotly debated topic on numerous television and radio talk shows and in popular magazines, giving rise to the "pronouncement by the mainstream media and conservative pundits that we are living in a 'postfeminist era.'" Moreover, Siegel notes that mainstream media's coinage of the "postfeminist" term roughly coincides with the publications of four of the most incendiary of 1990s feminist backlash texts: Christina Hoff Sommer's *Who Stole Feminism* (1994), Naomi Wolf's *Fire with Fire* (1993), Katie Roiphe's *The Morning After* (1993), and Rene Denfield's *The New Victorians* (1995) (Siegel 1997a, 75).

Hoff Sommers, Wolf, Roiphe, and others have been associated with Camille Paglia as "spokeswomen for the next feminist generation" (Siegel 1997b, 48). Although their writings, positions, and affiliations are hardly "symmetrical," many critical feminists emphasize that there are similarities in many of their "evaluations" of contemporary feminisms, as well as differences. The underlying thrust of their work has arguably underscored, framed, and helped structure the burgeoning "postfeminist" industry of the present.

Elaine Ginsberg and Sara Lennox identify one of the most fundamental and influential misrepresentations that has characterized postfeminist writings and now serves as one of the most capitalized themes of legions of imitators and progeny. In particular, Ginsberg and Lennox describe how various postfeminists have conferred a "clever rhetorical spin" to "the analytical term oppression," which is a central category of all genres of feminisms. The distorted notion of "oppression" that they advance portray "feminists' concern with the power men exercise over them as the whiney, self-centered obsession of privileged women with their own imaginary victimization—a defamation of feminist efforts to identify the nature and scope of male dominance that has fared very well indeed in the popular press" (1996, 188). Within this context, Nan Bauer Maglin and Donna Perry expand upon the necessity of recognizing the critical implications of underlying ideological similitude in disparate positions put forward by these 1990s backlash pundits:

> While their individual messages vary—Naomi Wolf's call for "power" over "victim" feminism seems less extreme than Roiphe's attack on what she calls "exaggerated" rape claims, for example . . . the overall effects of their work is to suggest that because some women have prospered, the systematic inequalities facing all women have vanished into history. Because they (or their friends) haven't been raped, sexual violence can't be endemic. They speak as though the difficult work of feminist transformation were over rather than continuing. (1996, xiv)

Yet postfeminist reductionist bifurcation of feminisms into two essentialized groups, of good and bad feminists, such as Wolf's delineation of "victim" and "power" feminists, has probably been one the most widely appropriated and influential ideas of these 1990s impersonator feminists by both imitators and "mass-marketed pop media." This false binary opposition has in fact been adopted and actually attained a measure of currency, by far too many anti- and postfeminists and, of course, much of media culture. As Ellen Willis so aptly describes it: "The complexities and contradictions of male-female relations . . . are flattened to caricatures of villains and victims. (Ironically, this flattening obliterates sexual abuse as a particular concrete reality . . .)" (1996, 49).

In later chapters, I challenge this victimization myth and analyze its pernicious effects, in particular, on feminist research and activism associated with violence against women, children, and the elderly as well as an all-encompassing globalized patriarchal violence, which I define as "family terrorism." In this chapter, I will argue that as part of a backlash against feminism in the 1990s, a wave of antifeminist pseudofeminisms have emerged, which have adopted various terms, and which attack the more radical feminisms that developed in the 1960s through the 1980s.

THE INDEPENDENT WOMEN'S FORUM (IWF) AND THE RIGHT'S ASSAULT ON FEMINISM

Conservative antifeminists, like Christina Hoff Sommers, who are associated with the right-wing Women's Freedom Network (WFN)[10] and the Independent Women's Forum (IWF), actively persist in exploiting the myth of a satanic academic feminist oligopoly. For example, in a spring 2001 university newspaper ad, entitled "Take Back the Campus" and sponsored by the IWF, "campus feminism" is described as "a kind of cult" that teaches "male bashing and victimology" (April 17, 2001, www.shethinks.org). It then goes on to cite a series of "Ms/ Information" composed primarily of so-called objective data, most of which involve issues that are complex, contentious, and highly contested. This right-wing assault on feminism, which is associated with the Bush administration, was characterized by Richard Cohen as "the tendency of the political right to seize on any scientific finding, no matter how tentative or, maybe, wrong, to support its ideology" (*The Washington Post, Online*, May 3, 2001). George W. Bush, one of the major promoters of conservative antifeminism, himself employs the manipulative technique of using pseudo-facts extensively.[11]

The Independent Women's Forum was "formed in 1992 by Republican women angered by the testimony of Anita Hill at confirmation hearings for Supreme Court Justice Clarence Thomas, and the prominent role played by the National Organization for Women and other feminist groups" (Moore and Deane, *Washington Post*, May 1, 2001, A1). Composed, primarily, of both politically prominent, successful right-wing women (many of whom hold, or are being considered for, high-level positions in the Bush administration) and the wives of powerful Washington conservative men, the IWF has been described as a "women's auxiliary of the conservative elite" (Kaminer, *The American Prospect*, Nov.–Dec., 1996). Indeed, the IWF's officials and sixteen hundred dues-paying members read like a "who's who" of some of the wealthiest, most reactionary careerist women (and men) who reflect the source of the IWF's financial support, which includes the conservative Olin, Bradley, and Carthage Foundations. Their ties with these kinds of organizations as well as their strong affiliations with the Bush administration and Republican political machine is evident given that: "Labor Secretary Elaine L. Chao is on its national advisory board. Linda Chavez, President Bush's first nominee for the Labor job, also is on the advisory board. Lynne V. Cheney, wife of the vice president, is a former member of its board of directors who is now listed as a member-*emerita*" (Morin and Deane, *Washington Post*, May 1, 2001, A1).

Zillah Eisenstein noted that the IWF has been "bent on dismantling many of the programs initiated by feminist reforms of the last two decades" (1996, 122). These include lobbying for "sex segregation at publically funded schools and the dismantling of affirmative action for women and people of color" (Jennifer Coburn, *The San Diego Union-Tribune*, Aug. 24, 1997). However, one of their most invidious causes, which speaks directly to the thesis of this text, is to destroy government programs related to violence against women. Not only does the forum oppose the 2000 revised 1994 Violence Against Women Act (VAWA), which it argues "is based on exaggerated claims of domestic violence and is being used by feminists as part of an ideological war against men" (Eisenstein 1996, 122), but they are actively attempting to substantively terminate it. "They have met with Justice Department officials and White House staffers to discuss what they said is a misallocation of resources directed through the department's Violence Against Women Office" (Morin and Deane, *Washington Post*, May 1, 2001, A1).

First passed in 1994, VAWA funding "supports battered women's shelters and rape prevention programs nationwide. It also provides the funding incentive for hundreds of cooperative initiatives between law enforcement, prosecutors, and victim services to stop violence against women" (Press Release, National Center for Victims of Crime, Sept. 7, 2000, www.ncvc.org). It is important to describe this act and its powers in detail given that it is one of the most significant U.S. social justice laws, especially in regard to violence against women, children, the elderly, indigenous, immigrants, and other marginalized peoples. Not only does it address social programs, government infrastructure, and institutions like women's shelters, but it also makes available funding for scholarly and professional research. The VAWA was "established within the Departments of Justice (DOJ) and Health and Human Services (HHS)" (Siskin 2001). The DOJ administers VAWA grants designed to assist legislative programs (for example, law enforcement and training programs for victim advocates and counselors), while the HHS grants "include funds for battered women's shelters, rape prevention and education, reduction of sexual abuse of runaway and homeless street youth, and community programs on domestic violence. Several studies of violent crimes against women were also mandated." As Siskin summarizes the act:

> On October 28, 2000, President Clinton signed into law the Violence Against Women Act of 2000 as Division B of the Victims of Trafficking and Violence Protection Act of 2000. . . . VAWA 2000 sets new funding levels and adds new programs. . . . VAWA 2000 reauthorizes most of the original act's programs, creates new grant programs to prevent sexual assaults on campuses, assists victims of violence with civil legal concerns, creates transitional housing for victims of domestic abuse, and enhances protections for elderly and disabled victims of domestic violence. In

addition to grants, VAWA 2000 authorizes a number of studies on the effects of violence against women, creates a domestic violence task force, and includes changes in federal criminal law relating to stalking, . . . intrastate domestic abuse, and immigration.

Between FY1995 and FY1999, Congress steadily increased funding for most of VAWA's grant programs. In FY2000 the amount appropriated for programs under VAWA was $435.75 million, *$3 million less than the FY enacted amount.* For FY2001, Congress appropriated $408 million, prior to the mandated rescission, for the programs that were authorized through VAWA 2000. (Siskin 2001)

The IWF has opposed the UAWA for years; with their rise to power in the Bush administration, the program is now seriously threatened.[12] In fact, the Independent Woman's Forum is neither independent (because it is funded by right-wing organizations) nor a forum (because it is controlled by Republican right-wing women who are now a force in the Bush administration). Like the IWF, the Women's Freedom Network also targets and attacks feminist campaigns and research that address issues of violence and abuse of women. As Wendy Kaminer puts it, "the Women's Freedom Network tends to minimize the problems of sexual violence, expressing particular contempt for protests of date rape and sexual harassment," which they claim to be issues that are fallacious or exaggerated by what they tender as an "extremist, ideological" feminist elite (Kaminer, *The American Prospect,* Nov.–Dec., 1996).

Hence, Ginsberg's and Lennox's warnings in 1996 (170) about "a new anti-feminism [that] appears to be part of a coordinated, well-funded, and highly visible conservative campaign to discredit scholarly and curricular changes in the academy since the sixties" seems particularly appropriate within the ultra-conservative backlash now under way in the twenty-first century. What is incredible about the IWF spring 2001 ad attacking feminism and women's studies, however, and much of the literature and public relations associated with conservative antifeminism, is that these women persist in voicing their accusations within a framework of elitism, condescension, and anti-intellectualism. They treat students and youth audiences, and basically the majority of feminists, as idiots or pliant dupes, as well as media illiterate, who fall prey to the seductions of radical feminists. Anita Blair, the Independent Women's Forum executive vice president and general counsel, described feminism today as "basically the tool, the servant, of elite women to get their way at the expense of less elite women—women who maybe don't have a lot of talent, brains, and money" (*New World Communications, Inc.,* Nov. 24, 1997). Yet the power of these right-wing antifeminist forces are escalating, confirming Ginsberg's and Lennox's foreboding assertion:

The *National Journal* observes that: "When it comes to women's groups, the fastest growth is among conservative and moderate organizations that reject 'feminist orthodoxy' . . . including the Women's Freedom Network, . . . the Independent Women's Forum, the Network for Empowering Women, and others." (1996, 189)

And, in fact, the Independent Women's Forum has become one of the most powerful right-wing forces in the United States, as it is now composed of numerous women officially associated with the Bush administration. It is hardly surprising that Christina Hoff Sommers heads the organization's national advisory board, which includes women members of the Bush administration such as labor secretary Elaine Chao, as well as other appointees and candidates:

> Today, the Women's Forum has become a favored venue for conservative scholars, writers, and policymakers to trade ideas and showcase their latest work on women's issues. Their reach inside the new administration exceeds the group's modest size. . . . Bush appointees who are not Independent Women's Forum members but must face Senate confirmation are dropping by its Arlington headquarters to be briefed on gender issues. (Morin and Deane, *Washington Post*, May 1, 2001, A1)

Not content to assail only mainstream feminisms, this odious organization attempts to malign and censure a multiplicity of dimensions of feminist thought and actions, through the antifeminist practice of reduction and one-dimensionalization. Once again, feminisms are depicted as a hotheaded, united, and liberal front that casts women as victims. "This has resulted, the group believes, in an angry intellectually rigid feminist viewpoint that believes affirmative action and other government programs are the only way to obtain true equality between the sexes" (Morin and Deane, *Washington Post*, May 1, 2001, A1). Hence, the invention of this fictitious authoritarian and sinister feminist hegemony allows the women associated with right-wing antifeminist groups to depict themselves as individualist champions dedicated to dismantling allegedly failed government programs, which have been implemented, they would like us to believe, by this rigid feminist intelligentsia (which also appears, in many instances, to be synonymous with the Democratic party).

The right-wing conservative assault on feminism, is not, however, the only manifestation of the backlash evident today. The rise of a variety of new styles of feminism adopted by younger women also adopt features of the backlash against the modes of political feminism associated with the 1960s and 1970s "second wave" of feminism.

ANTI-INTELLECTUALISM, LIFESTYLE FEMINISMS, AND THE BACKLASH

An anti-intellectual bias permeates much contemporary "postfeminist" literature that takes aim at various political and theoretical feminisms that have emerged since the 1960s. Postfeminist invective and scapegoating are targeted against an imaginary dominion of what Naomi Wolf characterizes as "insider feminists" and Hoff Sommers as "gender feminists," both of which are discussed in detail in the next chapter. They vilify an unspecified overseer sect of feminists who allegedly pose the greatest danger to the health of feminism. As Wolf imagines it: "The notion that all intellectual endeavors are collective and cannot go forth without the imprimatur of the self-appointed guardians of the Imprint of True Feminism will make feminism intellectually self-destruct" (1993, 117). This attack, which has been embraced by numerous 1990s and contemporary anti- and pseudofeminists, continues to pervert and devalue many key feminist "intellectual" undertakings. These include academic and nonacademic intellectual critical feminist endeavors such as women's studies programs, feminist pedagogy, activism, and a plethora of progressive writing and artistic projects (Keating 2000, 231). Yet many feminists and academic feminists, especially, are "hardly incapable of self criticism" and have been engaged in debates associated with formative and substantive difficulties associated with women's studies and feminist pedagogy for decades. This fact, however, seems to be disregarded and omitted from most of the criticisms of academic and intellectual feminists' intolerance and abuse, put forward by numerous antifeminists. Leora Tanenbaum is especially critical of antifeminists and pseudofeminists who one-dimensionalize and reduce the diversity and complexity of feminist academics and women's studies programs by insightfully pointing out that:

> [They] don't stop to consider the sexism pervasive in academia. If they sincerely cared about rehabilitating women's studies rather than scoring a few debating points, they would have examined the wider political context within which the discipline has emerged—and debates that have already taken place. (Tanenbaum 1994, 37)[13]

Within this context, Deborah Siegel also identifies an assault on theory (often under the guise of demonizing a fraudulent essentialized "academic feminism") as a corresponding theme of many of the seemingly divergent 1990s "feminist dissenters" and their various contemporary incarnations. Ironically, pseudofeminists like right-wing Christina Hoff Sommers and Democratic party partisan Naomi Wolf share this vilification of an alleged feminist intellectual elite. Carolyn Sorisio demonstrates how many antifeminists employed comparable arguments and decontextualized examples to characterize academic feminists "as out of touch, confining [themselves] to a realm of theory with no tangible significance in either the political or the personal sphere" (1997, 135). In fact, Siegel maintains that Roiphe, Wolf, and Denfield echoed the charges leveled by older reactionary antifeminists Camille Paglia and Christine Hoff Sommers in asserting that theory was "the refined instrument of academic feminist fascism" and have seriously impugned university feminist research and teaching, negated the consequential role of theory in multifarious dimensions of feminisms, as well as ignored and excluded ongoing debates on development and employment of feminist theory both inside and outside the academy (Siegel 1997b, 48).

While renegade conservatives such as Paglia and Sommers—themselves members of the academy—caricature and critique academic feminism and its advocates from within, the anti-intellectualism of the younger critics is differently motivated yet equally reductive. (Siegel 1997b, 47)

Indeed, the implications of this atheoretical form of faux feminism has provoked some younger generations of feminists to "reject the academy as a viable site for feminist activity" (Siegel 1997b, 48). Pseudofeminist discourse, which purports to be theory free, has been widely adapted by too many contemporary popular mainstream feminists (Siegel 1997a, 70). bell hooks has astutely identified the development and persuasiveness of this neutralized and commodified discourse as "lifestyle feminism." This is an apt description of the popularized, commodified, pseudofeminist discourses that dominate mainstream media culture. hooks argues that the politicized sisterhood of the 1980s "lost meaning as the terrain of radical feminist politics was overshadowed by a lifestyle based feminism which suggested any woman could be a feminist no matter what her political beliefs" (2000b, 11). And due, in large part, to dominance of hypermedia commercialization and backlash politics, this "mass-marketed popularized" lifestyle feminism threatens to replace oppositional and activist theoretical and practical feminisms from much of the public mind. As Eisenstein so aptly describes it:

The backlash today is deep and profound: it is against individualism as it operates *radically* for women. The market has to transform the militancy of this feminist individualism into consumerism. It attempts to do this by focusing on freedom, which the mass market absorbs, instead of equality, which the market rejects. Feminism gets redefined as an individualized consumer self-help market; and the politics surrounding the struggle for equality drops out the bottom. (1996, 113)

Ironically, what was originally called "third wave feminism" was completely at odds with the anti-, post-, and lifestyle (pseudo)feminisms of the 1990s and present. Third wave feminism was initially associated with women of color and those critical and oppositional discourses that I will later describe as "borderland feminism." However, many scholars argue that the revolutionary and critical feminist insights and significant contributions of many of these insurgent, often younger, writers of the third wave have been lost or forgotten due to the appropriation and commoditization of the third wave label by the younger generation of "lifestyle" feminists and pseudofeminists.

In fact, much of what is currently called "third wave" feminisms is indistinguishable from the popularized media marketed, atheoretical postfeminism that includes anti-, dissident, and what Michelle Goldberg describes as "shopping-and-fucking feminism" (2001). As she explains it: "This new shopping-and-fucking feminism is so ubiquitous right now in part because it jibes precisely with the message of consumer society, that freedom means more—hotter sex, better food, ever-multiplying pairs of Manolo Blahniks shoes, drawers full of Betsey Johnson skirts, Kate Spade bags, and MAC lipsticks."

Goldberg (2001) critically dissects the widespread appeal of a range of post-feminist writings that appeal to young women and the celebrity status afforded many of its authors in terms of the way in which they cleverly merge consumer values with atheoretical narcissistic individualism: "It's easy to swallow feminism, feminism that encourages you to pamper yourself and get rid of guilt and waltz through life. . . . Built on affirmations—'You go, girl! Work it!'—it doesn't make you feel bad about your vanity, as 70's feminism sometimes did, or hypocritical if you watch porn or wear glitter eyeshadow and miniskirts. It admits that consumer culture is often pleasurable and rewarding."

Indeed, this obsession with youth and beauty appears to be a major tenet of certain versions of "feminism" marketed and circulated today that reject so-called older feminisms. As she describes it: "by the 90s many younger women felt that the women's movement had betrayed them. Seventies feminism was perceived—however unfairly—as frowning dourly on make-up, romance, and shopping, all real pleasures in many women's lives" (Goldberg 2001). Although Naomi Wolf's informative and influential 1990 book *The Beauty Myth* (and, of course, Susan Faludi's revelatory, eminent 1991 text *Backlash*) did much to dispel these mythical depictions of feminism and "beauty," it was Wolf's reactionary 1993 *Fire with Fire*, and especially its reductionist premise of two essentialized groups of good/"power" and bad/"victim" feminists (which is discussed in detail in the next chapter) that is identified as being highly influential in the development of this "post–third wave feminism." Part of her appeal, according to Goldberg, was that the "power" feminism she advocated "embraced beauty, sex, and men, proclaiming 'male sexual attention is the sun in which I bloom'" (2001). Baumgardner and Richards, for example, identify Rebecca Walker and Naomi Wolf as two high profile representatives of third wave feminisms.[14] Indeed the deference paid to Wolf (which many feminists find shocking) raises serious questions about the ideology of some who define themselves as the new "third wave" especially in relation to their "feminist" epistemology and personal goals and objectives.

Although it appeared that the reality of an ongoing and escalating backlash against women and feminism had been widely accepted within scholarly, main-stream, and even popular cultural forms, anti- and pseudofeminists have not only embraced reactionary positions that deny the existence of any kind of backlash or, unbelievably, argue that the backlash is an invention, or the fault of a feminist conspiracy! "Dissident feminist" Cathy Moore, a journalist and author who is associated with the Women's Freedom Network and considers Hoff Sommers a role model, has focused on this notion of backlash in her antifeminist tracts, as well as attacking Pulitzer-prize winning journalist Susan Faludi and her 1991 text *Backlash*. She claims that Naomi Wolf asserted that " 'victim feminism' arose in the 1980s because feminists felt so besieged fighting 'the backlash.' "[15]

But perhaps it was the reverse: with most battles for equal opportunity won [*sic*], feminists came to be dominated by other goals and creeds. One could say that the movement had outlived itself and had to justify its existence, or that feminists were frustrated because, with the external barriers gone, women were still held back by more subtle obstacles. Or maybe feminists realized that equality wasn't what they wanted. (Moore 1999, 2)

Moore seems to be professing, in this bizarre and confusing assertion, that feminism became unnecessary because women had achieved equal rights in the United States. In order to survive they had to invent the backlash, as if the backlash was initiated by feminists to provoke problems for women. Regardless, aspects of this muddled explanation have become inscribed in much contemporary discourse about feminism and have been part up by popularized postfeminism. Catherine Orr contests this erroneous and dispiriting reading of the backlash advanced by many contemporary pseudofeminist perspectives that seem to be largely, but not exclusively, put forward by young women. Indeed, Orr goes on to argue that many of these supposed third-wave writings are fronts for more conservative antifeminist propaganda.

Convinced that feminism has become the cause of, rather than the solution to, women's problems, feminist dissenters are entangled in representations of third wave discourse. They frequently are touted and even supported by conservative constituencies and constructed as youthful rebels against "establishment feminism" in the popular media. (Orr 1997, 34)

However, rejecting "life-style feminism" and antifeminist postfeminism, other groups of younger women are continuing the tradition of critical feminism. Self-described "younger feminists" such as Leslie Heywood and Jennifer Drake condemn post- and antifeminists and "groups of young, conservative feminists who explicitly define themselves against and criticize feminists of the second wave" (1997, 1). They distinguish themselves from "postfeminists" like Katie Roiphe, Rene Denfield, and Naomi Wolf, who argued "against feminist critiques of rape [and] sexual harassment" and misrepresented themselves as spokeswomen for the "next generation," through their mutually exploitative relationship with mass media and popular culture, which transformed them into celebrity pundits (1997).

The younger generation of insurgent feminists further delineated their critical feminist epistemology, which they described as "the diverse activist work that terms itself 'third wave,'" from the more visible conservative postfeminism. Unlike the majority of what is commonly perceived as the third wave, which defines itself as "the core mass of the current women's movements in their late teens through their thirties, roughly speaking" (Baumgardner and Richards 2000, 401), the insurgent third wave did not identify themselves in accordance with age. In fact, "the 'definitional moment' of third wave feminism took place on the terrain of race in the early 1980s rather than age in the mid-1990s" (Orr 1997, 37).

But the younger oppositional and political feminists are almost invisible in the media compared to pseudofeminist and right-wing women. In fact, there is a discernable lack of critical feminist reporters and commentators in the popular media, while there seems to be a large number of right-wing women pundits in every media dimension. For as Laura Flandors reveals: "The right has some substantial help. A handful of ideologically driven funders underwriting these women's careers. Hours of research, then more of professional training have been bought and paid for on their behalf" (*In These Times*, Apr. 11, 1999).

Typically, right-wing groups who are heavily represented in the media include the Independent Women's Forum, the Women's Freedom Network, and right-wing institutes like Manhattan and American Enterprise. According to Flanders, media producers actively restrict feminists from television, using such justifications as "you're too close to the story to be a good source. Or you're too far from it" (and so on). Indeed, what has made life so much easier for backlash media producers to contract the right (wing) kind of women with the appropriate ideological beliefs and values is "the IWF directory of conservative women which was distributed free to the media" (*In These Times*, Apr. 11, 1999).

As Zillah Eisenstein notes (1996, 113ff), pop feminisms and antifeminisms simplify and caricaturize the feminist movement, depoliticize it, bury its complexities, conceal the "continuation of patriarchal structures," and veil the continuing violence against women and children. In addition, Isabelle V. Barker argues, "In its myopic and redundant insistence that women need to simply assert their sexuality and stop being victims, postfeminism callously ignores how sexualized violence has historically been deployed to reinforce social hierarchies" (2000, 647–48). Moreover, as Eisenstein puts it, conservative women who demean feminism ignore that

> Some 800 people are starving across the globe. Women and girls represent approximately 60 percent of the billion or so people earning one dollar a day or less. However, in countries labeled democratic, a new kind of excessive wealth exists in which billionaires are allowed to amass as much as they can with few limits. New levels of arrogance emerge just as the nation-state is being overshadowed by transnational corporations. (Eisenstein 1998, 1)

Indeed, it is the covering-over and denial of the prevalence of violence against women and children that is one of the most catastrophic effects of the antifeminist backlash. Thus, mass-marketed and popularized media feminism, which combines incessant attacks on so-called victim feminism with typical ideological messages and practices that "blame the victim," decontextualizes and individualizes pathological violent relations. As Eisenstein reminds us, the "absorption of mainstream," "post-" or "reformist feminism" has neutralized critical and even liberal feminisms because it depicts women as if they "were already equal and feminism was no longer needed" (1996, 113). This appropriation of what Eisenstein refers to as "mainstream equal rights feminism" and hooks calls "reformist feminism" is an apt description of many of the dominant hegemonic forms, such as popular postfeminism, that have gained such cultural prominence. hooks's description of "reformist feminism" captures the essence of much of the anti- and pseudofeminisms being investigated and critiqued throughout this text, as well as providing a revealing depiction of mass-marketed pop feminism:

> Reformist feminist issues centered on gaining social equality with privileged men within the existing social structure. These concerns neatly coincided with white supremacist capitalist patriarchal fears that white power would diminish if nonwhite people gained equal access to economic power and privilege. Supporting what in effect became white power reformist feminism enabled the mainstream white male patriarchy to bolster its power while simultaneously undermining the radical politics of feminism. (hooks 2000a, 104)

And most of the privileged women involved in media, who supposedly represent Western women, most certainly fit this norm and believe and act as if they had been afforded equal rights with professional men a long time ago. It is within this context that relations of violence against women and children become distorted. Eisenstein notes that

> depictions of women's victimization and powerlessness blanket the media. Talk shows are filled with concerns originally articulated by radical feminists: date rape, pornography, incest, sexual abuse, etc. But the media disconnects the original critique of patriarchal privilege from sexual battery. Whereas radical feminists connected the personal to the political, media depictions of sexual violence appear individualized and privatized. There is no politics to the personal because the personal is made private. "Sexual politics" and the uncovering of power-defined private moments is mass marketed. (1996, 113–14)

In fact, the discourse of "sexual violence and battery is used to catch women's attention," for commercial media have discovered "victimhood sells." And while "feminists are said to wallow in their victimhood," victim status is both attacked and exploited in that it underwrites "a huge industry." Ironically, television news, talk shows, newspapers, self-help books, videos, movies, tabloids, and MTV write their own texts with the words and images from feminist discourse, which has been completely depoliticized, especially by antifeminist and fashionable postfeminist pundits (Eisenstein 1996, 115).

Isabelle Barker discusses the manner in which contemporary postfeminists are collaborating in misleading and falsified characterizations of the concrete realities of male violence against women, propagating one-dimensionalized, stereotypical characterizations of antiviolence feminisms, as well as misappropriating much of their language and arguments to attempt to legitimate their often misogynist and antifeminist positions. In fact she identifies the legacy of 1990s antifeminists like Camille Paglia within much of their written work (Barker 2000, 646). She argues that the popularity of "the postfeminist challenge" in contemporary culture is largely due to its lack of substance and comments on the over-simplified naïveté, but seductiveness of its arguments in regards to victimization.

> In its myopic and redundant insistence that women need to simply assert their sexuality and stop being victims, postfeminism callously ignores how sexualized violence has historically been deployed to reinforce social hierarchies. The logic of postfeminism is one of simple inversion: "we are not the victims that feminists say we are," goes the message. Post-feminism tells women to stop their whining, suggesting that incidents of gendered violence are figments of feminist imagination. (Barker 2000, 647–48)

Barker goes on to identify a majority of postfeminists as primarily white, privileged women who came of age in the Reagan years, which picked up where Madonna (as the "material girl") left off. She sees this kind of "postfeminism" as primarily a creation of the mass media, which employed it as a "marketing ploy to advance the opportunistic concerns of individual women while simultaneously acting as an agent of antifeminist backlash by undermining feminism's radical/revolutionary gains" (2000, 647).

Therefore, this consumer backlash side of feminist discourse and "its commercialization operate both to publicize feminist concerns and to disconnect these issues from radical critique of male privilege" (Eisenstein 1994, 114). And it is this kind of decontextualization and apolitical individualism that "blames the victim" and ridicules and delegitimizes those who wish to recontextualize and change at least some of the violence of everyday life, which "is trafficked along lines of categories of sexual, racial, ethnic, national, and class difference" within the framework of contemporary global patriarchy. Hence the backlash, which owes much of its success to the employment of a divide-and-conquer strategy continues to flourish. However, feminists of all generations are beginning to recognize the folly of this kind of divisive tactic. As Heywood and Drake, who identified themselves as "third wave" feminists, put it: "Translation and backlash mean that we as third wavers have bought into the media demonization of 'sisterhood.' We are letting ourselves, to use Susan Douglas's word, 'catfight,' both with second wavers and across racial divides" (Heywood and Drake 1997, 49).

Camille Paglia is one of the major influences on the new pseudofeminist cadre and pop antifeminism. Accordingly, in the next chapter I provide a systematic critique of her work and other prominent 1990s feminist impersonators. My focus is on how these works decenter and attack the more critical and political versions of feminism that emerged out of the 1960s and 1970s and the ways that pseudofeminists like Paglia and Hoff Sommers deny, trivialize, or explain away violence against women and children.

NOTES

1. Two examples of contemporary media allegations concerning a postfeminist turn come immediately to mind. One is a cover story in *Time*, June 29, 1998, by Ginia Bellafante, entitled "Feminism: It's All about Me!" or "Who Put the 'Me' in Feminism," which I discuss in the text and which argues that much of contemporary feminism has "devolved" into a "postfeminist tic of offering up autobiography as theory" (58; 59). Another is the November 1999 *Vanity Fair* article, "Damsels in Distress" by Sam Tanehaus, which celebrates a "new wave" of conservative women, such as Wendy Shalit, Kanchan Limaye, Pia Nordlinger, Amity Shlaes, and Danielle Crittenden, who, he claims, are "the coming thing, heralds or sirens of a genuine conservative chic" (146). Much of the "antiestablishment" and "right-wing" "new sensibilities" of this new wave of writers, according to Tanehaus, are "unintended creations of that incubator of modern reactionism, the college campus, with its graying professoriat in thrall to New Left slogans, 'poststructuralist' curricula plying the invidious dogmas of race and gender 'difference,' and enfeebled administrators handing out condoms as a send-off to spring break" (148). And like their 1990s antifeminist predecessors, most are pictured or described as young, thin, drop-dead gorgeous, immaculately and expensively coiffed and dressed, predominantly white middle/upper class, media savvy and "sexy"—unlike their alleged (mythical) elderly, unattractive, feminist counterpart who Tanehaus describes in one of many characterizations as "stuffy and humorless" (1999, 148).

2. Lisa Palac is one of the many pseudofeminist authors who is taking advantage of the current publishing trend embracing "pro-sex" or "pro-porn" stances. In *The Edge of the Bed*, Palac "suggests that pornography can be liberating because X-rated movies were sexually freeing for her. 'Once I figured out how to look at an erotic image and use my sexual imagination to turn desire into a self-generated orgasm, my life was irrevocably and positively changed' " (Bellafante 1998, 59).

3. According to Jennifer Baumgardner and Amy Richards, "Bellafante's story [in *Time*] was pieced together from tabloids and women's magazines" and she and her editors ignored "hand delivered evidence" of "political activity relevant to the current [mainstream] feminist mandate." Richards is the cofounder of "the Third Wave Foundation, a national organization for young feminists" (Baumgardner and Richards 2000, 120–5; xxv).

4. Ferguson, Katrak, and Miner situate the particular 1980s backlash against feminisms within a specific contextual framework, noting:

> The 1980s backlash has a particular history, as do earlier ones in U.S. history. Each wave of antifeminism—1920s, 1940s, late 1970s—arises after certain gains in women's rights, and aims to erode such successes. . . . Lois W. Banner remarks how the 1920s antifeminism, though "extensive . . . rarely denied women the right to live their lives as they saw fit. But the anti-feminism of the postwar 1940s held women responsible for society's ills—either because they were failures as mothers or because they had left home for work." After the war, "Rosie the Riveter" was replaced by the homemaker as the national feminine model. Women were bombarded by jingoistic psychologists who declared with dubious "scientific" evidence that women working outside the home were playing havoc with their children's mental states. (Ferguson, Katrak, and Minor 1996, 50)

5. See below and chapter 2 for discussion of "next generation" and "new" feminism.

6. Leslie Heywood and Jennifer Drake attempt to make a clear distinction between the research and writings of young feminists (those they identify as coming of age in the late 1970s through the late 1980s) and that of women characterized in this text as antifeminists or feminist impersonators. As they put it:

Recently much media attention has been given to writings about third wave feminism, often labeled "postfeminism." In the perpetual battle of representation and definitional clout, the slippage from "third wave feminism" to "postfeminist" is important, because many of us working in the "third wave" by no means define our feminism as a groovier alternative to an over-and-done feminist movement. Let us be clear "postfeminist" characterizes a group of young, conservative feminists who explicitly define themselves against and criticize feminists of the second wave. . . . Not surprisingly, it is these conservative feminists who are regularly called upon as spokespersons for the "next generation." Writers such as Katie Roiphe, Rene Denfield, and Naomi Wolf argue against feminist critiques of rape, sexual harassment, and abortion. They publish books, appear on op-ed pages, and write for popular young women's magazines such as *Glamour* and *YM*. Conservative postfeminism is in every way more visible than is the diverse activist work that terms itself "third wave." (1997, 1)

7. As Ann Brooks explains it,

Postfeminism, as an expression of a stage in the constant evolutionary movement of feminism, has gained greater currency in recent years. Once seen, somewhat crudely, as "anti-feminist," the term is now understood as a useful conceptual frame of reference encompassing the intersection of feminism with a number of other anti-foundationalist movements including postmodernism, poststructuralism and postcolonialism. Postfeminism represents, as Yeatman (1994) claims, feminism's "coming of age," its maturity into a confident body of theory and politics, representing pluralism and difference and reflecting on its position in relation to other philosophical and political movements similarly demanding change. (Brooks 1997, 1)

8. As Kate Clinton describes it: "The D.C. Bush women are all playing their surrendered-wife roles very well. New Jersey's former racial profiler Christine Todd Whitman was forced to eat her pro-environment words and swallow her water with acceptable arsenic levels. Condolleeza Rice's solution to global warming is cold war, and so she defers to the Secretary of Defense." Clinton compares the current twenty-first-century mode of conservative behavior with Ira Levin's 1975 classic *The Stepford Wives*, where powerful men replaced their wives with "domestic sex robots" (*The Progressive*, May 2001; www.progressive.org). Clinton's insightful revelation of the overlapping and shockingly similar scenarios of these "horror" books is an apt description of escalating antifeminism and conservative backlash politics and attitudes.

9. As hooks explains it: "I liked this definition [of feminism] because it did not imply that men were the enemy. By naming sexism as the problem it went directly to the heart of the matter. Practically, it is a definition which implies that all sexist thinking and action is the problem, whether those who perpetuate it are female or male, child or adult. It is also broad enough to include an understanding of systemic institutionalized sexism. As a definition it is open-ended" (2000b, 1). Needless to say, an appropriate definition of femi-

nism necessarily involves the intertextuality of feminisms in relations to "gender" (tied in with sexual orientation), "class" (tied in with nationality and ethnicity), and "race" (tied in with nationality, ethnicity, and religion) (Segal 1999, 34).

10. Hoff Sommers was the leader of the Women's Freedom Network (WFN) when it was first organized. A statement from their newsletter captures the essence of this organization. "According to the *WFN Newsletter* (fall 1994), at the WFN's first national conference, entitled 'Taking Back Feminism,' the conference was distinguished by the diversity of the participants who were united by their independently achieved conclusions that: intelligent life can not [sic] continue under the presumption that all men are beasts and all women helpless victims, and journalists seeking commentary on gender issues require a third alternative to the radical feminist PC Left and the far-out Phyllis Schlafly Right" (Siegel 1997a, nn. 20, 80).

Rita Simon, the president of WFN in 1996, describes the philosophy and goals of this conservative-front group, which "purports to offer a moderate, alternative feminism": "What distinguishes WFN philosophically from mainstream feminist groups is a highly individualistic approach to equality, which disavows affirmative action" and opposes most legislation associated with women's civil rights. It is hardly surprising that at a 1994 conference sponsored by the Women's Freedom Network, the "superiority of free markets" and the celebration of entrepreneurship was advanced. Like the IWM, the WFN is an organization composed of, and which appeals predominantly to, white, upper-middle class, female professionals, including on its board of directors in 1996 "Harvard law professor Mary Ann Glendon, political scientist Jean Bethke Elshtain, and former U.S. Ambassador to the United Nations Jeanne Kirkpatrick" (cited in Wendy Kaminer, *The American Prospect*, Nov.–Dec., 1996).

11. Richard Cohen notes: "Bush is the near-perfect personification of the conservative tendency to make facts the servant of ideology—bend them, change them, invent them, but by all means make them politically acceptable" (*The Washington Post, Online*, May 3, 2001). In the same article, Cohen cites an example of this in regard to George W. Bush's obsession with a missile defense program in 2001: "This is not necessarily a bad idea—but it is certainly one whose time has not come. The technology for the system simply does not exist. But . . . Bush not only talked as if it did, he justified the system's rapid implementation by earlier reinstating North Korea as just the sort of totally nuts country that missile defense is aimed at deterring. Bush not only created a system, he created a need for it." For a systematic critique of Bushspeak, see Kellner 2001.

12. It was interesting when Hoff Sommers was asked on a Fox network television talk show whether she supported the Violence Against Women Act: rather than stating that she and her associates were opposed, she instead relied on typical double-talk. As she put it: "I would support it if it were improved" (May 22, 2001). And although much of its funding is used for women's shelters, Hoff Sommers went on to assert that although she supports the act, she is opposed to funding "feminist centers" and "women's studies." The IWF vehemence toward funding for women's shelters is offensive because they fail "to offer an alterative solution, specializing more in denouncing feminist ideas than presenting any of its own" (Jennifer Coburn, *The San Diego Union-Tribune*, Aug. 24, 1997). Given that there were only "approximately 1900 domestic violence shelter programs in the United States" in 1999, their views on this matter appear not only draconian but heartless (see National Resource Center Domestic Violence, 1999, in the National Center for Victims of Crime, www.ncvc.prg/).

13. Leora Tanenbaum notes that Ellen Willis, who was involved with one of the earliest radical feminist movements of the second wave, has been "unraveling the complicated causes of feminist intolerance since the second wave of feminism began" (1994, 38). Moreover, critical feminists, especially feminists of color such as Patricia Hill Collins (1998, 142–43), Gloria Anzaldua (in Keating 2000, 256), bell hooks (1994b, 61–68), and others have been involved in fascinating and highly complicated debates and critiques concerning elitism, exclusionary language, and colonialism within feminist scholarship and academic discourse.

14. Jennifer Baumgardner and Amy Richards, co-authors of *Manifesta: Young Women, Feminism, and the Future,* and associates of the Third Wave Foundation describe Wolf as "one of the first itinerant feminists of the Third Wave, Wolf traveled to college campuses across the United States, talking to young women." They go on to completely misrepresent and oversimplify her positions on contemporary feminism and themes of *Fire with Fire* and *Promiscuities* in a typical pop media style spin. "This touring led her to conclude that 'girls are still understood more clearly as victims of culture and desexuality than as cultural and sexual creators,' so she set out to change that assumption. Her next book, *Fire with Fire: The New Female Power and How It Will Change the 21st Century,* told women to embrace power, and *Promiscuities* recast the slut as rebel" (2000, 133). Although Wolf's *Fire with Fire* was criticized extensively by young feminists (many of whom were those who identified themselves as [insurgent] third wave feminists, cited in this text) Baumgardner and Richards scapegoat jealous "senior" feminists for taking (more than justifiable) exception to her text and her feminist celebrity status. Their distortion of Wolf's later positions is indeed indicative of how this mainstream third wave is provoking a mythical and counterproductive division in feminisms.

> Naomi Wolf was the good daughter, reaping accolades and the crown of Ms. Young Feminist in 1991, when her book *The Beauty Myth* critiqued the patriarchy's pressure on women to be beautiful. When she switched gears to challenging the old strategies of the movement and present a pragmatic "power feminism," she was quickly demoted. (Baumgardner and Richards 2000, 224)

See further discussion of Wolf in chapter 2.

15. Moore's interpretation of Naomi Wolf's alleged explanation of "victim feminism" as a response to the backlash is questionable given the manner in which Wolf discussed the backlash in *Fire with Fire*. Contrary to Moore's assertion, Wolf describes the backlash as an impediment to many women that has caused some to back "away from political power" (Wolf 1993, 259). Wolf comments that in response to the backlash, rather than developing or becoming actively involved in "victim feminism," some women have "lost the psychic energy to stand up in defense of their gains." Given that Moore is such a stickler for accurate "facts" and documentation, it is surprising that she fails to provide a reference to the statement she attributes to Wolf.

2

Culture Wars over Feminism:
Paglia, Wolf, and Hoff Sommers

The marketability of feminist-bashing "feminists" owes much to Camille Paglia. As bell hooks notes:

> Without Paglia as trailblazer and symbolic mentor, there would be no cultural lime-light for white girls such as Katie Roiphe and Naomi Wolf. And no matter how hard they work to put that Oedipal distance between their writing and hers, they are sing-ing the same tune on way too many things. And (dare I say it?) that tune always seems to be a jazzed-up version of "The Way We Were"—you know, the good old days before feminism and multiculturalism and the unbiased curriculum fucked everything up. (hooks 1994a, 86)

hooks's indication that the majority of these media stars are white reminds us that they also attempt to appeal to the media mandate that successful female entertainment personalities be "hot babes" who give great "sound bite." Indeed, Paglia does not hesitate to take credit for assisting in the development of "the reform movement in feminism," citing "Katie Roiphe's book *The Morning After* and Christina Hoff Sommers's *Who Stole Feminism?* as evidence that other people have taken up her call to *restore the original boldness and daring of the movement*" (*Toronto Star*, Nov. 8, 1994, B6; emphasis mine. See also Paglia 1994, xvi). Hence, I begin my critique with a dissection of the personae and presence of Camille Paglia before turning to in-depth examination of the views of a variety of other women writers who regularly attack her.

Indeed, the underlying stance of Paglia's "amazonian" feminism is highly ques-tionable, especially when presented within the context of critical feminist responses to her contentions and arguments. These kind of textual analyses and ideology critiques reveal a wide assortment of feminist interrogation and analysis of her work and its significance. However, such critiques are rarely acknowledged by Paglia or presented in media, culture or popular feminisms' assessment of her work. Moreover, Paglia's actual words are often reduced to abridgement and sound bites, especially in reviews of her work, which decontextualizes and often neutralizes the essence of her texts and contentions. Hence, I feel it is especially appropriate to incorporate Paglia's voice, which is quite unique in places, and the voices of those who appraise her writings in this section. It is in this light that the essense of her ideas and contributions to feminism can be addressed.

CAMILLE PAGLIA AND THE
NEW ANTIFEMINISM

Although Paglia often characterizes herself as one of the common folk, her background, education, and consequent writings are expressive of a highly privileged and elite milieu. Ironically, one of Paglia's favorite and frequently employed affronts of her feminist enemies, which denigrates them for being "white, middle class," is more than an apt description of herself. The oldest daughter of an Italian-born mother, who worked in a bank, and a first-generation American-Italian father, who was a professor of romance languages, Paglia attended the Harpur College, of the State University of New York, Binghamton. She was valedictorian and then did graduate work at Yale before going on to teach at Bennington, from where, she was dismissed for fighting with a student at a dance and other "scrapes and scandals" (Showalter 2001, 313; Findley 2000).

For years, Paglia taught humanities at the Philadelphia University of the Arts and likes to dramatize her academic woes and neglect (see 1992, 255ff.). With the 1991 publication of *Sexual Personae*, she was catapulted into media fame. Quickly taking advantage of the situation, Paglia churned out two volumes of popular essays, interviews, and other materials that publicized her views—*Sex, Art, and American Culture: Essays* (1992) and *Vamps and Tramps: New Essays* (1994). She became, as a result, a well-known media celebrity. Ginia Bellafante's 1998 *Time* magazine article on the purported death of feminism (previously referred to) identifies the alleged postfeminist shift from "intellectual undertakings" to "narcissistic ramblings" as "the Camille Paglia syndrome" (57, 58). According to Bellafante, Paglia's "landmark 1990 book *Sexual Personae* . . . helped catapult feminism beyond an ideology of victimhood" (58). And she goes on to report that writers like Katie Roiphe "launched careers by merely plucking from and personalizing Paglia's headline-making ideas" (59). While denigrating a number of these "Duh Feminists," who Bellafante blames for (yet, again!) the "death of feminism," she celebrates Paglia and her work as significant feminist icons.

However, it is highly unlikely that Bellafante has actually read Paglia's *Sexual Personae: Art and Decadence from Nefertiti to Emily Dickinson*, given her inaccurate depiction of the text. Indeed, bell hooks endowed the book with her personal annual award of "The Most Bought Least Read Books" (1994a, 83). As she describes it:

> An editor and reader of my work laments that not enough folks read me [or] know who I am. But she confesses, "It has to do, in part with the academic way you write! Why, if you let yourself go, you could be the black Camille Paglia!" This statement kept me laughing throughout the day. Though full of sass and wit, Paglia's *Sexual Personae* is tediously academic. (And no doubt as unread by mainstream reader[s] as most other English department literary criticism.) (1994a, 83)

Yet Paglia's credibility and prominence as a leading feminist critic and popular culture expert and the power she is afforded by the media is largely based on the supposed academic merits and on misconceptions of her first published book, *Sexual Personae*, a revised version of her Yale Ph.D. thesis. It is ironic that in actuality her magnum opus addresses neither popular culture nor feminism in any substantive manner. Yet these are the very topics on which Paglia pontificates in her numerous press releases, popular columns, published essays, interviews, and periodic news and magazine articles. And although neither her academic background nor her scholarly publications demonstrate any expertise in feminism, she has been misrepresented by herself and the media as an intellectual and scholarly expert in this arena. As I shall show, most of the reviews and analyses of *Sexual Personae* in popular media misrepresent the text as a significant contribution to contemporary feminism, when in fact it has little to do with feminist theory at all.

To understand how the media endowed Paglia with tremendous adulation and access on the basis of a largely unread academic book requires a brief description of Paglia's own sexual personae, much of which is revealed within *Sexual Personae* and her later published writings and interviews. Paglia cites an interview with a Canadian television program as evidence of her success in the development of her personae as a legitimate academic scholar, and hence expert, based upon the alleged intellectual significance of her "launching pad" *Sexual Personae*.

> She's been called "Hurricane Camille" and the "Joan Rivers of Academe." But make no mistake about it: it's her ideas, not her delivery, which have made her the hottest critic around, whether she's writing in *The New York Times* or in *Penthouse* magazine. She has provocative ideas on just about everything—from feminism to rock and roll and from Madonna to political correctness, and those ideas come at you like fire from a machine gun. Her book, *Sexual Personae*, took her twenty years to publish, and it's really become a launching pad for her, from where she now sits and takes critical aim at life. (Peter Downie, in Paglia 1994, 410)

It is due in large part to her style and a few outrageous "ideas" that Paglia owes her original celebrity status. Interestingly, she has constructed a presentational personae that closely parallels her discursive one. Paglia uses the dichotomies between her small stature and professional and tasteful attire (when not in costume, for media public relations) with her mode of verbal discourse to great advantage. Posing as the middle-aged, gray-haired professor, she contravenes that stereotype by speaking very loudly and quickly, in a fashion she has appropriated from Joan Rivers, Lenny Bruce, and drag queens. Indeed, her act is very astutely and self-consciously designed to take particular advantage of the contrast between her sexual personae and that of the stereotyped academic, which provides for a humorous and sometimes charming demeanor.

Moreover, her skilled employment of colloquial rhetoric, including "okay, all right?," "give me a break," or "pleeease," and constant interrupting style provide the audience with a false sense that she is "just one of the common folk." As she herself notes, "My characteristic American litany . . . of 'Okay, all right?,' . . . I tend to insert, in a rhythm borrowed from Lenny Bruce, when I have goaded the audience into a response" (Paglia 1992, 307).

This carefully orchestrated public sexual personae depends on the false depiction of Paglia as some kind of revolutionary or intellectual rebel. However, this is a thinly veiled sham invented to distract the reader or audience from fully comprehending her conservative and often reactionary agenda and attitudes. bell hooks captures this deceptive but effective technique, explaining, "Mass audiences fascinated with Paglia mainly heard sensational sound bites that often appear radical and transgressive for the status quo, or clever negative put-downs of feminism, so it may not be apparent to these groups that many of her agendas are utterly conservative" (1994a, 89). And hooks goes on to reveal that "Paglia's conservative sense of gender is coupled with an equally conservative take on race and issues of multiculturalism" (1994a, 89).

As mentioned previously, much of Paglia's carefully contrived public sexual personae she owes to early Joan Rivers, who at times she seems to be impersonating. As she describes it in her 1991 MIT lecture:

> Now, I really hit the wall of academe, boy, because no one could take me seriously. First of all, a fast-talking woman? Joan Rivers made my life a lot easier, when she appeared on the scene. Now when I talk, people go, "Oh, Joan Rivers." Before, they went, "Whoah—*freak!*" And, you see, people would discriminate against me because they thought, "Well, a fast-talking, little woman. She can't be serious." Because, you know, to be a deep thinker you have to be *slow*. So you'd notice this—like men at Yale were slow. You'd ask them a question and—[*long pause, staring*]. I could write a chapter in the time it takes them to answer a question. (Paglia 1992, 271)

However, it is the role of a particular stereotype of a gay man to which Paglia attributes the development of her iconic and discursive sexual personae that is integral to one of the major theses of *Sexual Personae* and her philosophy of life. Regarding her sexual personae, Paglia explains, "If you close your eyes while I'm on stage you may think I am a gay man. I have copied their manners, I do not move like a woman" (Paglia, in Iley 1994, D5).[1] Although Paglia describes herself conversely as bisexual or lesbian, she in fact thinks of herself as, and attributes much of her greatness to, this idealized gay man. As she puts it, "I seem to have the soul of a gay man" (Paglia 1994, 212). But her preferences appear to lie in a more stereotyped notion of homosexuality that crosses over into the arena in which she is particularly enamored. "My model of dualism is the drag queen, who negotiates between sexual personae, day by day. I sometimes call my system 'drag queen feminism' " (1994, 93).

As to her paradoxical perspectives on her own sexuality, she confesses, "I have lived most of my life as an open lesbian. I don't get involved with men, but I enjoy men's bodies. The erect penis is the ultimate symbol of sexual desire—there is no female equivalent, nothing that shows that complete excitation. If you live your life as a lesbian and don't react erotically to the penis you are closed down. And I have always said that I couldn't really be involved with a woman that couldn't understand this" (Paglia, in Iley 1994, D5).[2]

Not only does Paglia demean lesbian sex, she claims that the lesbian experience has not made any major cultural contributions: "[M]y experience of the lesbian world is not pleasant. . . . All this great talk about how wonderful and liberating lesbianism is, I am saying it is a disaster. No great art, great thought, great book has come of it in the last 20 years" (Paglia, in Iley 1994, D5). And it is this strange notion of coupling sexuality and male gay artistic superiority and female inferiority that underlies much of her philosophy of art and literature. Indeed, Teresa Ebert has identified this bizarre theory as central to the thesis of *Sexual Personae*:

> In order to create art or social order, the procreative (female) nature/body must be violently suppressed and abandoned. Thus she sees male homosexuality, as she argues in *Sexual Personae*, as "the most valorous of attempts to evade the femme fatale and to defeat nature" and create culture. For women to create, on the other hand, she must engage, accordingly to Paglia's reading of Emily Dickinson in *Sexual Personae*, in "self-hermaphrodization . . . an emptying out of female internality" and in "masculinizing her(self) into abstraction" (641)—which Paglia valorizes as a sadomasochistic undertaking in Dickinson. (Ebert 1996, 262)

Hence, Paglia and her writings cannot be ignored, as many feminists have done, since she has become an influential role model for a wide range of women and a media spokesperson for a virulent antifeminism. This seems to be the case, even though the first volume of *Sexual Personae* is an exercise in academic literary history that "examines antiquity, the Renaissance, and Romanticism from the late eighteenth century to 1900" through a study of particular genres or examples of art and literature (Paglia 1991, xiii). She primarily deploys a humanities perspective of art and literary criticism and, except for the first chapter (which replaced her longer "cancelled preface," later published in Paglia 1992, 101ff.), she does not address issues of contemporary feminism and has little on contemporary culture. A clear description of the text's central thesis is difficult to discover. This is in large part due to the nature and style of Paglia's discourse. Indeed, for Paglia, " 'Style' is an aspect of identification. For me, style *is* persona" (Paglia 1992, 115).

> My primary technique for revivifying interpretation is the metaphor. Bloom says the meaning of a poem can only be another poem. My practice is to meet metaphor with metaphor, fire lighting fire to rekindle an art work smothered by overfamiliarity and received opinion. . . . The metaphors of *Sexual Personae* mesh Freudian theory with the art work by providing a mediating link, a Janus-face looking two ways. The metaphors are notes toward a new art criticism, projecting tiny unsuspected movements into the still space between the lines of a text or between artist and work. The metaphors are subordinate dramas catching the artist midthought. My method is microscopic, showing an apparently smooth surface to be pitted by psychic abrasion, scourings of love and war. (Paglia 1992, 117–18)

This "metaphorical" method, especially in regard to her employment of analogies, may read expressively but poses serious problems for real understanding of her theoretical formulations, as well as grasping the context which is necessary to an understanding of her arguments and historical discussions. Indeed, her mode of discourse appears to be one in which form constrains or obscures clear argumentation and conceptual clarity. Her flamboyant style is arguably more appropriate within the dimensions of fictional writing, or her Internet columns in *Salon*, but becomes problematic when one is attempting to describe actual concrete human relations, historical fact, and scientific assumptions in a scholarly manner. Moreover, her employment of extravagantly rhetorical and metaphorical prose and discourse often seem intended to provide confirmation of her personae of intellectual and scholar. Her bombast, however, seems to have bamboozled some critics who should know better, as well as an unsuspecting public and media who do not share Paglia's elite educational and cultural background. Her avarice for academic success and celebratory status seems to underlie much of her misguided metaphorical machinations.

> Metaphor operates by simple analogy: this is that. My analogies may seem far-fetched. They have indeed been fetched from a far, a Magian gift-bearing by a scholar with stars in her eyes. My fetching—or schlepping, as I like to call it—is meant to demonstrate likeness, unity, and coherence where there was division, disorder, or irrelevance. I subscribe to a Renaissance cosmology, a divine network of correspondences, where everything is in analogy to everything else. (Paglia 1992, 118)

Her adaptation of this persona of rhetorical discourse and style may help explain many of the celebratory reviews of her text as well as the incomprehensibility of the text to so many of her readers. As she admits: "My metaphors are surreal visualizations or literalized cliches, concrete raids on the abstract. Cliche's are for me a comic folk poetry" (Paglia 1992, 118). Furthermore, "Throughout the book, anecdote, digression, and metaphor are used as bizarre juxtaposition or apposition, the surreal collage of dreamwork" (Paglia 1992, 119).

Many of the reviews of her text reveal that it is precisely her style (or personae) rather than content to which the critics are responding.[3] Teresa Ebert astutely classifies Paglia's style or personae as a mode of intentional farce combined with outrageous sensationalism.

> Farce is also its own mode of validation: it is a performative speech act that puts these scandalous proclamations beyond critique-al scrutiny. How can we take seriously a history based on ejaculation and the biology of urination? We do not need to. The logic of the outrageous works by preventing serious attention, by displacing critique. It works by titillating, eroticizing, and enthralling; it is a pornographic logic of simulated experience. Just as the excitement of an erotic image compels the viewer to suspend critical judgment so as not to interfere with the pleasure of the experience, so the pleasure of Paglia's texts reproduced the pornographic elation in the degradation of women through a sensational and imagistic prose. (Ebert 1996, 262)

Hence, the thesis of *Sexual Personae* must be somehow extracted from this farcical, metaphoric pastiche of sensationalist discourse. We must therefore go beyond Paglia's rhetorical facade to explicate the underlying themes and assumptions of her text. She claims to combine disciplines such as literature, art history, psychology, biology, and religion (1991, xiii), as well as astrology (1992, 254). Her book examines particular forms and genres of art and predominantly canonical literary figures like Spencer, Shakespeare, Blake, and other major writers. Indeed, in her original preface to the book, Paglia makes abundantly clear that "*Sexual Personae* accepts and reinterprets the canonical Western tradition. *It does not construct a feminist countertradition*—except with Sade and popular culture, which it pulls into the Western main line" (Paglia 1992, 123; emphasis mine). And except for a very few instances (such as a very brief reference to similarities between Elvis Presley and the English Romantic poet Lord Byron), Paglia's analysis of popular culture is reserved for the yet unpublished second volume of *Sexual Personae*. Even though "the second volume of *Sexual Personae* on modern popular culture, was completed in 1981 [it] is currently being revised to incorporate the thousands of note cards that have accumulated over the intervening decade and a half. That volume, like the first, will be released in hardcover by Yale University Press" (1994, xiv). As of fall 2001, it remains unpublished.

As Paglia explains it, "The second volume will show how movies, television, sports, and rock music embody all the pagan themes of classical antiquity" (1991, xiii). In fact, Paglia's project in *Sexual Personae* and her later collected essays is to ferret out "pagan" themes in Western culture from the Greeks to Madonna. Paganism, she claims, was never defeated by Christianity or Western civilization,

50   *Chapter 2*

but continues to nourish its culture to this day. It is within this context that Paglia
will come to attack contemporary feminism as a mode of puritanism that tries to
suppress pagan vitalism, and it is arguably these assaults against feminism that
are behind the media attention bestowed upon her.

Teresa Ebert points out that Paglia's attacks on feminism as puritanical and
repressive and her offensive conjectures about rape are the basis of "her more
popular texts and public behavior" (1996, 263). Sensation-mongering and playing
to crude media prejudice is a conscious strategy of Paglia, a "method" she
describes in the preface to *Sexual Personae* as "a form of sensationalism" (1991,
xiii). In fact, it was a December 1990 *New York Times* editorial on Madonna and
a January 1991 *Newsday* article on date rape that gained sustained media attention for her flamboyant and sensationalistic posturing as daring and outspoken
(collected in Paglia 1992, 303).

Hence, while mainstream media characterize Paglia as a feminist, in fact, *Sexual Personae* is an antifeminist and blatantly misogynist text. Indeed, Paglia herself admits in her later published original preface to *Sexual Personae* (1992) that
the domination of Western art and philosophy by men is in large part due to
ontological limitations of women:

> One of the themes of this book, unpalatable to liberal well-wishers, is woman's limi-
> tation by the body. It might seem that a battle-scarred veteran of the sex wars, born
> with a personality so ill-suited to the prescribed sex role, would have the most
> grounds for complaint against society. But the opposite is true: my noisy resistance
> to primary socialization brought me full circle back to biology. . . . The traditional
> association of assertion and action with masculinity and receptivity and passivity with
> femininity seems to me scientifically justified. . . . Biologically, the male is impelled
> toward restless movement; his moral danger is brutishness. Biologically, the female
> is impelled toward waiting, *expectancy*; her moral danger is stasis. . . . Sexual geogra-
> phy, our body image, alters our perception of the world. Man is contoured for inva-
> sion, while woman remains *the hidden*, a cave of archaic darkness. No legislation or
> grievance committee can change these eternal facts. (1992, 107–8)

Hardly a testament to women's "sexuality as humanity's greatest source," Paglia's misogyny belies her later claims of feminist status: "But women's maternal
fate, from which I made an Amazonian swerve has a darker side. From puberty
to menopause, women are hormonally mired in the liquid realm to which this
book gives the peculiar name the 'chthonian swamp,' my symbol for unregenerate
nature. Pregnant or premenstrual, the female body is slowed or even immobilized
by endemic engorgement, a Dionysian dowry" (1992, 109). And it is this biological imperative, according to Paglia, that impedes most women's cultural creativity; except, one assumes, for exceptions like Paglia herself, who has managed to
transcend this female fate and overcome her chthonian nature. As Ellen Willis
so astutely describes Paglia's peculiar form of pseudofeminism:

This is what Paglia's feminism comes down to: there are, or ought to be, two kinds of women. While most of us float tranquilized in the chthonian estrogen swamp, reveling in motherhood, "the primal source of life" with its "dark, ambiguous dualities," a liberated happy few will stand as shining moral examples to those who aspire to different paths. (Willis 1993b, 254)

Paglia herself admits, "Thus, despite my deviant and rebellious beginnings, I have been led by my studies to reaffirm the most archaic myths about male and female. I aim to recover the truth in sexual stereotypes" (1992, 108–9). And indeed she goes on to apply and legitimate these "archaic myths" about the nature of, and differences between, the sexes, which leads to another of her central theses and "landmark" conclusions:

Equality of opportunity, a crucial political ideal that all must support, should not be confused with sexual similitude, which remains a wishful fiction. Some past tests [sic] (never entirely reliable) suggested that female intelligence occupies the broad spectrum and that women do not reach the heights and depths of men, who may be genius or moron. This rings true to me. I do not believe that the historical absence of great women composers, mathematicians, and philosophers is entirely due to social factors, that is, to woman's lack of access to education and mentoring. Note, for example, in this liberated age, the rarity of world-class female chess masters. Chess shops and parks all over the world are filled with men, not women. Obsessed computer hackers are mostly male. Even sex crimes and mass murders demonstrate the greater conceptualism of men, who have a monopoly on fetishism and perversion. (1992, 109)

Paglia frequently employs these kinds of sensational and titillating analogies, without sources or grounding, as an excuse to confirm one of the multifarious imaginary oppositions and alleged binary forces that underscore her overall perspective. In this case, the preponderance of male serial or mass murderers is evidence of male intellectual superiority, for within Paglia's fractured, bifurcated worldview, such acts are the flip side of artistic genius. As she explains it:

Serial or sex murder, like fetishism, is a perversion of male intelligence. It is a criminal abstraction, masculine in its deranged egotism and orderliness. It is the asocial equivalent of philosophy, mathematics, and music. (1991, 247)

Paglia constantly tosses out such gross generalizations without supporting evidence or argumentation. Yet perhaps part of the reason for her popularity with the mainstream media—despite the long and often arduous, difficult, and demanding nature of *Sexual Personae*—is that it "makes good copy because it brims with caustic one-liners" (*People*, Apr. 20, 1992, 126). However, it is hardly necessary to actually read the text to retrieve these "caustic one-liners," because they are incessantly reiterated by Paglia in her interviews, press releases, and more popular writings as well as continually repeated within the myriad media reports that have provoked her celebrity status. And this is most certainly the case with her bon mot: "There is no female Mozart because there is no female Jack the Ripper" (Paglia 1991, 247). The influence of such statements on a host of reviewers has been especially effective. The pleasure afforded many of Paglia's fans by her sometimes outrageous and "pornographic logic" and style translates into the kinds of uncritical and celebratory analyses and evaluations of her work that have contributed much to her fame and fortune.

Teresa Ebert (1996, 263) cites Duncan Fallowell's July 1990 *Spectator* review of *Sexual Personae* as a "dramatic demonstration" of one such commentary that is especially revealing in that it epitomizes Paglia's ability to obscure substance with form. After conceding that he is "unable to critically evaluate, or even, as he admits, review the book; he can 'only attempt to digest it,' " Fallowell concludes his commentary with "a litany of sensuous descriptions of Paglia." As Ebert describes it:

> Each of these is followed by a quote from one of her "magnificent extemporisations." Thus he says, "She can be breathtaking: 'There is no female Mozart because there is no female Jack the Ripper.' " He consumes (and in turn reproduces) such statements without any critical or moral awareness; he simply relishes and savors the titillating pleasure of her sensational claims for male superiority and articulations for female debasement and degradation. (1996, 263)

Indeed, this revitalization of traditional sexual stereotypes both frames and punctuates Paglia's more widely publicized thesis regarding the combination of male and female sexuality that characterizes the great art, aesthetics, philosophy, music, and literature of Western society. Such stereotypes are backed up by unsubstantiated sociobiological explications and vulgar, overgeneralized (and often inaccurate) Freudianism.[4] Paglia constantly reduces the multileveled complexities of human culture and communication largely to the physical dimension of anatomical rationalization and distinction. In fact, her extended deliberations on the role of what she identifies as the "Dionysian," which she associates with femaleness and nature, are conflated with a biological essentialism concerning women's intellectual and artistic inabilities and limitations.

Paglia uses Nietzsche's distinctions between the Dionysian and Apollonian as her fundamental concepts for interpreting Western culture, without, however, properly attributing the distinction to Nietzsche or adequately clarifying the concepts herself.[5] In fact, Paglia is relentlessly dualistic, operating with dichotomies between nature and culture, the material and the ideal, female and male, and the rational, or Apollonian, and irrational, or Dionysian. She constantly elevates one set of her dichotomies against the other, valorizing, for instance, the masculine over the feminine. Or, she posits one side of her dichotomies, such as nature, as the ground of culture and art. Not only does she indulge in an outmoded metaphysical dualism, but she practices a relentless and monistic essentialism. Without qualification or evidence, she makes such dogmatic statements as "what is female comes from nature and not nurture" (Paglia 1992, 107), or "feminists, seeking to drive power relations out of sex, have set themselves against nature" (1991, 2). Essentializing the "masculine" and "feminine" (1992, 108), she cavalierly dismisses volumes of texts substantiating the social construction of gender.

Although she presents herself as "pagan" and "preEnlightenment" (1992, 118, passim), Paglia's grand (modern) theme is that of "the unity and continuity of western culture" (1991, xiii), thus occluding difference, heterogeneity, and breaks and ruptures within culture. Admitting to an "exceptional men" theory of history, the "greatness" in Paglia's (largely male) pantheon derives from genetic inheritance (1992, 102–3). Deploying an essentialist and biologistic theory of "hormones" and genetic determinism, the Marquis de Sade and the sadomasochistic, "Dionysian" or "chthonian" characteristics of "Sadean nature," appear as "the dark hero" of her book (Paglia 1992, 105). For Paglia:

> Lust and aggression are fused in male hormones. . . . The more testosterone, the more elevated the libido. The more dominant the male, the more frequent his contributions to the genetic pool. Even on the microscopic level, male fertility is a function not only of sperm but of their mobility, that is, their restless movement, which increases the chance of conception. Sperm are miniature assault troops, and the ovum is a solitary citadel that must be breached. . . . Nature rewards energy and aggression. . . . *Feminism, arguing from the milder woman's view, completely misses the blood-lust in rape, the joy of violation and destruction.* An aesthetics and erotics of profanation—evil for the sake of evil, the sharpening of senses by cruelty and torture—have been documented in Sade, Baudelaire, and Huysman. *Women may be less prone to such fantasies because they physically lack the equipment for sexual violence. They do not know the temptation of forcibly invading the sanctuary of another body.* (Paglia 1991, 24; emphasis mine)

But Paglia apparently does understand this "blood-lust," in that—as she redundantly reminds us—her special abilities are due to her "hormonal imbalance" and the preponderance of "testosterone" in her system (1994, 247). Or, as she put it in her 1994 television interview with Bob Costa, "my level of hormonal energy is male" (although she fails to back up any of these statements with any kind of empirical documentation). She also attributes her cognizance of male lust and aggression to her "male brain" (1994, 254), which, I assume, is somehow related to her allegedly high testosterone count, although Paglia has repeatedly failed to discuss the scientific sources of this relationship. The male *mind*, or *brain* (Paglia uses the terms interchangeably), she asserts, is "different" (from the female brain) and has "greater capacity for genius and deviation" (Bob Costa interview, 1994). Once again, however, she provides no documentation, references, or any findings from scientific or psychological studies to substantiate this claim.

Thus, ultimately, Paglia's work is a largely autobiographical testament to her

genius and testosterone, while her (successful) project was to gain public attention and become famous. She constantly attacks both academics and feminists,
as if she were the only contemporary writer to affirm popular culture, sexual liberation, and iconoclastic attitudes. Combining 1960s cultural libertarianism with
1970s "equal opportunities" (liberal) feminism, Pagalia's politics is a pragmatic
stew of conflicting motifs, while her theory is riddled with dualism, essentialism,
and unsubstantiated dogmatic assertions. Her success, I believe, is a result of her
own media manipulation in conjunction with a wide array of antifeminist positions that the media deploy to attack feminism.

And so we can next turn to Naomi Wolf, Camille Paglia's nemesis and another
media star who has successfully exploited both feminism and antifeminism in her
quest for fame and celebrity.

NAOMI WOLF'S "POWER FEMINISM"

Although Naomi Wolf wrote a popular, liberal feminist book entitled *The Beauty
Myth* in 1991, her second text, *Fire with Fire: The New Female Power and How
It Will Change the 21st Century* (1993), is an apt example of the co-opted perspective of collaborationist attacks on contemporary feminism. Wolf's third book,
Promiscuities: The Secret Struggle toward Womanhood (1997), although less incendiary toward feminism than *Fire with Fire*, expands upon many of the same
themes. Moreover, she manages to exploit the confessional narrative, narcissistic
form that became popular within the late 1990s as well as contemporary popular
culture, and is now often misrepresented as "new feminism" writing. In the past
years, she has been involved with the Woodhull Institute, a retreat in upstate New
York dedicated to training young women to succeed in corporate America.

On the whole, Wolf appears to have been granted a partial immunity from
critique by mainstream feminist critics of betrayal feminism like Susan Faludi, for
example, who excludes Wolf from reports of pod abuse. Following in the footsteps of Camille Paglia (who publicly trashes Wolf, probably due to competition
for the media spotlight),[6] Wolf has become, according to *Newsweek*, "one of the
best known feminists in the country" (Stark 1994, 139). And although, she
received good press and a positive reception from feminists after the publication
of her first book, *The Beauty Myth*, her subsequent text, *Fire with Fire*, contains
a wide range of attacks on contemporary and academic feminism that has helped
position her as an "feminist" expert of choice. Indeed, Wolf herself has become,
like Paglia, a major media celebrity, as well as an advisor to the Clinton administration and to Al Gore's presidential campaign, which, it was reported, was pay-
ing $15,000 a month for her services in November 1999.[7]

My discussion, however, will focus on Wolf's *Fire with Fire*, which advocates
a "power feminism" that is increasingly popular in various circles, ranging from
mainstream women to corporate and media groups. This text also contributes to

the false dichotomous paradigm, presented by most antifeminists, which includes the disparagement of so-called victim feminism, which Wolf criticizes from her own "power feminism."

What is so appealing about Wolf is not only her good looks, clear writing style, and highly trained media interpersonal and personal skills but her current philosophical take on women and power. Indeed, it is easy to see why she has been promoted to the media's personality *"A* list" in light of her imaginary dualistic portrayal of bad "victim feminism" and her consequent "self-help" therapeutic philosophy for change. Indeed, even the interviewer for an *Esquire* piece on Wolf acknowledged that *Fire with Fire* was a 180-degree turn from her earlier treatise.

Briefly put, in it, Wolf traces two separate histories of feminism, the "victim" school, whose beginning she locates in nineteenth-century morally superior separate-spheres reformism, and early "power feminism," which includes the Seneca Falls convention.[8] She advocates a "power feminism," asserting that (middle-class) women should use their money, their votes, and their inner nature (as aggressive as men's) to play equally in the arena of power. For Wolf, "this is not a call to be 'like men' but to [lay] claim to our humanity, all of it, not just the scenic parts" (Stark 1994, 139).

Wolf vilifies the "ideological" purist members of what she identifies as the "enemy" feminist camp of "victim" or "insider" feminism (Wolf 1993, xx). bell hooks aptly describes the basic epistemological premise of Wolf's conception as "[a misguided] insistence that capitalist power is synonymous with liberation and self-determination" (hooks 1994a, 97). Indeed, there is no question that economic parity is an essential element of contemporary feminism. However, to assume that to overcome the oppression of women is the fundamental principle rather than one of a variety of goals reduces the complexities and paradoxes that feminisms attempt to address. It also downplays issues such as the violence experienced by women at local and global levels. Hence, Wolf's highly questionable strategy for combating violence against women is worth pondering:

> Every woman is left to walk the front line of violence alone. . . . But why not be proactive? Why not publicize the fact that one woman out of nine carries a gun? I don't want to carry a gun or endorse gun proliferation. But I am happy to benefit from publicizing the fact that an attacker's prospective victim has a good chance of being armed. . . . What is keeping us from selecting a hundred women from every community, taking them on a two-week course in effective self-defense, and then publicizing the fact widely? Our cities and towns can be plastered with announcements that read, "A hundred women in this town are trained in combat. . . . The next woman to be assaulted might be one of these." Indeed, what keeps us from putting up those posters *without* doing the training? (1993, 314–15)

That Wolf could seriously advocate such an ill-advised and potentially hazardous proposal is not only a total disregard for the safety of real women but is also a cavalier lack of concern for the dangerous consequences of this recommendation if it were ever seriously acted upon. The mind boggles at the abundant potential for abuse if such an unconscionable plan was ever seriously realized. Although Wolf professes to have an opposition to gun propagation, the unmistakable subtext of her gun advocacy most certainly belies her protestation. Indeed, it is surprising that this statement did not achieve for Wolf some kind of endorsement or award from the National Rifle Association! As U.S. history can attest, the threat of armed potential victims is hardly a deterrent to violent crimes. Rather, organizations as radically divergent as the police to women's self-defense groups emphasize that arming oneself in this kind of situation not only might provoke or escalate violence but increases the chances of injury or death of the woman or an innocent bystander. Moreover, as has been demonstrated, the judiciary system is hardly sympathetic to women who kill or injure an attacker in self-defense. Further, in regard to "combat training," or the pretense thereof, women's self-defense organizations, like the Canadian *Wen-Do* Association, assert that it is the element of surprise that provides women trained in these skills with any realistic advantage for escaping, relatively unharmed, any potentially violent situation. To advertise gun training, as Wolf so irresponsibly suggests, would seem to be tantamount to goading or inciting attacks on women.

Ironically, Wolf's position on power feminism is shared by a variety of conservative pundits. In particular, her advocacy of female empowerment and neglect of the structural bases of inequality and oppression is shared by such outspoken opponents of progressive feminism as Mary Matalin. Matalin, who was the political director of the failed 1992 Bush presidential campaign and is currently Vice President Cheney's press secretary, stated in a 1993 *Newsweek* cover story entitled "Sexual Correctness: Has It Gone Too Far?" (which is obviously intended as an indictment rather than a question) that "Women want equality. Equality in a capitalist society means economic equality. Money is power. Power is equality" (Matalin 1993, 62).

This simplistic axiomatic mantra, however, misrepresents the multidimensional and contradictory terrain of feminisms with such unsubstantiated cliches as: "Though feminist leaders are mostly aligned with those sentiments, they can't separate their quest for economic equity from the inane political correctness of their extremist sisters" (Matalin 1993, 62). But in true 1990s collaborationist fashion, Matalin supplements her commentary with typical, and highly quotable, pop sound-bite-style wisecracks, which include: "Well, get those moody girls a prescription of Motrin and water pills quick" (Matalin 1993, 62).

Wolf's curious breed of feminism is predicated on the question of "how to get more power into women's hands—*whoever they may be, whatever they may do with it*" (Wolf 1993, 127; emphasis mine). This mandate, however, would appear to celebrate such women as Margaret Thatcher and Heidi Fleiss as leading contenders of power feminism. For as Wolf puts it in her self-help style, media friendly text *Fire with Fire: The New Female Power and How It Will Change the 21st Century*:

"I am a feminist" should be like saying "I am a human being." . . . On this level women should be free to exploit or save, give or take, destroy or build, to exactly the same extent that men are. This is the level of simple realization of women's will, whether we like the result or not. (1993, 139)

The need for what she has labeled "power feminism" was apparently revealed to Wolf through a recognition of what she perceived as a serious lacunae in feminist thought. This lack was made apparent, she claims, in response to repeated pleas, throughout her travels, of women who "felt estranged from a women's movement that sometimes uses rigid women-versus-men language, and presents only one set of attitudes as correctly 'feminist' " (1993, xvi). Thus, her decision to "give voice to the unlabeled feminism of the majority of women who long for equality but shun the movement" inspired her to found a sorority for bad girls— "power feminism." Her inspiration would serve as a necessary and purportedly altruistic response to the mythical, inflexible organization of "politically-sexually correct" feminists (1993, xvii).

Wolf's paradoxical shift from her previous position expressed in her best-selling text *The Beauty Myth* makes sense in light of Phyllis Chesler's insightful analysis.

Women have not won the war against women; we have only begun to fight. The heat of battle is intense. Many women are running scared, smiling as fast as they can. Clearly, it's too hot in the kitchen for Naomi Wolf and she's made her exit; that she insists on describing her departure as "*radical* feminism" is sheer Newspeak. While Wolf's first book, *The Beauty Myth*, exposed how media images of "perfection" were harmful to women, *Fire With Fire* seems to be written *for* the media—as if Wolf's applying for a job as a news anchor or syndicated columnist. No crime, by the way, but no book either. (Chester 1994, 56)

Moreover, Wolf's born-again polemic against the feminist movement is an apt illustration of why the revisionist discourse of betrayal feminists is so persuasive, as it reduces the complexities, diversity, and contradictions of the feminist movement to an imaginary domain of good versus bad feminisms. Paglia, Wolf, and other "feminist" critics of contemporary feminism tend to construct oppositions that denigrate and even demonize feminist positions, groups, and theorists that they oppose and contrast with their own views. The result is both an imaginary bifurcation of the women's movement and oversimplification of the issues facing women and other victims of oppression. Wolf's denunciation of "victim feminism," for instance, covers over the fact that women are oppressed victims of social inequality and injustice *as well as* active agents of struggle and empowerment. Wolf's dichotomizing position thus downplays both the importance of analysis of forms of oppression of women and the reality of such things as inequality, poverty, racial and sexual oppression, and violence. A more expansive feminist analysis would thus *combine* the discourse of oppression with empower-

ment and calls to action. Both disclosure of oppression and valorization of struggle are powerful organizing tools. However, the discourse of empowerment
without realistic depiction of the obstacles to overcoming oppression can lead to
an idealized belief in the power of the will, thus fostering an individualism that
undermines women's solidarity.

Indeed, elevating "empowerment" as an ideal while downplaying oppression
not only transforms the discourse of empowerment and agency from a collective
organizing discourse into an individualist one but also provides a conservative
coding to the term. In fact, the right has regularly appropriated terms like
freedom, individualism, and *empowerment,* associated with 1960s oppositional
movements, for their own purpose. Teresa Ebert describes this process as "retro-
feminism":

> [R]etrofeminism turns the empowerment of women into its other. Empowerment
> no longer means the collective ability to transform economic, political, and cultural
> conditions affecting women because, according to Wolf, economic *opportunity* is
> already here. All that stands in women's way is their "lack of a psychology of female
> power to match their new opportunities." In short, all women need to do is realize
> their innate *feminine power.* . . . There is surprisingly little difference between retro-
> feminists like Wolf and such advocates of traditional femininity as Georgette Mos-
> bacher (whose fame derives largely from her marriage to Texas oil millionaire and
> Republican power broker, Robert Mosbacher) and New Age feminists like Marianne
> Williamson—all three of whom appeared together to promote their books to a lun-
> cheon of society women at New York's 21 Club and to participate in the broad cul-
> tural move to counterfeminism. As noted by two critics who witnessed the event, all
> three advocate the power of "sheer feminine will" in their books (Wolf's *Fire with
> Fire,* Mosbacher's *Feminine Force,* and Williamson's *A Woman's Worth*), and all are
> putting forth "empowerment as the ultimate form of do-it-yourself therapy." (1996,
> 254)

Hence, once again, we are witnesses to one of the pseudofeminist's most effective deceptive devices, the co-optation and distortion of feminist discourse; in
this case that of the term *empowerment.* Not only do they manage to strip it of
its powerful, radical, political meaning by reducing it to the individualized pop-
psychological domain, but they also manage to associate it with pseudo-solutions
designed to divert attention away from evaluation and criticism of institutional
injustice or abuse. Accordingly, in the next section, I will examine some of the
rhetorical strategies deployed by the feminist impersonators who divide the feminist movement. In particular, I will borrow a term from Alfred Hitchcock—who
was a master at fooling his audience—to examine how duplicitous antifeminist
attempts often succeed in doing the same.

THE "MacGUFFIN" TECHNIQUE

The widespread technique of misrepresentation, employed by betrayal feminists
proves to be a clever and seductive tactical maneuver to validate the feminist

impersonator's bifurcated ideology (e.g., of "good" and "bad" feminisms), while at the same time clouding and mystifying the contextual reality of their various purported concerns. The invention of an evil totalitarian regime of "femi-nazi" enemies (which is only one of the many prejudicially memorable sound bite–like terms employed by different impersonator feminists to describe this alleged hegemonic feminist conspiracy) is best understood in Hitchcockian terms, as a "MacGuffin." Loosely put, a "MacGuffin" is "the vaguest us-versus-them plot to be somehow foiled" (Taylor 1978, 119).

> The word is derived from a shaggy dog story Hitch [Alfred Hitchcock] liked to tell which, briefly summarized, concerns an inquisitive chap in a Scottish train and a taciturn fellow traveler. There is a large, mysteriously shaped parcel on the rack, and the inquisitive passenger asks the other what it is. "A MacGuffin" is the reply. "What's a MacGuffin?" "It's for trapping lions in the Highlands." "But there are no lions in the Highlands." "Well, then, there's no MacGuffin." (Taylor 1978, 119)

Consequently, "a MacGuffin is something totally irrelevant and nonexistent which is the subject of conversation and action and which everyone within the drama believes to be very important" (Taylor 1978, 119–20). It is an empty plot device that distracts the audience from recognizing a complex array of pressing issues. I am suggesting that the arguments against feminists by antifeminist feminist impersonators are, in actuality, largely MacGuffins. One of the consequences of the colonized mentality that characterizes the collaborationist pseudofeminist rhetoric is that it has created a false stereotype of the feminist as a "femi-nazi." The construction of this mythical, MacGuffinesque creature—and the imaginary, monolithic, dogmatic hive, from which she purportedly hatched—owes much of its credibility to the works of feminist impersonator celebrities like Camille Paglia, Naomi Wolf, and Christina Hoff Sommers. Indeed, even though the label *femi-nazi* is in itself an oxymoron, its linguistic similarities to the word *feminist*, as well as its profound sensationalizing effects, make it a perfect vehicle of contempt and derision for those who are fighting for humanitarian ideals and principles. For as Marilyn Friedman explains it, feminism, in fact, celebrates and encourages debate and appraisal, rather than—as the pseudofeminists would have us believe—censuring criticism. Despite, however, the familiar caricature of the intolerant "femi-nazi," feminism does not close down the public forum of ideas, but, rather, enlarges it by insisting that it include women's voices. True, some individual feminists are personally intolerant of the views that they regard as clearly wrongheaded and dangerous for women. More often, however, it is feminists—tolerant as well as intolerant—who find themselves harassed and slandered by their own adversaries (Friedman and Narveson 1995, 24).

Indeed, feminisms allow for many conflicting positions and extensive areas of study, thus generating differences and factionalization. Ideally, such diversity fosters and does not censure debate, though in the stereotypes of pseudofeminist antifeminists, femi-nazis stifle debate while they themselves proliferate imaginary oppositions and divisions. This promotes what colonization theory sees as a typical "divide and conquer" strategy in which collaborators sow disunity and undermine solidarity. Although many of these impersonator feminists provide ostensibly different labels for what they identify as "bad feminists," the MacGuffin remains the same. Central to their arguments is the invention of a mythical group of allegedly fascistic feminist organizations attempting to indoctrinate others into a state of victimhood and passivity—often with Andrea Dworkin and Catherine MacKinnon as central figures, due, in large part, to their well-publicized antipornography positions. This MacGuffin, in turn, is used to mask and subliminally sell the real underlying argument of the various betrayal feminists' particular stance and thus transforms their individual texts into marketable, lucrative best-sellers. In the case of Wolf, for example, the MacGuffin of "insider," or "victim," feminism includes the following phantasmagoric litany of self-defeating, dogmatic, and substantively fictional characteristics (for which she provides no documentation, references, or citations):

> Charges women to identify with powerlessness.
> Is sexually judgmental, even antisexual.
> Idealizes women's childrearing capacity as proof that women are better than men.
> Exalts intuition, "women's speech," and "women's ways of knowing," not as complements to, but at the expense of, logic, reason, and the public voice.
> Denigrates leadership and values anonymity.
> [T]ends toward groupthink, as well as toward hostility toward individual achievement.
> Is judgmental of other women's sexuality and appearance.
> Is obsessed with purity and perfection, hence is self-righteous.
> Has a psychology of scarcity: there is only so much to go around, so one woman's gain is another's loss. If there is inequity, wants women to "equalize downward"— e.g., to give up "heterosexual privilege" by not marrying, instead of extending civil rights; to give up beauty, instead of expanding the definition.
> Wants all other women to share its opinions. (Wolf 1993, 136–37)

Wolf relegates "difference,"[9] or "separatist feminists," to the regimes of "insider" or "victim feminism" but also applies the label to Marxian academic feminists, because of their emphasis on the analysis and critique of capitalism as well as their failure "to figure out ways for women to use it to their own advantage" (1993, 247). Thus, in her polemic, Wolf appears to include liberal feminists with Marxist feminists in this victim/insider feminist category. In her attack on so-called Marxist feminists, whom she further faults for what she perceives to be their misdirected strategy for women's economic empowerment, Wolf claims:

> Insider feminism often seems to be more comfortable with the important tasks of pointing out economic discrimination against women, or with legislating more

money for women, as in equal-pay campaigns, than it is with the "masculine," potent act of putting the means to generate profits in women's own hands. In its hangover hostility to capitalism, it has not yet made the jump from asking to taking. (1993, 247)

Wolf's conception of a victim feminism cohort with shared philosophical and political positions is an imaginary proposition. Indeed, there is hardly a definitive agreement on the meaning of "feminism," never mind a collective agenda of feminist principles, shared by the rich diversity of schools and genres of feminist thought and practice. In fact, this promotion of the MacGuffin of victim feminism is central to the success of the feminist impersonator's mandate and is extensively employed by a number of these betrayal feminists. As "next-generation" feminist Carolyn Sorisio makes effectively and lucidly clear, feminist impersonators have hit the proverbial media jackpot with their usage and exploitation of the "victim" metaphor:

> The charge of "victim feminism" seems to have generated the most attention. To attribute this recognition solely to an antifeminist backlash ignores other aspects crucial to the debate. Let's be clear here. The language of "victimization," much like "political correctness" several years ago, has been co-opted for a political agenda that goes far beyond gender. Critiques of "victim feminism" appeal to the myth of rugged individualism, the belief that anyone can overcome obstacles and succeed in American society. Pouring historically exploited groups into one victimization mold enables some Americans to disclaim any debt we may have as citizens who greatly benefit from gender, class and race inequity. *It obscures the true dynamics of power and absolves responsibility.* (Sorisio 1997, 140–41; emphasis mine)

Indeed, it is precisely this kind of pervasive "blaming the victim" colonial mentality that is becoming an escalating theme of contemporary ideological thought. Concurrently, it is being misapplied to discredit many disparate issues and struggles that the terminology of *victim feminism* manages to obscure. The projection of a reductive and grossly oversimplified vision of the feminist movement manages to effectively decontextualize feminist positions and struggles from the environment of the multileveled sets of relations that mediate and constrain women. Sorisio, in fact, goes on to demonstrate how manifestly important and effective the designation of "victim feminism" has been to the success of the feminist impersonator literature: "George Will [an influential conservative critic] hailed [Katie] Roiphe for challenging the 'victimization sweepstakes' that the government and media allegedly award" (Sorisio 1997, 141).

It is within this context, then, that the deceptive practice of inaccurately lumping together diverse and often unaffiliated and even oppositional feminist schools, theorists, and practices with one another and presenting them as one heterogeneous organization called "victim feminism" emerges as a rhetorical ploy to discredit a wide range of feminist theory and practice. In fact, Wolf is hardly alone in her fallacious coalescence of academic Marxist feminists (as she often erroneously identifies them) with liberal feminists, mainstream feminists, and alternative feminisms to support her ridiculous invention of a hegemonic evil-feminist conspiracy. Indeed, most of the impersonator feminists misidentify and confuse the multifarious theories and practices of both contemporary and classical feminist positions in their texts and rhetoric. This is especially evident in the collapsing of multiple—and often contradictory—theoretical visions, which are generally misclassified as "academic feminisms." The noncontextual nature of antifeminist discourse is particularly evident in this regard in that they often mistake and muddle up fundamentally different theoretical feminisms, such as traditional Marxist, radical, liberal, and more current strains of poststructuralism, postmodernism, and postcolonial feminisms to further their unsubstantiated charges of a victim feminist conspiracy.

Sorisio's specific criticism of Katie Roiphe for these kinds of errors is also applicable to the majority of pseudofeminist feminist impersonators. For their intentional failure to identify differences between feminist theorists and specific schools of thought demonstrates their lack of literacy in the field. Yet it also safeguards them from appropriate critiques of their work, while concurrently perpetuating the MacGuffin of victim feminism: "By refusing to name the feminist theorists she implicates or to analyze their ideas seriously, Roiphe creates an inaccurately monolithic portrayal of what is a very complex, dynamic, and contentious field. She repeats the common pattern of replacing specific people and arguments with the all-encompassing category 'feminists' " (Sorisio 1997, 140).

Another MacGuffin stigmatized by pseudofeminist antifeminists is the stereotype of the antisex, puritanical, man-hating woman. Indeed, monolithic depiction of feminism as puritanical and antisex is not only inappropriate but outrageous, given what have been called the "sex or gender wars," within the feminist terrain as well as the growing prominence of "prosex" ("sex-radical," "radical-libertarian," or "sexual liberal" feminists). Arguments and debates regarding women's sexuality, sexual pleasures, erotica, and pornography have constituted an area of contention and deliberation since at least the dawning of the second wave of feminist theory (Tong 1998, 64).

Debates over women and sexuality became especially apparent during the mid-1980s, and Lisa Duggan provides a context for these feminist controversies.

> During the decade from 1980 to 1990, a series of bitter political and cultural battles over issues of sexuality convulsed the nation—battles over the regulation of pornography, the scope of legal protection for gay people, the funding of allegedly "obscene" art, the content of safe-sex education, the scope of reproductive freedom for women, the extent [of] sexual abuse of children in day care centers, the sexual content of public school curricula, and more. (Duggan and Hunter 1995, 1)

Numerous texts, articles, and essays elucidating multiple dimensions of feminist studies and theories in relation to women and sexuality in both theory and praxis abound. And many of these discuss and debate issues of pornography, from a number of perspectives. It is impossible to even begin to summarize the quantity and quality of this body of feminist literature, and it is not necessary for the central argument of this text. However, no one writing on feminism should be unaware of this arena of discussion, especially after the so-called gender or sexuality debates that exploded in the aftermath of a controversial conference on sexuality held at Barnard College in April 1982. According to Lynn Chancer:

> The disagreement revolved around interpretation of sadomasochistic sexual desires as experienced by women across diverse sexual orientations. Again, feminists tended to divide according to whether they stressed sex or sexism. On one side, were Gayle Rubin, Pat Califia, and other feminists who argued that freedom to practice sadomasochistic sexuality was a necessary component of ensuring sexual freedom in general. On the other side were feminists such as those who contributed to a volume starkly entitled *Against Sadomasochism* (1982), who linked sadomasochistic desires with gendered relationships structured around experiences of dominance and subordination; thus being against sadomasochism meant being against gendered oppression. (Chancer 1998, 11)

The hypocrisy of the impersonator feminists whose credibility, in large part, depends upon a mirage of a puritanical antisex feminist cabala is even more laughable given that, as Rosemarie Tong's delineation of this conference made clear, a wide variety of feminists have been prosex. Moreover, issues of sexuality are hotly debated within contemporary feminism, which contains a variety of positions on the topic (Tong 1998, 68–69). In fact, in the late 1990s, *Lingua Franca* reported the rising popularity, within the academic realm, of a new breed of "corporeal feminists" who study and defend pornography (Lord 1997). As M. G. Lord describes it: "For [Constance] Penley, [Laura] Kipnes, [Linda] Williams and their allies, porn is an unruly force that promises to unsettle social conventions, and studying it is a radical political act" (1997, 41).

Furthermore, some feminists claim that feminist research and study within the domain of the "pleasure and danger of sexuality" are privileged and given more support in women's (or gender) studies programs (Barry 1996, 190). Barry goes on to argue that there are more publishing opportunities and contracts for prosex feminist treatises than are available to those she calls (antisex) radical feminists. She identifies this lack in relation to publication of both radical feminist thought in general and works that focus on issues of male violence against women and pornography (Bell and Klein 1996).

In addition, sexual harassment policies have been widely debated by various mainstream and academic feminists. Indeed, feminist criticisms of interpretation and application of many aspects of sexual harassment legislation has become especially fashionable. Some debates in the 1990s were provoked by the multiple official and unofficial allegations against former president Bill Clinton for sexual harassment, abuse of power, and sexual misconduct (and in the context of the right-wing's exploitation of these issues and the attacks on his presidency that they have inspired). Jane Gallop, an academic feminist in the fields of literary criticism, pedagogy, and sexuality (who, as she puts it, aspires to "sexualize the atmosphere in which I work"), has written a book—in response to charges and findings against her for sexual harassment of students—criticizing what she calls current "antiharassment rhetoric." Gallop claims that many university sexual harassment policies address and condemn issues of sexuality rather than discrimination (Gallop 1997, 10–11; 21).

Yet impersonators continue to exploit the myth of feminism's antimale and antiheterosexuality platform. In a book whose title says it all (*The New Victorians: A Young Woman's Challenge to the Old Feminist Order*) Rene Denfield claims that feminists today are advocating the Victorian-era belief that sexuality is inherently evil and any display of it must be squashed, ultimately portraying women who enjoy sex as complicit whores. But Denfield uses a term with which no contemporary women would wish to be even remotely associated—"the *New Victorian*," who basically "*advocate[s] abolishing heterosexual sex*" (see Faludi 1995, 38; emphasis mine).[10] However, Denfield was not the first of the impersonator feminists to apply this analogy. As Faludi points out, characterizing contemporary feminist positions as prudish Victorianism has become a common and effective charge of antifeminists in general who "paint feminists as 'neo-Victorian' prudes terrorizing gals with rape tall tales" (Faludi 1993, 61). In fact, Denfield's text, according to a variety of critics (including Victorianist scholar Gertrude Himmelfarb), not only presents "representations of Victorian culture [that are] historically inaccurate" (Siegel 1997b, 69) but also surprisingly (given the competitive nature of publishing) offers no new or original insights or incriminations to this extensive body of literature.

Although Denfield's boxing background does give her a unique public relations profile and perhaps helps explain her more pugnacious proclivities, her book was just another in a series of treatises that basically reiterate and recycle the same common one-dimensional, antifeminist theme that puts forward contentions of the alleged existence and hegemony of a powerful order of "bad feminists." Indeed, "next-generation feminist" Deborah L. Siegel's careful reading of Denfield's missive reveals that she essentially "repackages Wolf's 'victim feminist' by dressing her up in Victorian garb" (Siegel 1997b, 69). Denfield then once again argues "that an 'antimale sentiment has led to what amounts to victim mythology, a set of beliefs that promote women as the helpless victims of masculine oppression'" (69). Hence, regardless of the prose or the form, the substance remains remarkably similar, whether it underlies the rhetoric of the young feminist impersonators, the pseudofeminist wannabes, or the mother pod feminist pundits. For as Siegel describes it:

In their attempts to master (and bury) the would-be past of feminist history, Wolf, Roiphe, and Denfield create sensational, fictional accounts of a demonized feminism to satisfy a "progressive" narrative structure that might be summarized (pace each author's respective rhetorical flourish) as, "Down with the 'bad' feminism and up with the 'good!'" Their critique of the "bad" is often based upon a presupposition of a preexisting ideal of a public sphere that claims to represent all women and can be criticized and made answerable for its failure to do so. (1997b, 67)

However, the antifeminists' high visibility and multiple publishing and interview opportunities stem, in large part, from their understanding and manipulation of the American ideological dream, made so recognizable through the Hollywood film. Indeed, a story or myth—especially one that is as simplistically bifurcated as the one the pseudofeminists profess—cannot introduce black hat despotism without enlisting the white hat saviors to defeat the evil and institute goodness in its place. And it is at this juncture that the pseudofeminists proclaim their own personal salvation or gospel, which they describe as some prefixed form of feminism, particular to themselves.

Call it "power feminism," call it "babe feminism," call it "feminism for the majority," today's populist feminists are rejecting the "obsolete" and "maladaptive," the "Victorian" and the "stock plot fantasies" of their feminist foremothers—and their progeny. (Siegel 1997b, 64)

And cleverly and seductively in its stead they present or attempt to substitute themselves and their particular "alternatives" or "answers."

Armed with this explanatory device and inspired by the mission of recuperating feminist agency for the good of all, these . . . dissenting daughters set out to reclaim the label "for the majority." In their campaign against "victim mythology" that they argue pervades current organized feminist activism, Roiphe and Denfeld [for example] appropriate the phrase "taking back" feminism, a parodic play on the "Take Back the Night" rallies organized by campus rape crisis centers in the 1980s. (Siegel 1997b, 63)

The victim feminism argument thus rests on a highly problematic, but unarticulated, essentializing of a certain type of "bad" feminism. While the antifeminists rarely engage the essentialist versus nonessentialist arguments concerning the nature of women, or social construction of women, which tend to characterize an important current of contemporary feminist theoretical and practical debate, they assume a covert essentialism of feminist thought. Indeed, a kind of vulgar-essentialist character is attributed to all feminist diversity in its reduction to an evil, victim feminism. Sorisio points out that "Wolf's 'victim feminism' is really another way of discussing essentialism" and goes on to identify Wolf's outdated definition of victim feminism as a vulgar-essentialist version that "claims a universally passive, nurturing female nature" (Sorisio 1997, 144).

NAOMI WOLF'S DEMONIZING DUALISM

Such demonizing of "bad/victim feminism," however, is a necessary oppositional ploy for Wolf's presentation of a binary, and thus purported alternative, agenda of power feminist standards, which contrasts her mythical doctrinaire MacGuffin of insider feminism. And it is this description that is the substantive aspect of her text; the real story, if you will. According to Wolf, the power feminist program:

Examine[s] closely the forces arrayed against a woman so she can exert her power more effectively.

Knows that a woman's choices affect many people around her and can change the world.

Encourages a woman to claim her individual voice rather that merging her voice in a collective identity, for only strong individuals can create a just community.

Is unapologetically sexual; understands that good pleasures make good politics.

Knows that poverty is not glamorous; wants women to acquire money, both for their own dreams, independence, and security, and for social change.

Acknowledges women's interest in "signature," recognition, and game, so that women can take credit for themselves and give generously to others.

Is tolerant of other women's choices about sexuality and appearance; believes that what every woman does with her body and in her bed is her own business. (Wolf 1993, 137)

At first blush, Wolf's mandate appears relatively harmless, seemingly encompassing a Frank Capraesque form of liberal capitalism, mediated by the patriotic dictum of the American dream. This mythology of rewarding inherent worth coupled with hard work as well as the belief that those chosen are obliged to condescend responsibly and charitably toward the less fortunate seems to underlie Wolf's dogmatic dualisms. Yet Phyllis Chesler, like Carolyn Sorisio, identifies an insidious avaricious tendency inherent in Wolf's individualistic, self-serving power feminist agenda.

Wolf's message, to women only, is: Improve yourself, your self-esteem, your appearance, your attitude—and pay no attention to the high female body count. Don't analyze it or draw political conclusions. All is sunny, couldn't be better. No pain, all gain. (Chesler 1994, 57)

Moreover, underlying Wolf's vision is a recycled version of realizing success through literacy and advocacy of the dominant patriarchal code, or "rules of the game"; in other words, excelling in collaborationist techniques. Indeed, this is hardly a new idea and was probably best expressed in the early 1980s in a highly popular best-seller by Colette Dowling, entitled *The Cinderella Complex: Women's Hidden Fear of Independence* (1981). It is not surprising that the woman-as-victim thesis resonated throughout this dated text in a fashion more similar than not to what the 1990s betrayal feminists claim to be a daring new discovery. As Dowling expounds:

> I've learned that there are other women like me, thousands upon thousands of us who grew up in a certain way and who have not been able to face up to the adult reality that we, alone, are responsible for ourselves. . . . But it was not until the Seventies that a cultural shift occurred, and women were looked at, thought about, and treated differently than ever before. Different things were expected of us. Now we were being told that our old girlhood dreams were weak and ignoble, and that there were better things to want: money, power, and that most elusive of conditions, freedom. . . . But freedom, we soon found out, frightens. It presents us with possibilities we may not feel equipped to deal with: promotions, responsibility. . . . Freedom demands that we become authentic, true to ourselves. And this is where it gets difficult, suddenly; when we can no longer get by as a "good wife," or a "good daughter," or a "good student.". . . *In fact we were not trained for freedom at all, but for its categorical opposite—dependency.* (Dowling 1981, 2–3)

Although Dowling concentrates on the notion of dependency rather than victimization, the only real difference between her analysis and many of her impersonator feminist sisters is her identification of the potency of childhood socialization of girls in producing dependency, primarily in the form of the mother's influence. Yet if one replaces the notion of the disempowering "mother" with that of the "feminist" nemesis, a disturbing resemblance to the vitriolic campaign of 1990s betrayal feminism is revealed. (Dowling, however, credits feminism with facilitating her liberation from "the Cinderella complex.") Thus pseudofeminists depend upon the MacGuffin of an evil feminist conspiracy to sell their underlying, often recycled, arguments as new and improved.

As bell hooks points out, the establishment of a false dichotomy between "good" and "bad" feminists allows for the creation of "a competitive area . . . where all feminists who do not agree with [their] thinking are either shown to be lacking, lined up in a kind of metaphorical firing squad and shot down . . . or simply ignored" (1994a, 94). This is hardly a testament to Wolf's power feminist claims of tolerance in that:

> Any reader schooled in radical or revolutionary thought would understand this insistence on competition to be a mirroring of internalized sexist thinking about power, about the way in which women have traditionally been socialized to relate to one another in patriarchal society. Rather than offering a new vision of female power, Wolf transposes the old sorority girl, dog-eat-dog will to power away from the arenas of competitive dressing and dating onto feminism. (hooks 1994a, 94–95)

Ironically, although a central argument concerning the MacGuffin of dogmatic feminism is their alleged failure to engage in debate and criticism, this is the rudiment of all forms of critical feminism. In reality, it is the pseudofeminists who have constructed a barricade against meaningful, challenging discussion, which, as bell hooks argues (1994a), is often self-serving.

Even though she is critical of "insider feminism," Wolf has used power garnered after writing the bestselling *The Beauty Myth* to network, to create a support structure that makes feminist individuals fear reprisal if they publicly criticize her work—power that could have been used to establish forums for progressive debate and dissent. (hooks 1994a, 94)

The hypocritical nature of Wolf's power feminist is evident in her declaration that "it is not dissent which is harmful to feminism, but consensus." Indeed, hooks notes that Wolf's "work reveals no evidence that she constructively engages ideas that are different from her own" (94). Wolf's celebration of dissent and denigration of consensus reveals once again the one-sidedness of her positions. For while in some contexts dissent is salutary, in others it is consensus that is needed to organize and carry through a course of action.

Indeed Wolf's blindered power feminist agenda neutralizes the reality of the diversities of feminisms and omits some of the most significant feminist contributions, especially those of or concerning multicultural women and women of color. Instead, she sets up a MacGuffinist imaginary opposition between two mythical, nonexistent groups and ignores the real, concrete, practical, everyday relations and problems of contemporary women. In this sense, her narrow, elitist vision of the world of feminist thought is a great disservice to those who want to learn about the eclectic and exciting contradictory arena of feminism. Impersonator feminists also neglect those women who do not share the "privileged backgrounds" and who require pedagogical assistance at both the educational and grassroots levels, free of the conscious and unconscious condescension and patronization of pseudofeminists. This attitude of condescension is especially apparent in the impersonator feminists' attitudes toward the young female masses, whom they deem to be so highly susceptible to the brainwashing techniques of the "granola" feminist cabala. "In our cities, on our campuses far from home young women are vulnerable and defenseless" (Paglia, *The Buffalo News*, Apr. 2, 1995).

Critical younger feminists, like Paula Kamen, however, take offense at such ageist, elitist, and derogatory attitudes toward the cognitive and critical abilities of young women. This patronizing stance illuminates the pernicious elements of the betrayal feminists' platform, which purports to protect these young women from insidious evil forces. They are covertly depicting young women as stupid and helpless (a stereotype, one might add, that mirrors the manner in which they are classified within the dominant code). As Kamen puts it, "All of us [younger generation feminists and potential feminists]—even the college students at the most elite schools—aren't as sheltered as we look" (Kamen 1991, 6).

Yet the impersonator feminists' Manichaean position depends on the myth of a mass of witless, irresponsible, sheep-like young women who must be protected and saved from the MacGuffin of victim feminism. In this sense, a certain smugness, self-righteousness, and downright conceit permeates and pollutes the purported altruistic stand and heroic actions espoused by betrayal feminists. Within this context, a pattern that connects the impersonator feminists to one another is revealed. For their supposed passionate concerns regarding the dangers of a nazifeminist order provokes a one-dimensional response, which is then supplemented by particular critiques of aspects of a variety of feminist positions, of which each antifeminist feminist fancies herself an expert. These targets include assaults on women's studies programs, empirical findings concerning issues related to rape, harassment, poverty, and so on. These types of indictments, one must add, cast aside central concerns of feminism and the concrete practical realities of the plight of multiplicities of women.

The majority of the billion human beings suffering starvation in the world are women and children, who live in a state of chronic undernourishment, and the majority of the fifty thousand people a day who die of starvation and malnutrition are women and children. Even in rich countries, "chronic malnutrition afflicts millions, mainly old people and families headed by unemployed women with dependent children" (French 1992, 38). On July 24, 2001, the Economic Policy Institute released a report stating that 29 percent of American "working families with as many as three children under age 12 do not earn enough income to afford basic necessities" (www.epinet.org/epihome.html).

Hence, Wolf's criticisms and so-called alternative program resonates as elitist insensitivity if not a laughable solution in light of the reality of the feminization of poverty. It is also unlikely that Wolf's and her followers' advocacy of middle-class power feminist resolutions will have any significant impact on the 39 million Americans officially living in poverty as of 1993; 77.4 percent, more than three-quarters of which are women and children (Sidel 1996, 70). The appalling acceleration of the numbers of women and children living in poverty is hardly restricted to the United States and has, in fact, become so great a problem in "every late capitalist welfare state in Western Europe and North America" that the term *feminization of poverty* has been coined to describe this alarming phenomenon (Fraser 1989, 144).

As Ruth Sidel has so painstakingly documented, even official U.S. policies proposed to assist middle-class families "will not be sufficient to help poor women and children overcome the pernicious effects of poverty. A combination of universal entitlements and targeted programs for poor families is therefore urgently needed" (1996, 219). Nancy Fraser goes even further in her dialectical clarion call for a radical practical "challenge to the dominant policy framework" (1989, 145), which must necessarily be "a theoretically informed but practice-oriented way of thinking about social-welfare [by] feminist scholars and activists" (1989, 12).

These kinds of deep structural changes are urgently needed, given the findings of the 1995 United Nations sixth annual Human Development Report (which is prepared by independent experts for the development agency)—the theme of which was the status of women on a global level—"hundreds of millions of women in both rich and poor nations are still significantly undervalued economically, denied access to political power and kept down by crippling inequalities under the law. . . . Seventy percent of the world's poor are women, and women and children make up 80 percent of its refugees and a disproportionate number of the casualties in dozens of small-scale wars [while] 'violence stalks women's lives, in peace and in war' " (*New York Times*, Aug. 18, 1995). Within this context, the individualist and altruistic program proposed by Wolf's power feminism platform demonstrates she is someone seriously out of touch with reality and sensitive to the needs of only those whose race, class, and affluence she shares.

Although Wolf purports to eschew the dimensions of Katie Roiphe's and Camille Paglia's writings, which trash the work of rape-crisis feminists because of their "taking the occasional excesses of the rape crisis movement and using them to ridicule the entire push to raise consciousness about sexual violence" (Wolf 1993, 135), her analysis shares similar qualities. As an example of victim feminism, Wolf describes her personal experience working at a rape crisis center. Although it would seem that the very idea of a rape crisis center and the courage and commitment involved in this kind of work would represent power feminism incarnate, according to Wolf, the evils of victim feminism resided in such sites. Curiously, her harshest criticism seems to be reserved for the aesthetic nature of the center.

> The physical surroundings were like a stage set for the evocation of grief. You walked up a flight of damp concrete steps sticky with trash. Once inside, you were met by the sight of sofas with their stuffing spilling out, rickety folding chairs flung on their sides, and bare light bulbs casting shadows over it all. The light made people's skin look dead white or liverish gray-brown. One wall held nothing—not a cheap reproduction from a passing art exhibit, not a fruit or a flower, only a pockmarking of gouges from thumbtacks. The other wall held only a relentless battery of bulletins from the war [*sic*]: "*Jamais encore*! Women say NO to the shame of rape!" (Wolf 1993, 150)

Wolf continues to argue that the "shabbiness" of the center was not due to lack of finances as "there was money enough for a softer lightbulb, a reproduction of Cezanne's apples," but to a concerted effort on the part of "insider feminists" to construct a defeatist and self-serving atmosphere. As she puts it:

> the rape crisis center was staffed by a core collective with its own ingrained ways of doing things; the insufficiency, the misery were almost beloved, for they underscored how much we had suffered, how pitiful were our resources in the face of the mighty opposition, and how good we were to volunteer our time in such conditions. . . . The shabbiness of the center reinforced the "moral" of the rape: You were made to feel

like nothing by the crime; now come try to recover in a place where we treat ourselves like nothing, too. (Wolf 1993, 153)

Wolf's other complaint, shared by a number of antifeminists, is the consensus mode of decision making and discussion that is employed my many of these kinds of feminist (and "grassroots"/community) organizations. Although this is a time-honored process that finds its basis in democratic principles, the pseudofeminists find it a heinous practice, designed to undermine individualism and promote a movement of automatons. These impersonator feminists, in true binary fashion, appear to be confusing consensus with conformity or conversion. However, the uncomfortable resemblance to "red-baiting" that underlies the nature of these charges cannot be ignored, because it supports the unstated assumptions that prove central to the success of the betrayal feminist's platform on contemporary feminists: that insider feminist epistemology is decidedly "un-American."

In her analysis of the failure of Shannon Faulkner—the first woman allowed to enroll as a cadet, in 1995, at the all-male U.S. military academy, the Cita-del—to survive the initiations of "hell week," Susan Faludi focuses on the delete-rious implications of this individualistic platform. As she explains it, one of the greatest contributing factors in Shannon Faulkner's defeat was her embrace of the popular myth "that history is driven not by the actions and changing beliefs of large numbers of ordinary people, but by a few heroic giants who materialize out of nowhere to transform the landscape" (Faludi, *New York Times*, Aug. 23, 1995). In retrospect, Faulkner, who claimed to be an individualist and not a feminist, declared that "It would be different if there had been other women with me." In this light, [i]t is especially ironic that what she perceived as a personal failure was transformed into the collective failure of the women's movement. For "once Shannon the individual stumbled, her humiliation instantly became all women's." Shannon Faulkner's example is like far too many others in that she became involved in the paradoxical illusion where "women are condemned to fight alone and condemned to fail communally."

> Solidarity is fostered in men—whole state-supported academics teach it to them—but it is suspect in women. Lately, that message has been reinforced by so-called feminist pundits, from Camille Paglia to Christina Hoff Sommers, who tell women over and over: "You can do it on your own. You don't need any help from the orga-nized women's movement." (Faludi, *New York Times*, Aug. 23, 1995)

Indeed, Naomi Wolf's power feminism personifies the mythical ideology of individualism, thus further provoking the divide-and-conquer mentality that poses one of the largest threats to organized feminisms and a genuinely feminist agenda and practice. This is exemplified by one of the criteria of Wolf's power feminism that "encourages a woman to claim her individual voice rather than merging her voice in a collective identity, for only strong individuals can create a just community" (1993, 137). In this sense, Wolf seems to have lost sight of one of the central tenets of feminism, which necessarily "involves women supporting women. . . . The early feminist notion of 'sisterhood' reveals this aim. Feminism seeks to promote women's support, care, nurturance, respect, and esteem *for women*" (Friedman and Narveson 1995, 31).

A favorite technique shared by the impersonator feminists involves projecting onto the "imaginary other" feminists allegedly pathological positions and behaviors that they themselves embrace. Such projection further erects the MacGuffin mythology, which veils the true nature of contemporary feminism as well as the self-serving agenda mediating the betrayal feminists' mandate. In this sense, Faludi contends that:

> If pod feminists have adopted the strategy of cooptation pioneered by conservative advisers to George Bush, they also have echoed another behavioral pattern of recent vintage among right-wing pols: projection of their sins onto their opponents. (1995, 35)

Faludi goes on to document specifics of this enterprise of projection—which include the accusations that feminists "stifle the views of dissenting women," are "paranoid whiners" who deem all women to be passive victims, and propagate lies about the reality of the conditions of women. bell hooks, however, identifies one of the most effective of these projection techniques, which is a revelatory observation into the underlying reductionist nature of the betrayal feminist epistemology (hooks 1994a, 81). Indeed, hooks recognizes the irony that "[t]his kind of either/or binary thinking mirrors the narrow-minded dogmatic thinking it claims to critique" (hooks 1994a, 81).

CHRISTINA HOFF SOMMERS'S MacGUFFIN FEMINISM

This mixture of co-optation and projection, within a dualistic frame, to escalate the MacGuffin of a grand victim, or "insider," feminist conspiracy, also characterizes right-wing ideologue Christina Hoff Sommers's work. In fact, Hoff Sommers provides one of the most blatant examples of the exploitation of the MacGuffin technique in regard to the antifeminist backlash as well as exhibiting an apt adaptation of the arts of projection and collaboration in advancing ideological arguments. Her text *Who Stole Feminism? How Women Have Betrayed Women* (1994) is, in fact, mostly MacGuffin, incorporating a critique of allegedly flawed feminist empirical research techniques and statistical findings as the justification for a particularly nasty attack on a mythical organization she has labeled sex/gender feminists (gender feminists for short) (22). Although the betrayal feminists have participated in one of the most effective backlash campaigns launched against contemporary feminisms, Hoff Sommers begins her text with the classic projection—shared by many of her pseudofeminist cohort—that the gender feminists sow division in the movement. This is hypocritical, because it is actually the betrayal feminists whose success depends on the promotion of a division within feminism (especially in relation to their own bifurcated positions). Consequently, the propagation of a mythical erasing of real differences in feminisms enhances a reactionary response and justification for their stance. Indeed, Hoff Sommers's purported rationale for writing her book is that she is a "a feminist who does not like what feminism has become" and passionately believes that "[t]he new gender feminism is badly in need of scrutiny" (1994, 18). This description is hypocritical, however, in light of the perks and benefits she has garnered because of her status as a betrayal feminist pundit.

In fact, her text and related writings have transformed Hoff Sommers from an undistinguished associate professor of philosophy at Clark University into a "betrayal feminist" media star. Her promotion by right-wing groups has paved the way for a lucrative position as a Brady fellow at the American Enterprise Institute and "Chairman" of the "National Advisory Board" of the Independent Women's Forum (IWF), which is connected with the Bush administration (see chapter 1). Her crusade against the "feminist menace," which she characterizes as being "backed by well funded, prestigious organizations as well as individuals," is a classic example of impersonator feminist projection. For Hoff Sommers admits that she has received funding from the Lynde and Harry Bradley Foundation, the John M. Olin Foundation, the Carthage Foundation, and other grant sources (Hoff Sommers 1994, 33). Hence, her assertion that "it is not so easy to receive grants for a study that criticizes the feminist establishment for its errors and excesses" (1994, 8) is an apt reflection of the hypocritical nature of Hoff Sommers's attack.[11]

Moreover, Hoff Sommers argues that "feminist ideologues" are "quietly engaged in hundreds of well-funded projects to transform a curriculum that they regard as unacceptably 'androcentric,'" covering over that she is part of a right-wing campaign to attack and undermine women's studies programs (see chapter 1). Hoff Sommers's further claim that anti-intellectual feminists are "driving out the scholars on many campuses" is only one of many unsubstantiated claims with which the "big lie" rhetorical structure of her indictment is constructed.[12] Carl Boggs angrily refutes Hoff Sommers's assertion that "[i]t is now virtually impossible to be appointed to high administrative office in any university system without having passed muster with gender feminists":

Hoff Sommers appears oblivious to the fact that the upper levels of academia—presidents, administrators, deans, departmental chairs—remain largely bastions of male power. As Laura Flanders reports in the September/October issue of *EXTRA!*, this ridiculous claim is just one of many unsubstantiated charges that fill Sommers' book. (Boggs 1995, 8)

Yet the basic premise of Hoff Sommers's argument is especially appealing to the widespread binary-oppositional perspective. For she affirms that " 'the gender' feminists [who] lack a grassroots constituency [and] blame a media 'backlash' for the defections of the majority of women . . . have stolen 'feminism' from a mainstream that had never acknowledged their leadership" (1994, 18). Thus, the title of her book is one of the most blatant examples of projection, in that it is, in actuality, Hoff Sommers and her impersonator feminist colleagues who are trying to steal the complex, multidimensional, and empowering feminist movement. In fact, the reductionistic, binary, oppositional, mythical paradigm that they assault most accurately describes their own simplistic position. In this sense, betrayal feminists have epitomized what Susan Faludi has identified as "a kind of pop-culture version of the Big Lie that stands the truth boldly on its head and proclaims that the very steps that have elevated women's position have actually led to their downfall" (1991, xviii).

Like her colleagues', Hoff Sommers's MacGuffin hinges on the fantasy that there exists a unified vanguard of staunch feminist ideologues, with a shared platform of beliefs. This cadre is allegedly actively involved in a covert operation of indoctrination that is "carried away with victimology . . . seeing our society as hopelessly compromised by sexism . . . [they] haven't read the great books. They haven't learned to think, to reason, to argue. They've learned to be offended" (Hoff Sommers, interviewed in *Rocky Mountain News*, Jul. 16, 1995).

> The pseudofeminists maintain that [feminists] . . . bellyache about a fantastical conspiracy plot hatched behind the scenes by mustache-twirling misogynists who have succeeded in brainwashing a mass female population. (Faludi 1995, 36)

To perpetuate this gross oversimplification, however, Hoff Sommers goes beyond many of her pseudofeminist sisters in identifying particular members of this supposed conspiracy who, in reality, are associated with some of the most divergent schools of feminism, thus collapsing significant epistemological and political differences into one homogenized feminist ideology. It is especially ironic that she misclassifies feminists (such as Gloria Steinem and Susan Faludi, to name two) who are, in fact, at the forefront of mainstream feminism as "gender-feminist" enemies. Indeed, anyone possessing a rudimentary knowledge of contemporary feminisms would immediately recognize the inappropriate and impossible nature of her so-called feminist alliances. She purports that Marxist feminists share the same epistemological perspectives with difference feminists, socialist feminists, postmodern feminists, and liberal feminists, to name a few.

> Lumping together all kinds of feminists, from Marxist to cultural to radical, her argument boils down to an advocacy of a feminism rooted in traditional liberalism as opposed to all others. (*Kirkus Reviews*, Apr. 15, 1994)

Hoff Sommers's proposition is so laughable that it is reminiscent of another alleged conspiracy that supposedly occurred over thirty years ago, when a group of 1960s radicals were called before the House Un-American Committee. At that time, Abbie Hoffman, one of the defendants who was the cofounder of the Youth International Political Party (Yippie), was accused on the stand of conspiring to "enter into an agreement with David Dellinger, John Froines, Tom Hayden, Jerry Rubin, Lee Weiner, or Rennie Davis to come to the city of Chicago for the purpose of encouraging and promoting violence during the [Democratic] Convention Week." His answer to this charge would seem to be an apt one for those put on trial by Hoff Sommers et al.:

A. [Abbie Hoffman] An agreement?
Q. Yes.
A. We couldn't agree on lunch. (Levine and Greenberg 1970, 148)

Of course, this does not mean that there are not many shared assumptions among members of the dialectically shifting feminist schools of thought. However, universal agreement within a supposedly monolithic feminist movement is not only a ludicrous notion but also is at odds with the very essence of feminisms that celebrate and embrace difference and debate. Indeed, the internationalist feminist collective agreement to disagree was demonstrated at the Fourth United Nations Conference on Women in Beijing in September 1994. Janet Wilson describes the import of this essentially conflictual stance—in relation to a variety of matters—for both the maintenance and development of global sisterhood as feminisms necessarily recognize different, and often divergent, contextual realities.

> While women share many of the same problems, such as poverty and lack of access to education, health care and family planning, we come to the table armed with views as divergent as our backgrounds and cultures. (*Austin American-Statesman*, Feb. 24, 1994)

Susan Faludi provides us with what appears to be an accurate appraisal of how antifeminists employ an imaginary logic to make it appear as if "insider feminists" do not thrive on debate, dissent, and conflict for necessary dialectical change, which is the essence of progressive feminism.

> Heated exchanges, not censorship, characterize feminists' approaches to difficult subjects like pornography, surrogate motherhood, or RU 486. These differences of opinion—and willingness to argue passionately over them—are precisely what strengthen the vitality of the women's movement. But these points are quickly lost in the pods' endless loop of logic, which goes something like this: the antifeminist feminists say feminists stifle disagreement. A feminist disagrees with this statement. She must be trying to stifle dissent. And so on. (Faludi 1995, 36)

Moreover, because mainstream feminists are incorporated into Hoff Sommers's feminist blacklist, it is unclear as to how these feminists have stolen feminism from themselves. Her own celebration of equity feminists following in the footsteps of the "old feminist" principle admits that many of the feminists Hoff Sommers attacks are in fact following the traditional equity principles that she is herself espousing.

> The old feminism has had many exponents, from Elizabeth Cady Stanton and Susan B. Anthony in the middle of the nineteenth century to Betty Friedan and Germaine Greer in our own day. It demanded that women be allowed to live as freely as men. To most Americans, that was a fair demand. The old feminism was neither defeatist nor gender-divisive, and it is even now the philosophy of the feminist "mainstream." (1994, 24)

Elizabeth Cady Stanton's response to Hoff Sommers's curious depiction of her perspective might be, "Come, come, my conservative friend, wipe the dew off your spectacles, and see that the world is moving" (Stanton, part 1, *The Women's Bible*, 1895, cited in Partnow 1992, 811). Especially given that one of Cady Stanton's least inflammatory statements, included in the *History of Women's Suffrage*, which she coauthored with Susan B. Anthony and Mathilda Gage in 1881, asserts "But standing alone we learned our power; we repudiated man's counsels forevermore; and solemnly vowed that there should never be another season of silence until we had the same rights everywhere on this green earth, as man" (cited in Partnow 1992, 811).

However, Elizabeth Cady Stanton seems a curious hero for Hoff Sommers, given the "old feminist's" position on women's superiority, which bears a remarkable similarity to that of difference feminists, who are near the top of Hoff Sommers's gender/insider hit list. For example, in one of her diary entries in 1890 Stanton wrote:

> Our trouble is not our womanhood, but the artificial trammels of custom under false conditions. We are, as a sex, infinitely superior to men, and if we were free and developed, healthy in body and mind, as we should be under natural conditions, our motherhood would be our glory. That function gives women such wisdom and power as no male ever can possess. When women can support themselves, have their entry to all the trades and professions, with a house of their own over their heads and a bank account, they will own their bodies and be dictators in the social realm. (cited in Partnow 1992, 182)

Such a dramatic misunderstanding of a central historical feminist icon would be shocking in the case of a popular-journalistic style antifeminist. However, it is inexcusable in the works of an academic philosopher with a supposed expertise in the area of feminist philosophy. Yet this type of conceited disregard for the appropriate scholarship necessary for the credibility of her academic credentials, as well as her argument, underlies Hoff Sommers's writings in general.

Indeed, she has demonized so-called gender feminists whose liberal philosophies, in actuality, would fit with what is deemed to be the true principles of equity feminism, even though Hoff Sommers, as demonstrated, partially misrepresents their positions (to expand upon her enemies list, one can only assume). Hoff Sommers describes her preferred "equity feminists" as a group who "believe that American women have made great progress and that our system of government allows them to expect more. They do not believe that women are 'socially subordinate'" (Hoff Sommers in Susan Jacoby, *Newsday*, May 22, 1994).

Yet even Susan Jacoby, who appears to subscribe to an element of Hoff Sommers's depiction of two oppositional feminist groups, takes issue with what she discerns to be an erroneous description of an equity/mainstream feminist position (although she prefers the term *egalitarian feminists*). Jacoby agrees with Hoff Sommers's contention that equity feminists "hold a more optimistic view of the progress women have already made than gender feminists do. However, the one conviction that has united feminists across the ages is the belief that women, as a group, are indeed subordinate—even though their second-class status is now a de facto rather that a de jure phenomenon [and] the true differences among feminists involve the means they advocate to end female subordination" (Jacoby, *Newsday*, May 22, 1994). Thus, those who perceive themselves as part of the equity club, designated by Hoff Sommers, take issue with her very definition of its liberal epistemological foundations. As libertarian feminist Wendy Kaminer reminds us, "The popular image of feminism as a more or less unified quest for androgynous equality, promoted by the feminist nemesis Camille Paglia, is at least ten years out of date" (1993, 59).

Consequently, Hoff Sommers's assertion of a unified gender feminism covers over the diversity of contemporary feminisms and richness of its debates. She is so out of touch with current feminist discussion that she blames this alleged takeover of mainstream feminists on "feminist ideology . . . divisive, gynocentric turn, and the emphasis now . . . on women as a political class whose interests are at odds with the interests of men" (Hoff Sommers 1994, 24). This claim is so outrageous precisely because anyone at all versed in current feminist theory is aware that the notion of women as a "class" has evoked some of the most extensive debate in the past decades of feminism. Moreover, the notion has been revoked publicly by those feminists most directly targeted by Hoff Sommers. Note Michele Barrett's eloquent observation on this major shift in feminist epistemological thought in response to accusations against Western feminisms' appearance "to speak for all women when in fact it spoke only for certain women" (Barrett 1988, vi).

Hence there is an alignment between a political recognition of differences of power and resources between women—exemplified by the racism of white feminists and all that this reveals about the impossibility of sisterly solidarity—and more philosophical criticism of the integrity of the category "women." (1988, vi)

Barrett manages to capture the essence of one of the most contentious, empowering, and critical issues in contemporary feminist literature and research. Yet the pseudofeminists (and many mainstream feminists, I must add) seem to have little if any awareness of the real struggles and provocative changes taking place within the feminist terrain especially in relation to transformative and global feminisms. Indeed, as Barrett simply puts it, "it embodies an insight of a very general nature: that the perception of significant differences *between* women is in itself a challenge to the grand feminist claims of an unshakable identity *as* women" (1988, vi–vii).

It is indeed fantastic that these antifeminist feminists, like Hoff Sommers, seem to be blind to one of the most significant issues in contemporary feminist thought: insurgent multiculturalism and debates concerning difference and alliance at a variety of levels. Instead, the feminist impersonators seem to be obsessed by a narrow, eurocentric caricatured stereotype of feminism and constantly reveal their ignorance of the current variety and diversity of contemporary feminisms.

Yet Hoff Sommers and many of the other antifeminist feminists would have us believe that a central issue, distinguishing insider/gender feminists from the power/equity team, is related to the argument, most commonly associated with Faludi's *Backlash*, that there is a contemporary resurgence of a backlash against women in general and feminism in particular. Once again, Hoff Sommers's one-dimensional, bifurcated ideology poses serious problems for the credibility of her argument. One of her claims, in regard to equity feminists, concerned their "optimistic view" concerning women's progress in contrast to the alleged pessimism of "gender feminists" who supposedly exaggerate the backlash against women and feminist defeat.

Cogently answering this argument, Elayne Rapping, whose political writings would situate her within Hoff Sommers's camp of gender feminists, recontextualizes the reality of "backlash" while critiquing the pessimism that the betrayal feminists insist is embraced by all insider feminists. Rapping stresses positive developments in relation to women's position, as well as setbacks, thus undercutting Hoff Sommers's intractable gender feminist stereotype. Rapping's explication is worth quoting at length.

While I don't deny the existence of a backlash against feminists' gains (which would be absurd), the overly reductive and pessimistic understanding of what that backlash actually means and how it should be talked about and responded to troubles me. . . . The backlash model of media dynamics assumes an ahistoric, one-dimensional, either/or, them/us, then/now (in current academic jargon, "binary") playing field. According to backlash theorists, feminists made certain strides in the late 1960s and then, in the 1980s, were pushed back to point zero by the monolithic, misogynist forces of the backlash. (1994, 9)

Rapping, to the contrary, stresses continuing gains and strengths of the feminist movement, as well as defeats and problems. It is also highly unlikely that Hoff Sommers would position bell hooks, a revolutionary African American feminist, within the equity feminist domain. However, hooks is hardly an advocate of the backlash/defeat model either, although she also provides a contextual translation of the realities of backlash.

[Black women's] challenge to the status quo has generated serious anti-black female backlash. The kind of backlash that combines fierce racism with anti-feminism, the kind Susan Faludi does not even begin to consider in her best selling book *Backlash: The Undeclared War Against Women*. Indeed, Faludi's work erases any focus on the way in which race is a factor determining degrees of backlash. (hooks 1993, 2)

hooks's harsh review of Faludi's backlash model, which the betrayal feminists claim unites so-called victim feminists, further fractures Hoff Sommers's "gender feminist" myth, while pointing to the complex and dialectical conflicts and debates that characterize the diverse and transdisciplinary feminist terrain. For as hooks continues in her critique of Faludi's argument:

That she could completely ignore the specificity of race, and once again construct women as a monolithic group whose common experiences are more important than our differences, heralds the acceptance of an erasure within the realms of popular feminist books—works written to reach mass audiences—of all the work black women and women of color have done (in conjunction with white allies in struggle) to demand recognition of race. (hooks 1993, 2)

Ann Jones, a feminist whose concerns are primarily within the area defined as violence against women, is another who, it would seem, fits neatly into Hoff Sommers's definition of gender-victim feminists. Yet Jones advances a potent and angry critique of the "backlash model," which the betrayal feminists insist is a universal theme underlying the victim-feminists platform, writing: "Even feminists sometimes seem to have forgotten about violence against women . . . the two best-selling feminist books of 1991–1992—Susan Faludi's *Backlash* and Gloria Steinem's *Revolution from Within*—scarcely mention it, perhaps because the threat of violence to women is now so pervasive as to be part of the very air we breathe" (1994a, 16).

Once again, we are confronted with the paradox that many of those identified by betrayal feminists as gender feminists are considered by large numbers of feminist theorists hardly as fanatical extremists, but rather as mainstream feminists. In the next chapters, I will continue this discussion of contemporary antifeminist assaults on feminism by discussing the backlash against the F-word and how the victimization debate plays out in the light of actual violence against women and what I call "family terrorism."

NOTES

1. Paglia consistently celebrates gay men: "Is there something innately different about the gay male brain? And do family factors and gay culture reinforce that difference? . . . What I do know is that gay male consciousness, as I have experienced it, is stunningly expansive and exquisitely precise. Gay men have collectively achieved a fusion of intellect, emotion, and artistic sensibility that resembles Goethe's or Byron's integration of classism and Romanticism. The intellectual of the twenty-first century, trained by an academic system I am trying to reshape, will think like a gay man. . . . The effeminacy of gay men—which emerges as soon as macho masks drop—is really their artistic sensitivity and rich, vulnerable emotionalism" (1994, 75).

2. Paglia also confesses, "Male homosexuality is not encumbered by the ideology that lesbian feminism is. I don't believe that you are born gay, it is [a] ridiculous, absurd statement. Most women are bisexual, they can succeed bisexually in a way men can't. . . . I think lesbian sex can be wonderful, but it's lacking in many ways. . . . Man and woman can have wild primitive sex. You don't get that with lesbians—there's something lacking. It's so tiring, making love with women, it takes forever. I'm too lazy to be a lesbian" (Paglia, in Iley 1994, D5).

Paglia also likes to point out that her current partner Allison is bisexual, has dated men, and is "equally attracted to men" (cited in Findley 2000). bell hooks makes the astute comment that: "Lesbian women who have a patriarchal mindset are far less threatening to men than feminist women, gay or straight, who have turned their gaze and their desire away from the patriarchy, away from sexist men" (hooks 200b, 97). For dissection of Paglia's history, sexuality, personae, and writings, see Showalter 2001.

3. Judy Stoffman epitomizes the critics' praise of Paglia, which focuses on style over substance: "There is no doubt that [Paglia] is one of the great prose stylists of our time, unmatched in the vigor of her arguments, even if some of them do not stand up to close examination" (*Toronto Star*, Nov. 8, 1994, B6). Or, "[Paglia's] style is marked by angry exhilaration, brittle epigrams and acid paradoxes, a combination that bullies rather than persuades. The posturing is hard to take seriously, indeed may well be a literary game, a tongue-in-cheek performance to rile the various critical camps." (Rachel Clare, *The Times Literary Supplement*, www.barnesandnoble.com, Dec. 17, 1998). Paglia's pugnacious polemics are, however, obviously entertaining, enabling *Sexual Personae* to win a *Lingua Franca* poll as the best academic book of the 1990s (October 2000). In a response to an e-mail, *Lingua Franca*'s editors admitted that such online polls "are never without flaw" and conceded that there might have been an organized e-mail campaign to select Paglia by her friends and fans.

4. Kathleen Higgins (1993, 370), in her review of *Sexual Personae*, notes that Paglia's "cavalier" attitudes toward appropriate explication and substantiation apply even to the works of her "heroes." In regard to Freud, in particular, Higgins notes: "Although operating on a largely Freudian map she conflates the erotic and aggressive instincts as Freud does not" (1993, 370). Indeed, it is safe to say that Paglia has extremely limited knowledge of psychology and biology, despite posturing in both areas. As Robin Lakoff notes, "Paglia spends a good part of her article venting spleen at her target. But to disguise the pure venom of her attack, Paglia claims the 'objectivity of science and medicine' by couching it in psychoanalytic terminology" (Lakoff 2000, 185).

5. Belatedly, Paglia calls attention to the Nietzschean roots of her distinctions in the "Cancelled Preface" to *Sexual Personae* that appears in Paglia 1992, 101ff.

6. Paglia herself, in a *Toronto Globe and Mail* interview, reveals that her differences with Wolf are more personal and competitive than theoretical or political: " 'I'm not like Naomi Wolf,' she declares, referring to the best-selling author . . . and a *major nemesis of Paglia on the New-Age-Feminist circuit* [emphasis mine]. 'I'm not like Naomi Wolf who, when she was being interviewed by a reporter, received him alone in her apartment wearing orange see-through harem pants, okay? Now *ex-cuse* me, okay? . . . Naomi, like, she's the perfect example to me of what's wrong with white middle-class girls, batting her eyes at men, never able to live a day without a man, not for one day has she been without a man, and I, on the other hand, an open lesbian with a bisexual history have never used men as an escort service, never taken advantage of men' " (Dec. 7, 1994, C1). Interestingly, as Deborah Siegal notes, the subtitle of Wolf's *Fire with Fire* "underwent a transformation from the first to the second edition. Whereas the original subtitle reads, *The New Female Power and How It Will Change the Twenty-First Century,* the revised version reads, *The New Female Power and How to Use It.* . . . Wolf's new title places additional emphasis on the reader's agency (and responsibility) to practice what Wolf preaches; the new title suggests that this is, indeed, a how-to book" (Siegal 1997a, 80n22). Meanwhile, as Showalter notes, Paglia "was having a field day, calling Wolf 'a *Seventeen* magazine level thinker' " (2001, 319).

7. See the op-ed piece by Maureen Dowd on Wolf, "The Alpha Beta Macarena" (*New York Times*, Nov. 14, 1999), which reports that Wolf was advising presidential candidate Al Gore, allegedly a "beta male," to become an "alpha male" (i.e., more macho and assertive). Such counsel is homologous with Wolf's "power feminism" advice to women and was widely ridiculed in the media, forcing the Gore campaign to distance itself from her "counsel." Dowd reported previously on Wolf's position with President Clinton's 1996 reelection campaign. At that time, Wolf assisted in the promotion of the image of the "president-as-good-father," which would present Clinton as "a comforting authority figure who builds and defends the family home" as a strategy "to help lure women voters" (*New York Times*, June 2, 1996, E 15). Indeed, *lure* most certainly seems to be the operative word, given not only Clinton's adventures with Monica Lewinsky but his support for draconian cutbacks in welfare and AFDC (Aid to Families with Dependent Children) programs. While such welfare programs are flawed, they have arguably "saved millions of families from hunger, homelessness, physical assault and total despair" (Sidel 1996, 84). In fact, widespread attacks on Wolf for her advice to Gore to be "Alpha male" and her subsequent distancing from the Gore campaign led Elaine Showalter to suggest that Wolf had failed "Power 101" (2001, 319). In fact, Marjorie Williams blames Wolf for the increasing gulf between Clinton and Gore which some believe was a major cause of Gore's failure to win the presidency in Election 2000:

> In addition to hardening Gore's growing fury (against Bill Clinton), Wolf had another important effect. Up to that time, success within GoreWorld, as it had come to be known by the White House, was defined by how well you could work with (and work) ClintonWorld. Wolf's example taught people coming into the Gore campaign that the fastest path to the candidates' heart was now anti-Clintonism. And within the White House, presidential staffers watched the shift in sentiment around Gore with growing alarm. (Williams 2001, 135)

8. It has been claimed that "The Seneca Falls Declaration is the single most important document of the nineteenth-century American women's movement. It was adopted at a meeting called to consider the 'social, civil, and religious rights of women,' which assembled at the Wesleyan Chapel at Seneca Falls, New York, on July 19, 1848" (Schneir 1994, 76).

It was at this famous women's rights meeting in Seneca Falls, New York—which was organized by leading U.S. feminists, Elizabeth Cady Stanton, Susan B. Anthony, Lucretia Mott, and others—that a "Declaration of Sentiments and Resolutions," drawn up by Stanton and others, which used the American Declaration of Independence as a model, was presented for ratification to over 300 people. (Schneir 1994, 76–77)

A close reading of the Seneca Falls Declaration, however, reveals resolutions, and an underlying spirit, which appear to be at odds with Wolf's so-called power feminist epistemology, especially in regard to the individualistic bias of her approach. For example, included in this call for women's equality is the more inclusive demand for women's commitment and promotion of "every righteous cause by every righteous means" (Schneir 1994, 82). Indeed, the altruistic essence of the Seneca Falls Declaration is a characteristic blatantly lacking from Wolf's individualistic "power" feminism.

9. "Difference feminism" refers to a school of writings and research that celebrates traditional female qualities as at being at least the equivalent—if not more valuable—than those generally ascribed to men; see Pollitt 1994, 42ff.

10. Denfeld joined Wolf, Hoff Sommers, and Paglia on the lecture circuit as women who attacked mainstream feminism for being irrelevant to most women. Her second book *Kill the Body, The Head Will Fall* (1997) describes her boxing experience and provides fragmentary reflections on violence, aggression, sports, and men and women. A *Salon* reviewer described it as "an inelegant mongrel of memoir and commentary . . . with long passages arguing that women are more violent than is ordinarily thought" (Feb. 26, 1997). Such views play into those that symmetrize male and female violence, as I discuss in the next chapter. Interestingly, it is conservative women like Wendy Shalit who have been arguing for more prudish sexual behavior, attacking feminism for going too far in advocating sexual liberation (Shalit 1999).

11. As discussed in chapter 1, Hoff Sommers connected with the right-wing Women's Freedom Network (WFN) and the Independent Women's Forum (IWF), which is now the major policy center for women's issues in the Bush administration. She acknowledges that her 2000 book *The War Against Boys* was funded by the rightwing W. H. Brady Foundation that underwrote her position as Brady Fellow at the American Enterprise Institute. Curiously, while Hoff Sommers called herself an "equity feminist" and presented equity as a positive ideal in her 1993 book, in her 2000 book she attacks "equity specialists" and those who militate for "gender equity," perhaps reflecting the views of her rightwing sponsors who are themselves enemies of gender, race, or class equity.

12. Hoff Sommers's unsubstantiated charges against an academic feminist elite appear particularly callous in light of the reality of the current condition of many of the feminist activists of the 1960s and 1970s. Indeed, Phyllis Chesler has carefully documented the contemporary plight of some of these women and has subsequently observed, "I am saddened and sobered by the realization that no more than a handful of feminists have been liberated from the lives of grinding poverty, illness, overwork, and endless worry that con-

tinue to afflict most women and men in America" (1994, 67). Chesler goes on to demonstrate that rather than being members of an imaginary well-funded monolithic
organization of feminist elders, dictating gender-feminist policy, "I have seen the best
minds of my feminist generation go 'mad' with battle fatigue, get sick, give up, disappear,
kill themselves, die, often alone, and in terrible isolation, as if we were already invisible:
to each other, and to ourselves, our role as pioneers . . . diminished, forgotten" (1994, 67).
Chesler poignantly documents her own problems in this regard. Indeed, Michele Landsberg reported that feminist pioneer Kate Millet circulated a desperate plea on the Internet,
stating that she could not get jobs, invitations to speak, or published and was living in
extreme poverty (*Toronto Star*, July 5, 1998). Since then, Millett's classic text *Sexual Politics*, which was out of print, has been republished.

3

The F-Word and the Victimization Debate

In this chapter, I focus on aspects of violence in the family and discuss how various schools of contemporary feminist thought confront, explain away, or challenge the issue of violence against women and children. The Hedda Nussbaum/ Joel Steinberg case from the late 1980s provides a useful test of how mainstream approaches to wife abuse and what I call "family terrorism" fail to address the complexity of the issue and demonstrate the need for perspectives such as those I propose in this study. The case is important because it first put on the media agenda—before the O. J. Simpson trials—the issue of male violence against women. The Nussbaum/Steinberg case also helped provoke productive debates within the feminist movement, which was divided over the issue of whether Hedda Nussbaum should be seen primarily as a victim of wife abuse or as a participant in her child's murder. Most crucially, I hope to reveal how the case shows both problems in formulating issues of family violence or dimensions of family terrorism and the ways that the antifeminist pseudofeminists mystify and obscure these issues. I believe the Nussbaum/Steinberg case dramatizes the need for the contextual and dialectical forms of critical feminism that I am trying to develop within this text. Moreover, the case has had major effects on arguments over violence against women and children, victimization, and legislation concerning family violence.

Following the themes of the first two chapters, I also engage debates over the F-word and discuss in detail the ways that feminist impersonators like Hoff Sommers manipulate statistics to downplay violence against women. This involves the complex issue of the use of statistics and empirical studies in debates over family violence and which studies are privileged. I highlight the importance of Linda Gordon's history of family violence, Ann Jones's books on violence against women, the classical research of R. Emerson and Russell Dobash in their *Violence against Wives*, and present the salutary warnings of Darrell Huff's classic text *How to Lie with Statistics*.

THE F-WORD

Another of the central themes of the pseudofeminists' assault on the feminist movement, which is exploited by Wolf, Roiphe, and, especially, Hoff Sommers, concerns the exploitation and reduction of a highly complex issue regarding many women's aversion to the feminist label. The question of young women's (in particular) identification with, and as, feminists is a contentious one. However, on close examination, this situation is far more contested than the betrayal feminists and traditional media would lead us to believe.

Hoff Sommers has emerged as a leading contender in promoting hostility toward "feminism" through her inflammatory misrepresentations of the nature of the contemporary feminist: "Their primary concern is to persuade the public that the so-called normal man is a morally defective human being who gets off on hurting women" (*The Washington Times*, June 5, 1995). This theme, which Hoff Sommers has been promoting for years, is again the focus of her recent book, *The War against Boys: How Misguided Feminism Is Harming Our Young Men* (2000). Once again, it is feminists and their complicit male colleagues that are the origin of societal problems, in this case mistreatment of boys within educational institutions and not institutional or social structures and relations.

The dominant media, of course, promotes this image of the man-hating feminist witch, while assisting in legitimating betrayal feminists as a credible antithesis. These "newest feminists," like Hoff Sommers, according to *The Washington Times* (June 5, 1995), "worst of all . . . like men and are willing to work with them rather than against them." Even though feminists, women's liberationists before them and suffragettes even earlier, have demonstrated diligently and repeatedly that this provocative antimale stereotype is simply that, it appears to be a myth that enjoys a periodic revitalization. "Ever since the media discovered feminism in the mid-nineteenth century, they have been more inclined to denounce it than study it" (Faludi 1995, 33). Needless to say, the impersonator feminists are taking full advantage of the dominant media (as well as other hegemonic societal institutions) to sell themselves:

> Theirs is a beguiling line of argument because it is (a) positive, in a rah-rah "Year of the Woman" way, and (b) nonthreatening. [They] aren't encouraging women to pursue social change, and they certainly aren't asking men to change. It is no-risk feminism for a fearful age: just post your achievements, make nice with men, and call it a day. The Power of Positive Thinking will take care of the rest. (Faludi 1995, 32–33)

Although a vitriolic attitude toward individual men is espoused by a small minority of feminists (within a particular theoretical framework), the majority of feminisms distinguish between individual men and the collective system of patriarchy. However, the fantasy of the man-hating feminist plays a fundamental role in the betrayal feminists' indictment against "gender feminism." They are, in fact, exploiting and embracing the new right's take on feminism, which equates "all feminism with hatred of men, sex, marriage and family" (*Newsday*, May 22, 1994). bell hooks identifies the sheer lunacy of this notion, especially in regard to the historical antecedents of the actual nature of feminisms' position on the so-called man question.

> [W]e are witnessing a new generation of women, who, like their sexist male counter-parts, are aggressively ahistorical and unaware of the long tradition of radical/revolu-tionary feminist thought that celebrates inclusiveness and liberatory sexuality. Both these groups prefer to seek out the most conservative, narrow-minded feminist thought on sex and men, then arrogantly use these images to represent the move-ment. (1994a, 78)

Indeed, hooks pulls no punches when it comes to shattering the myth of the rabid, man-hating feminist stereotype exploited by the feminist impersonators and their media pimps.

> [M]any sexist men remain unable to accept that women (and our male allies) who repudiate patriarchy assert sexual agency in new and exciting ways that are mutually humanizing and satisfying. It has always served the interest of the patriarchal status quo for men to represent the feminist woman as antisex and antimale. Even though the real lives of women active in feminist movements never conformed to this repre-sentation, it continues to prevail in the popular imagination because the subjugated knowledge that embracing feminism intensifies sexual pleasure for men and women in this society, no matter our sexual practice, is dangerous information. (1994a, 78)

Once again the pseudofeminists are depending on an either-or vision of reality to distort public opinion as well as to reinforce dominant myths regarding femi-nisms. Marilyn Friedman attacks the opportunistic attempt of betrayal feminists to perpetuate this stereotypical male-bashing depiction by eloquently describing the legitimate underlying philosophy of feminisms' take on the nature of male behavior in relation to individual men, the collective male, and patriarchy:

> [F]eminists in general do not promote an attitude of resentment against individual men unless those men, as individuals, abuse, exploit or oppress women (as rapists, batterers, harassers, misogynists, etc.). A great deal of feminist theory is devoted to analyzing institutions and practices as social wholes, along with their characteristic male biases and the individual men who rise within them to positions of power and authority. This sort of analysis is hardly identical to promoting resentment against all individual men. (Friedman and Narveson 1995, 30–31)

Moreover, betrayal feminists are also perpetuating the fiction that men do not and cannot profess a profeminist philosophy. In fact, the underlying humanitar-ian essence of feminisms demands men's involvement and recognition of the disenabling nature—for all peoples, at different levels and dimensions—of patriarchal relations of domination and oppression. For as Friedman reminds us:

[S]ome men enjoy, exercise, and promote "male privileges" a good deal less than do other men. Feminists recognize these differences (often based on race and class identities) and modify their reactions accordingly. In addition, many feminist women feel a solidarity with profeminist men who challenge male-biased and male-dominated social practices. (1995, 31)

Unfortunately, however, those men engaged in feminist praxis are often categorized as "wimps" (rhymes with limp) and are susceptible to some of the most denigrating insults perpetuated against contemporary men in that their "cocksmanship" and "manliness" are impugned (i.e., they are impotent, "pussy-whipped," "henpecked," etc.). Katie Roiphe devotes a particularly mean-spirited chapter of her book *The Morning After*, which caricaturizes and often cruelly stereotypes academic feminists and "profeminist" men. Her description manages to encompass the scorn and derision heaped upon men who demonstrate feminist sympathies, and she incorporates an insidious homophobic subtext in her characterizations. Indeed, her portraits simultaneously reveal and reinforce many of the dominant ideological prejudices employed against these supposedly pathetic, ugly profeminist men. Moreover, Roiphe confirms the ever-present myth that the realm of feminist men is inhabited by geeks and losers.

Peter is not conventionally handsome. He is short, plump, and wears glasses. He looks nervous, years of facing schoolyard bullies still show on his face. . . . Peter tells me that his closest friends in high school were women. He says that he never really went through a hanging-around-and-drinking-beer-with-the-guys phase. . . . In Marc's image of the ideal world, people exist along a bisexual continuum. He says that as far as he is concerned, Robert Bly's "soft man," with his quiche-loving seventies sensitivity, should be an ideal. (Roiphe 1993, 131–32, 135)

This form of mockery, directed toward those who exhibit feminist-type leanings proves to be a convincing deterrent to many men—and women—from either publicly or privately investigating or associating themselves with the empowering principles of feminist theory or practice. Indeed, the fear of ridicule proves to be an effectual obstruction to critical engagement with feminism. Paula Kamen identifies this as fear of "the stigma" of feminism.

The twisted, all-too-common logic about feminists goes like this: If you stand up for women, you must hate men. Therefore, you must be angry. Thus, you must be ugly and can't get a man anyway. Hence, you must be a dyke. . . . Under these conditions, the feminist stigma is powerful and self-perpetuating. It blocks people from raising their consciousness, discovering the fundamentals behind feminism and taking a stand. In a way the stigma acts like barbed wire around the real issues, the real problems, the real history and the real connections. (Kamen 1991, 7)

Moreover, the antimale stereotype has been highly effective in provoking prejudice toward feminisms, which the feminist impersonators have exploited, especially in the case of young women. Indeed, impersonator and postfeminists continue to hit the college and professional tour circuit—appropriating and co-opting Catherine Stimpson's original telling, tongue-in-cheek phrase describing the dominant equation of feminism with "the F-word." Regina Barreca (1991) in her brilliant and often hilarious text on women's humor, *They Used to Call Me Snow White . . . But I Drifted*, provides a clear description of Stimpson's position.

Catherine R. Stimpson wrote an article in *Ms.* in 1987 about how important it is for women to learn to say the "F Word" in public. Stimpson, who is the dean of the graduate school at Rutgers University, was of course referring to the word "feminism" when she used the term the "F Word." We know well enough that nobody's embarrassed to say the word "fuck" anymore, but a lot of women are still hesitant to say the word "feminism" in mixed company—as if saying "Yes, I'm a feminist" is much more unladylike than telling somebody, for example, to "fuck off." (1991, 177)

It is indeed unfortunate that the label "feminist" has a pejorative meaning for many. Katha Pollitt, a prolific feminist writer, describes the duplicitous and complicated role of the media in reinforcing antifeminist bias.

It's important to see how much of our ideas are constructed for us by the world around us, by the media. . . . And when it comes to feminism . . . the media has portrayed it inaccurately. Feminists are portrayed as man-hating—in two contrary ways. One is the woman who is sexual the way a man is sexual—too aggressive and demanding. And then there is the contrary stereotype which is feminism as man-hating lesbian. (Katha Pollitt, *The Baltimore Sun*, Jan. 8, 1995)

Indeed, feminist scholar Susan Douglas expands upon the deleterious effects of the media's long-term denigration and perpetuation of the feminist stereotype. In her fascinating and entertaining overview of the contradictory nature of images of women in popular culture, *Where the Girls Are* (1994), Douglas demonstrates that:

The moment the women's movement emerged in 1970, feminism once again became a dirty word, with considerable help from the mainstream news media. News reports and opinion columnists created a new stereotype, of fanatics, "braless bubbleheads," Amazons, "the angries," and "a band of wild lesbians." The result is that we all know what feminists are. They are shrill, overly aggressive, man-hating, ball-busting, selfish, hairy, extremist, deliberately unattractive women with absolutely no sense of humor who see sexism at every turn. They make men's testicles shrivel up to the size of peas, they detest the family and think all children should be deported or drowned. Feminists are relentless, unforgiving, and unwilling to bend or compromise; they are singlehandedly responsible for the high divorce rate, the shortage of decent men, and the unfortunate proliferation of Birkenstocks in America. . . . As recently as 1989,

Time announced that "hairy legs haunt the feminist movement" and concluded that the women's movement was "hopelessly dated." (7)

The result has been that for many young women, the term *feminism* has suffered the worst possible fate that can be afforded one in this media culture: it has become "unfashionable." As Paula Kamen puts it, "Before a few years ago, like many of my generation, I had vague images in my head—from the media and hearing people talk—of lunatic, testosterone-crazed lesbians burning their confining underthings in garbage-can bonfires. They were wearing something masculine and practical, like flannel lumberjack shirts. Toughskin jeans from Sears—the kind we had to wear when we were little—and, of course, combat boots (Kamen 1991, 9).

Barreca goes on to explain how this erroneous notion of feminism is not only out of touch with the reality of the term but is also a male defined concept. She talks about her horror, initially, at being identified with the F-word.

> I thought being a feminist meant I couldn't wear lipstick or crave men with small behinds. . . . I thought "feminist" meant no more steamy flirtations or prolonged shopping trips. I thought it meant braided hair and short nails, maybe mandatory tofu. I certainly associated feminism with humorless, dour, and—worst of all—unblinkingly earnest women. That was sort of like believing the mouse's version of the cat, since it entails being given access to a vision that could see nothing besides teeth and claws. . . . I was warned about so-called feminists. I was told by boyfriends, friends, relatives, professors, and other disreputable sources that such women were ambitious, sharp-tongued, a little too smart for their own good. They told me that only women who couldn't get laid got political. They told me what was perhaps the biggest and most interesting lie of all: that independence and ambition were unattractive in a woman. (Barreca 1991, 174)

Further, many young women reveal that any demonstration of assertiveness, in relation to sexism, is often deemed so unfashionable by not only one's peers but also by those in positions of authority that it can provoke others to bully and ridicule them.

> At my school, when boys put girls down or make sexist remarks, some of the girls even laugh. And whenever I say anything, everyone tells me not to take things so seriously. Girls who stick up for themselves are called "femi-nazis" by the boys. When we were having a class discussion, even one of the supposedly "cool" liberal female teachers laughed at the guys' attitudes. (Abigail Ryder, sixteen, Wellesley, Mass. In *Parade Magazine*, Nov. 5, 1995, 6)

Yet despite the barriers constructed against them, scores of younger women are combating this stereotype by speaking up and espousing feminist positions. For example, writings like the 1995 anthology *Listen Up: Voices from the Next Feminist Generation* include such heartening and optimistic statements as those provided by Barbara Findlen in her introduction to the text. She, along with a number of other feminists from her generation, discuss the excitement of being given the opportunity to be "a part of a massive, growing, vibrant feminist movement at the age of eleven—something that literally had not been possible for . . . my older sisters, my mother, or any of my other feminist role models" (xi).

> To me, the existence of feminism—and a feminist movement—meant that the rage I felt was no longer impotent. . . . The legacy of feminism for me was a sense of entitlement. . . . While this is certainly not the kind of experience every young woman, or even every young feminist, has had, the point is that it's the kind of experience *only* a woman of this generation could have had. We are the first generation for whom feminism has been entwined in the fabric of our lives; it is natural that many of us are feminists. (Findlen 1995, xii)

Within this context, unsubstantiated claims by betrayal feminists like Naomi Wolf that "most American women of all races and classes—and younger women, in particular—really dislike the word 'feminism'" (1993, 60) must be seriously questioned. The false claim reveals the propensity of betrayal feminists to exaggerate, distort data, and fail to provide credible documentation to support their so-called facts. Paula Kamen provided a far more sophisticated analysis, in her contextualized, well-documented, and statistically sound study. While readily identifying "the older generation's" need "to recognize the special threat of the feminist stigma to people of our age group" (1991, 7) as well as building better bridges between these two generations, she discovered:

> In the interviews I conducted, as well as in polls by publications such as *Time* magazine and the *New York Times*, young women have shown they support the feminist political agenda [and] appreciate the strides made by the women's movement. Since 1989 young feminist activists have been awakened and galvanized by threats to abortion rights. . . . Other action by young feminist activists—most of it not taking the visible form of protests—is steadily increasing: working within older women's organizations, educating and lobbying from campuses, mobilizing communities at a grass-roots level and taking the lead in other progressive struggles, including environmental and antiracism work. (1991, 3–4)

Contrary to the popular myths perpetuated by the impersonator feminists, many of these young women were and are attracted to, and involved in, feminisms precisely because they understand that it is a multidimensional contested domain rather than a universalized totalitarian regime. Moreover, young feminists welcome these differences as a reflection of the diversities of the realities of their own personal and collective experience and context. As Barbara Findlen puts it:

> Generation X, thirteenth generation, twentysomething—whatever package you buy this age group in—one of the characteristics we're known for is our disunity. . . .

Even in eras that offer unifying forces more momentous than *The Brady Bunch*, each individual's personal experiences define the time for her. Women's *experiences* of sexism are far from universal; they have always been affected by race, class, geographic location, disability, sexual identity, religion and just plain luck. How patriarchy crosses our paths and how we deal with that can also be determined by our families, school systems, the degree and type of violence in our communities and myriad other factors. So what may appear to be a splintering in this generation often comes from an honest assessment of our differences as each of us defines her place and role in feminism. (Findlen 1995, xiii)

In fact, the impersonator feminists' claims concerning the general public's—and women's in particular—dismissal of contemporary feminisms, as well as their assertions concerning the majority of women's disavowal of the feminist label, appears to be yet another in a series of misrepresentation, omission, or inadequate research. Surprisingly, 1996 studies demonstrated the inaccuracy of betrayal feminists' charges in these matters.

The latest Harris poll on the subject, a nationwide sampling of 1,364 people that was released last summer, found that not only do 71 percent of Americans (men and women) support the women's movement, a majority of women identify themselves as feminists. (Faludi 1996b, 26)[1]

VICTIMIZATION AND THE MYTH
OF VICTIM FEMINISM

Yet the betrayal feminists continue their public campaign to distort the realities of feminisms by painting feminists not only as male-bashing, ball-breakers but also as whining victims. Although at odds with the depiction of man-hating, competitive, vindictive, sexually dominating bitches—like the Glenn Close character, Alex Forrest, in the 1987 film *Fatal Attraction* (and all her various media incarnations)—women-as-victim has become a common theme of the feminist impersonators' supposed disenchantment with the feminist autocracy. It complements their accusations of the pervasion of puritanism and Victorianism within the movement. More importantly, however, the betrayal feminists alleged animus against "victimization" allows for highlighted, sound bite–style discussion involving what they have deemed to be exaggerations and gerrymandering in relation to issues concerning violence, rape, harassment, and a number of other issues. Camille Paglia labels feminists who address these types of violence as "Infirmary Feminists."

Let's get rid of Infirmary Feminism, with its bedlam of bellyachers, anorexics, bulimics, depressives, rape victims, and incest survivors. Feminism has become a catch-all vegetable drawer where bunches of clingy sob sisters can store their moldy neuroses. (*Toronto Star*, Nov. 8, 1994)

In fact, within feminisms' multivalent theories, the notion of victimization is a contested domain, to say the least. The issue has sparked a wealth of theoretical debate and practical responses in a variety of schools associated with a complexity of philosophical and scientific debates and issues within the biological, psychological, anthropological, sociological, and ideological realms. However, criticism of feminists for what some believe to be an exaggeration of women's status as victims has been appropriated, reduced, and one-dimensionalized by the betrayal feminists' pundits in order to advance their dualistic good versus evil argument (see chapter 2).

Teresa Ebert provides an insightful elucidation of the *retrofeminists'* (her term for identifying those she describes as reactionary counterfeminists) Manichaean projection technique in this regard: "retrofeminists translate the very meaning of feminism into its other: turning a liberating feminism into victim feminism. They blame feminism for *causing* women's oppression, for producing victims" (1996, 254). The result of the stigmatization of "victim feminism" downplays the violence against women and makes it appear that those who are fighting against it are whiners who exaggerate women's victim status and demean women into a subordinate role.

Katie Roiphe, a twenty-something Princeton graduate student, became a flavor-of-the-month betrayal feminist celebrity by deploying this tactic. In her book *The Morning After: Sex, Fear, and Feminism on Campus* (1993), she claims that "rape-crisis" or "campus feminists" have convinced many young women to cry "rape" the morning after a night of "bad" or coercive sexual relations, thus exploiting the victimization ploy to the max. Apparently, according to Roiphe, devious feminists have constructed an insidious campaign, which finds its basis in distorting "facts" and presenting women as passive victims, thus reinforcing "traditional views about the fragility of the female body and will" (154).

> Preoccupied with issues like date rape and sexual harassment, campus feminists produce endless images of women as victims—women offended by a professor's dirty joke, women pressured into sex by peers, women trying to say no but not managing to get it across. (1993, 149)

Roiphe does not deny that rape and violence against women exist, but argues that feminists are presenting an exaggerated account of such actions and not only misrepresent the related statistics but also use faulty methodologies.[2] Her argument rests on the MacGuffin principle, in that she has invented a malicious feminist terrorist organization, committed to stealing the hearts and minds of young women. This insidious victim feminism supposedly transforms young women into cringing, mindless, victims who can be controlled by the rape-crisis, campus feminist elite who are using "rape as a red flag . . . to rally the feminist troops" (1993, 151).

Rape is a natural trump card for feminism. Arguments about rape can be used to sequester feminism in the teary province of trauma and crisis. By blocking analysis with its claims to unique pandemic suffering, the rape crisis becomes a powerful source of authority. (1993, 151)

The outrageous claim that feminists are conspiring to block analytic discussion of crucial issues like rape is, once again, an apt example of how betrayal feminists rely on classic projection techniques to advance their binary oppositional logic. Moreover, they are able to appear convincing through cloaking their reductionist and oversimplified notions within a poetic, polemical, and often sarcastic discourse. As Faludi puts it:

The pod feminists argue that the feminist "establishment" exaggerates women's inferior social and economic status to generate attention and support for its cause. From sexual harassment to eating disorders to rape to adolescent girls' low self-esteem— you name it, the pods say, it's all hot air and hype. Furthermore, they say that feminists manage to pass off this malarkey as truth because the feminist-blinded media just buy what the women's movement has to sell without examining it. (1995, 36)

Yet that Roiphe, like so many other pseudofeminist pundits, is more form than substance seems to enhance—rather than detract from—the media celebrity status afforded her. Indeed, her work has been criticized by numerous critics as problematic in a variety of areas. According to Katha Pollitt, for example, "it is a careless and irresponsible performance, poorly argued and full of misrepresentations, slapdash research and gossip" (1995, 163–64). Yet, as Faludi has pointed out, the dominant media is resistant to presenting information that reveals the feminist impersonators' falsification of facts concerning violence against women. As Faludi notes, "The media continue to pass along without question bogus findings promoted by right-wing foundations while going on high alert whenever a feminist writer fumbles a statistical footnote" (1996a, 10).

However, critiques of their positions have hardly stopped betrayal feminists from citing the same erroneous sources as well as each other's arguments as credible, legitimate findings.[3] That these often unsubstantiated or imprecisely documented claims are given credence is even more offensive, given recent reports by such well-established and professional nonfeminist organizations as the U.S. Justice Department and the American Medical Association. Of course, all statistical studies of human behavior are not absolute but only representations that need to be qualified and interpreted, a position that seems not to be grasped by many researchers, including antifeminists. Indeed, those anti- and postfeminists who seem fixated with numbers do not seem to recognize that stats and data are contextually mediated. Consequently, they become obsessed with enumerations that neutralize and dehumanize the real material human relations, which these women should actually be addressing. Instead, data is too often employed, by antifeminists, as foils to provoke division and promote counter-productive arguments that distract from and damage the legitimacy of feminist scholarship and activism, especially in relation to issues of family terrorism.

Indeed, there are profound problems associated with dependence upon statist-istal evidence as definitive, especially given the abundance of diverse and contra-dictory findings due to differing methods, data samples, and other factors (as discussed later in this chapter). For example, a U.S. Department of Justice report stated that "Findings of intimate partner victimization vary widely from study to study" and "there are many gaps in the scientific literature on intimate partner violence" (Tjaden and Thoennes 2000, 1). Unfortunately, disparate, decontextua-lized and sometimes illegitimate findings can be easily cited and are often employed to back up fallacious claims. Even cases of "scientific studies," like those conducted by the Department of Justice, demonstrate serious inconsisten-cies and indicate the enigmatic nature of empirical research which is so often treated as "objective." For example,

The new Justice Department report, covering 1992–1993 . . . concluded that there were 500,000 incidents of sexual assault a year. These included 310,000 rapes or attempted rapes—twice as many as published in the previous reports—and 186,000 other sexual assaults. (*New York Times*, Aug. 26, 1995)

These figures are double those of the Justice Department's previous report (which had been cited by many of the betrayal feminists to discount so-called exaggerated statistics referred to by some feminist scholars). The doubling of these numbers reflected that in 1995, for the first time, people were asked spe-cifically about rape (*New York Times*, Aug. 26, 1995). Moreover, the report found that 80 percent of rapes were perpetuated by someone known to the assailant and, in many cases, "rape victims [did] not label themselves as such because they mistakenly believe that forced sex can be rape only if the rapist is a stranger" (*New York Times*, Aug. 26, 1995) Many of these attacks would thus fall into the catego-ries of "date" or "acquaintance rape," which betrayal feminists are most apt to criticize as being inflated incidents, brazenly misrepresented by rape-crisis femi-nists to provoke a "hysterical" climate. As Camille Paglia explains it:

I think the definition of rape has gotten much too broad. I would prefer to confine rape to either stranger rape or to the intrusion of sex into a nonsexual situation. I am a 60's radical. I believe in the free love ideals of my own generation. What I don't like is a kind of reactionary turn toward puritanism that current feminism has taken. (*Crossfire*, CNN, November 26, 1993)

Within this context, the findings of both the Justice Department and the American Medical Association (AMA) would fall into the realm identified by Paglia as "feminist hysteria." The AMA's 1995 release included such devastating findings as "61 percent of rape victims are under the age of 18; three-quarters of sexual assaults are committed by a friend, acquaintance, intimate partner or family member [and] males are the victims in 5 percent of reported sexual assaults" (*New York Times*, Nov. 7, 1995). This so-called feminist hysteria about rape of women would seem to also apply to a 1998 collaborative study jointly funded by the U.S. Department of Justice and U.S. Department of Health and Human Services:

> Using a defintion of rape that includes forced vaginal, oral, and anal intercourse, nearly 18% of women in the United States said they had been raped (14.8%) or the victim of an attempted rape (2.8%) in their lifetime. Based on these survey figures, 17.7 million women are projected to have been raped. More than half of rape victims said they were under age 17 when first raped. Of the women who reported being raped at some time in their lives, 22% were under 12 years old and 32% were 12 to 17 years old when they were first raped. (Siskin 2001, 2)

Moreover, the AMA also reported on the pathological reality of contemporary family relations in that:

> [F]amily violence—domestic violence, child physical abuse and neglect, child sexual abuse and mistreatment of the elderly—was widespread. Each year in the United States, it said, two million to four million women are battered, 1500 women are killed by intimate partners, 1.8 million elderly people are mistreated and 1.7 million reports of child abuse are filed. (*New York Times*, Nov. 7, 1995)

According to a study published in the *Journal of the American Medical Association*, one in five high school girls has been physically or sexually abused by a dating partner, a statistic supplemented by recent estimates from the U.S. Centers of Disease Control and Prevention that indicates 22 percent of high school students are victims of nonsexual dating violence (*AP*, July 31, 2001). Accordingly, the American Academy of Pediatrics has recommended that doctors screen teens for sexual assaults (*Los Angeles Times*, June 11, 2001). Earlier, the AMA concluded that "this crime [sexual assault] is shrouded in silence, caused by unfair social myths and biases that incriminate victims rather than offenders" (*New York Times*, Nov. 7, 1995). And this silence is encouraged and perpetuated by self-righteous, collaborationist feminists who are, in fact, contributing to the escalation of sexual violence through their assaults on feminist critiques and techniques designed to address and publicize these matters.

The co-optation and reduction of antirape feminist positions and the polemic against victimization by the pseudofeminists have serious deleterious consequences for the struggles against violence toward women, children, and the elderly. Furthermore, the impersonator feminists depiction of so-called rape-crisis feminist's maintenance and perpetuation of victimized behaviors is sheer fabrication. Indeed, as the AMA justifiably points out, it is silence that preserves and provokes a victimized mentality; and it is precisely the termination of this silence that underlies progressive feminist theoretical and practical epistemologies.

As Faludi has accurately stated, "If feminism stands for anything, it is the belief that women can and must stand up and speak out. Feminism identifies victimization not so we can wallow in it, but so we can wallop it" (1995, 36).

Yet, collaborationist feminists continue to demonize and confuse processes designed to combat victimization with submission to victimization. As Marty Langelan astutely points out, "women are anything but passive when it comes to assault and harassment" (*The Arizona Republic*, Nov. 30, 1993). Not only is there an increase in women fighting back in cases of rape and attempted rape, but there is also a general escalation among women and girls in combating and confronting harassment and sexual violence in schools, the workplace, and the public arena (*The Arizona Republic*, Nov. 30, 1993). Michele Landsberg, a Canadian feminist activist, writer, and journalist, astutely notes that the popularization and appropriation of serious feminist critiques of "victimization" by antifeminists and the media's exploitative misrepresentation of the notion are linked to the unifying escalation of feminist concerns and public critiques of violence against women.

Not coincidentally, as the anti-violence campaign gains force, numbers and clout, a neat little parallel industry of female anti-feminist commentators has sprung up to give comfort to those who would like to deny or downplay the troubling specter of male violence. (*Toronto Star*, Nov. 28, 1992)

She goes on to aptly describe the self-righteous and opportunistic attitude that permeates the collaborationist antifeminists' arguments in this regard.

Their theme is that women aren't victims. Not at home, not on the job. Feminists should just stop whining. They base this wholesale dismissal on their own happy accomplishments—"Hey, I look at me, I'm a chemical engineer! No more need for feminism!" Seeing the world through Me-colored glasses, they're a good example of the Reagan-Bush triumphalists, the "I'm O.K.; You can drop dead" crowd who celebrated their own greed and trashed the poor as "losers." . . . Not only is the analysis wretchedly lacking in the economic sphere—no one can rationally dispute the fact of women's unequal pay opportunity and access to justice—but when it comes to the issue of violence, it's breathtakingly insensitive. (*Toronto Star*, Nov. 28, 1992)

In truth, victimization is preserved and enhanced through shame and silence, and feminist demands for women to speak out and publicly demonstrate their outrage is not only an empowering process but also one of the best defenses against a victimized mentality. In fact, "across the country, in university dorms, high-school gyms, libraries, church basements and rec rooms, it's those dreadful 'rape-crisis feminists' who have been doing the one thing that works: teaching women and kids how to defend themselves" (*The Arizona Republic*, Nov. 30, 1993).

Betrayal feminists, however, choose to ignore and misrepresent the gains for women in the struggle against violence, in part, by nitpicking over numbers applied to document cases of sexual violence. But, "denying the numbers and denouncing feminists won't make those statistics disappear. And dealing realistically with the risks does not make women weaklings" (*The Arizona Republic*, Nov. 30, 1993). Katha Pollitt provides one of the most reasonable contextualizations of this issue when she asserts, "One in five, one in eight—what if it's 'only' one in ten or twelve? Social science isn't physics. Exact numbers are important, and elusive, but surely what is significant here is that lots of different studies, with different agendas, sample populations, and methods, tend in the same direction" (1995, 168).

Moreover, as Susan Faludi points out, feminists are hardly infallible in this regard and usually make every effort to correct these errors when they become apparent. However, "[e]veryone makes mistakes, and feminist writers are no exception, as any feminist will tell you. But what happens to a mistake once it's made—whether it is decried or adopted, vilified or glorified—depends less on its magnitude than on its political utility" (1996a, 10).

The collaborationist feminist impersonators, however, do not confine themselves to the area of empirical findings. One of the most deceitful and appalling techniques, employed by Roiphe in particular, is her attempt to impugn so-called victim feminists concerns over date rape in a way that suspiciously resembles classic racist assumptions. In this sense, Roiphe argues that the term *date rape* is often a misnomer for what are, in actuality, "miscommunications" due to "differences in background" and "cultural mixing" (1995, 158).

> Not so many years ago . . . [s]tudents came from the same social milieu with the same social rules, and it was assumed that everyone knew more or less how they were expected to behave with everyone else. Diversity and multiculturalism were unheard of. . . . With the shift in college environments, with the introduction of black kids, Asian kids, Jewish kids, kids from the wrong side of the tracks of nearly every railroad in the country, there was an accompanying anxiety about how people behave. When ivory tower meets melting pot, it causes tension, some confusion, some need for readjustment. (Roiphe 1995, 157–58)

Nelson W. Aldrich Jr. (1995) takes Roiphe to task for this outrageous analysis, criticizing the insular provincialism of her position while calling attention to its bigoted fear of cultural and racial diversity.

> For if it's true that our erotic mayhem, such as it may be, is a consequence of crossed cultural signals, then all we have to do to fix matters is a little cultural cleansing. Schools, single bars, neighborhoods, municipal swimming pools, cruise ships, wherever people meet to date and mate (and possibly rape) need only be segregated by village culture, that is, by the variety of second-nature nurture they received at birth, merely because of their birth, and all will be well. (183)

That Roiphe is taken seriously at all is even more outrageous, given the medley and span of her misrepresentations, which are hardly restricted to the sociological or empirical domain. Ever diligent in her mission to name and vilify "feminist prophets of the rape crisis," she identifies Susan Brownmiller as a leading figure in the rape-crisis feminist conspiracy to propagate victimization (Roiphe 1995, 151). Brownmiller indeed brought the politics of rape into the mainstream with her 1975 best-seller *Against Our Will: Men, Women and Rape.* However, Roiphe presents a complete distortion of Brownmiller's position on battered women and victimization by claiming that Brownmiller is a "victim feminist." Indeed, if Roiphe had done even her rudimentary homework and bothered to read the afterward to *Waverly Place* (1989), Brownmiller's fascinating and often gut-wrenching best-selling fictional account of the case of Hedda Nussbaum, she would have discovered that Brownmiller is sharply critical of both the presentation of Hedda Nussbaum as a "victim" and the employment of the "battered wife syndrome" argument as a justification for Nussbaum's criminal behavior.

Moreover, Brownmiller provides a balanced analysis of women as objects of oppression and subjects of struggle while arguing against conceptualizing women merely as victims. However, as bell hooks demonstrates, betrayal feminists employ the imaginary argument of a monolithic reductive feminism for their own personal advantage in an attempt to bolster their own image as courageous, independent, individual insurgents.

> The absence of our works and our words makes it appear that Roiphe stands alone in her will to name and critique aspects of feminism. Forget the nature of her argument, the underlying message irrespective of the issues she raises is that most feminists refuse to embrace any form of dissent, are rigid and dogmatic—with the exception of herself and perhaps Camille Paglia. Had she insisted on acknowledging the range of dissenting voices within feminism, the multi-dimensional critiques that already exist, the underlying premise of her book would have lost its bite. (hooks 1994a, 105)

Not only do impersonator feminists misrepresent feminist activists' attempts to address important women's issues such as rape and violence, they also systematically misrepresent feminist attempts to set forth facts on these issues, accusing them of exaggeration and misrepresentation. In the next section, accordingly, I want to address the way that empirical studies concerning violence against women are abused by betrayal feminists and used to deny or minimize the nature and extent of rape and other forms of brutality.

EMPIRICAL STUDIES AND THE MISREPRESENTATION OF REALITY

In her enthusiasm to vilify gender-feminists for their perpetuation of "lies" in relation to the abuse of women, Christina Hoff Sommers exploits a controversial and widely debated finding regarding a 1993 FAIR publication that claimed that violence against women increased during the annual Super Bowl Sunday football game.[4] The contentious issue revolved around a statement by Sheila Kuehl of the California Women's Law Center, citing a study that found that in 1988–1989, reports of women-battering in northern Virginia escalated by 40 percent in conjunction with the Super Bowl. Unfortunately, it appears that Kuehl misrepresented the study, and when Ken Ringle of the *Washington Post* discovered the error, he confronted Linda Mitchell of FAIR for her failure to denounce Kuehl's assessment of the findings (Wolf 1993, 99–100; Hoff Sommers 1994, 190–92). Hence:

> The Ringle story, "debunking" feminists' claims of violence against women on Super Bowl Sunday, was national news; Alan Dershowitz attacked "self-proclaimed women's advocates" and what he called their "reliance on hearsay" in the *Los Angeles Times*. *The Wall Street Journal* compared FAIR's campaign to Orson Welles's "The War of the Worlds," a hoax about invasion from another planet. (Wolf 1993, 99)

As far as Hoff Sommers is concerned, this is the end of the story, and she presents it as one of the most glaring examples of gender feminists duplicity in proclaiming erroneous empirical facts, providing her with another notch in her campaign to discredit the movement (Hoff Sommers 1994, 190–92). Yet, further investigation of this issue reveals, once again, that Hoff Sommers is engaging in what seems to have become her favorite pastime of projecting onto the other the sins of the self. Hoff Sommers blatantly and dogmatically claims that "No study shows that Super Bowl Sunday is in any way different from other days in the amount of domestic violence" (1994, 15). But Hoff Sommers's dubious choice of this event to back up her attack on "gender feminism" reveals the shoddiness of her own scholarship and failure to address the literature that put in question her dogmatic claims. For this intrepid would-be scholar has omitted scrutiny of subsequent follow-ups to the Super Bowl Sunday scandal and has ignored a variety of studies that document increased violence against women during the Super Bowl. Indeed, Naomi Wolf,[5] whose "power feminism" earns Hoff Sommers's praises, cites statistics and studies that confirm the alleged "fallacy" of Super Bowl Sunday violence:

> But after the explosive coverage of FAIR's alleged shortcomings, the other side of the story went largely unremarked. The *Los Angeles Daily News* also found that calls went up markedly at at least two shelters after the game. When the *Portland Oregonian* investigated at the Portland Women's Crisis Line, it learned that on Super Bowl Sunday the information clearinghouse had taken thirty calls—three times the average number. "We could go to fifty or sixty calls," said Tess Wiseheart, the crisis line's executive director. "We've always noticed a climb on Super Bowl Sunday, and we always put on extra help." (Wolf 1993, 100)

Once again, we are reminded of Faludi's contention that the media emphasizes and exploits errors, no matter how trivial, in feminist empirical research while ignoring erroneous statements that support antifeminist bias. Moreover, it is interesting to note that both Hoff Sommers and the dominant media conveniently avoided citing other empirical studies that would put the emphasis where it belongs. In other words, although the specific figure of 40 percent may have been erroneous, the fact is inconsequential in light of the evidence presented by a variety of Super Bowl violence studies, which identified an increase in the battery of woman with this particular sports event. As Dobash and Dobash revealed as long ago as 1979:

> Many women reported that when the husband returned home after being in [a] predominantly male setting he expected her immediately to meet his every need. Demands for the performance of wifely duties, sexual and/or domestic, might be refused, with the result that the husband becomes violent. (121)

There is no doubt that researchers like Dobash and Dobash (1979), Enloe (1993), McBride (1995), Gordon (1994), and others account for, and make sense of, the increase in male violence against women, not only during Super Bowl Sunday but also during similar kinds of events that are experienced in particular kinds of male environments. Furthermore, Hoff Sommers's and others' failure to acknowledge research that contravenes findings of so-called scientific studies they choose to cite demonstrates how subjective bias is consistently employed to shore up allegedly neutral, objective facts of life and "commonsense" arguments.

Given their goals of discrediting feminism, it is hardly surprising to find betrayal feminists, like Hoff Sommers, embracing and promoting the ideological myth of pure "objectivity" to shore up their propagandist stance regarding "victim feminists"—itself a myth constructed by critics of feminism. It is also typical that Hoff Sommers et al. refuse to acknowledge the role of their own subjective bias in deciding which of the supposedly "objective" empiricist studies they will cite to support their arguments. Indeed, both Hoff Sommers's motives and scholarship are suspect, given that her chapter "Noble Lies" in *Who Stole Feminism* is dedicated to dispelling the quantitative and qualitative dimensions of women-battering and undermining the credibility of those she demonizes as gender feminists. However, it is based on two scandalous lies of her own.

I have already punctured Hoff Sommers's alleged "Super Bowl Sunday" "lie," by showing that there is a wealth of evidence correlating the event with increased violence against women. The second lie is an attempt to complement her version of the Super Bowl story as a "bald faced untruth" with her distortion of the historical reality of a law known as "the rule of thumb," which she cites as an example of feminist "revisionist history" (1994, 203). Hoff Sommers vehemently argues that the "rule of thumb," which stipulated that, in accordance with British law, a man could legally beat his wife with a switch or rod no wider than his thumb, is a feminist fiction. Moreover, she goes on to boldly assert that "On the contrary, British law since the 1700s and our American laws predating the Revolution prohibit wife beating, though there have been periods and places in which the prohibition was only indifferently enforced" (1994, 204).

Hoff Sommers provides no documentation for this "fact," which is hardly surprising, given there are no grounds for her claim. Linda Hirshman's angry response to Hoff Sommers attempts to set the record straight:

> Contrary to Christina Hoff Sommers' contention in her book *Who Stole Feminism?*, the origin of the expression "rule of thumb" as it applies to wife-beating is not a "feminist fiction." The authoritative collection of English common law, Blackstone's *Commentaries on the Laws of England*, records that wife-beating was allowed as long as the man did not exceed the reasonable bounds of "due governance and correction." Several nineteenth century U.S. cases . . . cited the "old law" that a husband had the right to whip his wife provided that he used a switch "no larger than his thumb." . . . The ancient license to chastise one's spouse rested on and reinforced another legal abuse—that women lose their separate identities upon marriage. Thus, according to the *Commentaries*, since men were answerable for their wives' acts, they should be able to "chastise" them. (Hirschman 1994, 44)

Moreover, even rudimentary research reveals the outrageous falsity of Hoff Sommers's claims. For example, her failure to consult Blackstone's commentaries on English common law regarding wife-beating (which is a widely acknowledged and referenced source of this law) demonstrates either a willful obscuration of the facts or gross scholarly negligence and ignorance. This is even more outrageous given that, as Faludi reminds us, Hoff Sommers's specialty is in "feminist-error identification" (1996a, 10). In addition, her further dogmatic and unsubstantiated statements concerning British and U.S. legal prohibition of wife abuse (cited above) are also patently false (e.g., Hoff Sommers 1994, 204). For as Dobash and Dobash (1979) establish:

> It was not until 1891, in the case of *Reg. v. Jackson*, that the legal right of the English husband to restrain his wife's liberty by physical means may be said to have been completely abolished.
>
> In America, wife beating was made illegal in Alabama and Massachusetts in 1871. It was ruled that "the privilege, ancient though it be, to beat her with a stick, to pull her hair, choke her, spit in her face or kick her about the floor, or to inflict upon her other like indignities, is not now acknowledged by our law." By the end of the nineteenth century, the right of chastisement was expressly rejected. (63)

Given the extensive documentation readily available on these matters, it is mystifying why Hoff Sommers's glaring errors and unsupported assertions were not "fact-checked," at least by her editors before publication. And it is furthermore baffling as to why her text continues to be heralded by dominant media, antifeminist pundits, and others as a reputable source of information.

Moreover, Hoff Sommers, incredibly, employs these two "noble lies" to present the research of sociologists Richard Gelles, Murray Straus, and Suzanne Steinmetz—which is widely cited and often used to confirm misogynist attitudes toward the battered woman—as authoritative "objective" studies of "domestic violence." Indeed, her use of this study is a glaring example of how "scientific" empirical surveys—which are purported to be "value-free"—are employed to legitimate highly subjective and often biased assumptions. Interestingly, the deleterious implications and problematic nature of this work, in particular, as well as other studies of the same ilk, were critiqued at the time by the editors of *Ms.* magazine:

> What's appalling is that . . . there are much quoted "experts" out there, claiming that women are as much to blame as men: women "provoke" the beatings—there's that old sick refrain. And the newest twist on equality: women are beating men just as often. How do they figure that? By relying on devices like the "Conflict Tactics Scale" developed by sociologists *Murray Straus and Richard Gelles*. The scale measures family violence; attacks are weighted by severity, but the results are generally reported as though a slap on the wrist by a woman is the same as a kick in the head by a man. (Golden 1994, 3a; emphasis mine).

Although the Conflict Tactics Scale (CTS) and the paradigmatic framework (defined as a "family systems" perspective) that mediates their methodology have been highly criticized as flawed and biased, "Straus, Gelles, and Steinmetz have published the largest body of social science research on domestic violence" as they "have been substantially funded by the U.S. National Institutes of Mental Health" (Kurz 1993, 253). And given the nature of their findings, it is hardly surprising that Straus et al. are afforded such prominent positions in the writings of antifeminist proponents, despite the fact that critics such as R. Emerson Dobash and Russell Dobash, two distinguished researchers and activists in the field of women abuse, take much of Straus's research to task, for a variety of reasons.[6]

The Dobashes' work is taken as a foundational classic in studies of violence against women. As Ann Jones notes:

> The work of feminist researchers and activists bears out the thesis sociologists R. Emerson Dobash and Russell Dobash developed in 1979 after studying violence against wives in Scotland; namely, that violence between husbands and wives is an extension of the historic domination and control of husbands over their wives and should "be understood primarily as coercive control." In other words, family violence is *not* just a series of isolated blow ups, the result of anger or stress or too much to drink, though it often looks that way to the woman who is its target. Rather, family violence *is a process of deliberate intimidation intended to coerce the victim to do the will of the victimizer.* (1996, 336)

In the course of my studies, I will provide supporting evidence and arguments to bolster this position.

First, the Dobashes identify what they deem to be unsubstantiated biases in regard to the tendency in these studies to find women at least partially responsible for the abuse they endure at the hands of their lovers or partners. Further, critics of Straus et al. indicate that their findings are based on faulty sampling techniques: "Based upon the results of his quasi-experimental study of a few families and the results of a survey of high school graduates' perceptions of violence between their parents, Straus argued that 'the level of violence is greatest when the wife is dominant in decisions' " (Dobash and Dobash 1979, 23).

Moreover, critics like the Dobashes cited many fallacies and problematic aspects of Straus et al.'s controversial study.

[T]hey have failed to distinguish qualitatively different types of physical force between various family members. They have mistakenly inferred that attitudes toward the use of violence are equivalent to its actual occurrence, and they have erroneously attempted to explain away the greater use of violence by husbands by arguing that men and women have an equal potential for violence. . . . Straus, Gelles, and Steinmetz have suggested that findings that indicate greater and more severe violence on the part of men in the family arise "only because women are on average weaker than their husbands and hence have more to lose by such acts." The implication of this statement is clear: women could or would be just as violent as men but because they are different (weaker) they are less violent. *Interestingly, this argument suggests its own refutation. [Moreover] . . . their supposition that women could be just as violent as men is not supported by any evidence.* (Dobash and Dobash 1979, 19–20; emphasis mine)

This failure to differentiate between disparate forms of violence, as well as the intensity and consequent effects of these attacks, is not uncommon, as Dobash and Dobash point out, to a number of so-called objective surveys on wife abuse, even though in the case of the Dobashes' own studies, and numerous other surveys that they cite, there was little evidence of women assaulting their partners. When this did indeed take place, it was usually in response to their husbands' offensive actions. The pure quantification of violence prevalent in studies put forward by Straus et al. reinforced common myths about husband battering. According to their findings, "Only a few women on very infrequent occasions responded to their husband's verbal aggression by initiating violence" (Dobash and Dobash 1979, 105).

Jones argues that "[Straus and Gelles'] research continues to mislead the public and policy makers alike and to mask the real nature and severity of male violence against women" (1994a, 155). Indeed, such dubious "empirical" studies that minimize violence against women have the unfortunate effect of dehumanizing and desensitizing the grisly reality of battery and abuse, hence, neutralizing and negating the gravity of the problem. Moreover, "The dynamic aspects of violence to wives cannot be captured in a gross quantitative manner" (Dobash and Dobash 1979, 107). What abuse activists are advocating, then, is not a ban on empirical research per se, but rather the putting in question of certain flawed studies that purport to be scientifically objective or neutral. Studies of violence in the family cannot help but reflect the biases of the scientists or funding agencies that support them. Consequently, as Dobash and Dobash point out, such studies can only be valid and useful if they contextualize the relations they are attempting to investigate. As they explain it, "Gross categories such as slapping or punching fail to provide any real clues into the nature and severity of attacks. . . . In order to understand precisely what constitutes a physical attack we must turn to the detailed accounts of women subjected to these attacks" (Dobash and Dobash 1979, 106).

It cannot be too strongly emphasized that realistic and utilitarian research into human experiences and pathologies necessitates situating them within the concrete relations of everyday life. Contextualizing and accompanying such examinations with living, breathing, human, face-to-face revelations about such episodes advances the kinds of understanding and change that only empathy can truly promote. For example, note if you will, the manifest shift in our comprehension of the horrific reality of wife-battering when a quantified account of numbers of "slaps," "punches," and "kicks" are replaced or supplemented with accounts like the following:

He punched me, he kicked me, he pulled me by the hair. My face hit a step. He had his bare feet, you know, with being in bed, and he just jumped up and he pulled on his trousers and he was kicking me. If he had his shoes on, God knows what kind of face I would have had. As it was I had a cracked cheek bone, two teeth knocked out, cracked ribs, broken nose, two beautiful black eyes—it wasn't even a black eye, it was my whole cheek was just purple from one eye to the other. And he had got me by the neck and, you know, he was trying, in fact, practically succeeded in strangling me. I was choking, I was actually at the blacking out stage. I was trying to pull his fingers away, with me trying to pull his fingers away, I scratched myself, you know, trying to get his fingers off. He hit me and I felt my head, you know, hitting the back of the lock of the door. I started to scream and I felt as if I'd been screaming for ages. When I came to he was pulling me up the stair by the hair. I mean, I think it was the pain of him pulling me up the stair by the hair that brought me round again. (Dobash and Dobash 1979, 107)

Further clarification of the obfuscating nature of decontextualized, (pseudo)-scientific studies of "domestic violence" could perhaps be obtained by proposing that in a quantified form, O. J. Simpson's report of his alleged abuse at the hands of his wife, Nicole, would be equivalent to the well-documented violence he exercised against her. Hence, an "objective" empirical study of "spousal" or so-called husband-battering requires qualitative and contextual analysis. Quantitative statistics do not get at the heart of the issue of violence within the family, although properly interpreted, statistical and empirical evidence are extremely useful.

Yet despite widespread denunciations of the validity of the Conflict Tactics Scale, Straus et al. continued to receive lucrative funding, and warm receptions, for their further statistical surveys of "family violence," which employed the CTS technique to summarize their findings (Jones 1994a, 155). This is in spite of the astonishing reality that one hardly needs expertise in empirical analysis to ascertain the problematic nature of a scale in which "hitting your 'partner' with a pillow counts the same as hitting him or her with a sledgehammer, and two slaps on the wrist count the same as two knife attacks" (Jones 1994a, 155)!

It is precisely this specious decontextualized quantification that Dobash and Dobash identify in their condemnation of another seriously flawed aspect of Straus et al.'s empirical technique. In particular, this is in regard to the employment of what Dobash and Dobash call "the general systems model," which underlies Straus et al.'s "family systems" methodology.[7]

> The general systems model removes people from the family setting, human beings with historically shaped motives, values, and intentions, and relates abstract concepts to other concepts, ignoring the historical and interactive aspects of the family. When one examines Straus's model or any other systems model, one sees that it is preeminently a metaphysical argument in the sense that an analysis lacking in substantive content is an analysis of relationships between abstractions and is little more than relationships between words. (Dobash and Dobash 1979, 25)

Dobash and Dobash are arguing the ineffectiveness of so-called scientific methods that attempt to apply objective, quantitative, mathematical equations to the elaborate and multileveled complexities of any mode of human interpersonal relations. As they put it, "We reject this extremely abstract method and think that the more general and abstract the approaches to interpersonal violence become, the less useful they are in the understanding of violence" (25).

The oversimplified, one-dimensionalized quantification of complex realities is not restricted to Straus et al.'s "family systems model" but is a prevalent component of the writings of many impersonator feminists like Hoff Sommers. It is also apparent in the frameworks of other scholars' (both feminist and nonfeminist) analytical attempts to minimize the problem of violence against women, as this text will demonstrate. Moreover, the dangerous reductive and biased qualities of these studies are further realized through their tendencies to concentrate on the recipients of the violence rather than on those who do the battering. The bias of such research is evident and provokes one to ask why so much time and money is exerted on studying the recipients rather than the perpetuators of such attacks.

> "[E]xperts"—psychologists, psychiatrists, and sociologists mostly—fortified with government grants, busily study why women stay. Naturally they study the question, and the whole problem of male violence, by studying women, thereby managing to

blame women while turning "their problem" into a tidy profit, generously provided by your tax dollars and mine. (Jones 1994a, 152–53)

In contrast, many feminist researchers of family violence argue for the implementation of a paradigm that does not decontextualize the power relations between men and women and family members. They advocate, instead, the employment of a paradigm that places "male-female relations at the center of their analysis and view[s] inequality between men and women as a key factor in violence" (Kurz 1993, 253). Dobash and Dobash, for example, provide a convincing and eloquent argument that clearly identifies both the serious deficiencies inherent in decontexualized empirical studies of wife abuse and the merits of a dialectical, multidimensional approach that takes into account mediating social, political, and economic factors for any credible and responsible investigation into these kinds of relations. They go on to demonstrate how their own examination of wife-battering necessarily begins with a premise that recognizes the role of inequitable divisions of power and cultural status in male violence toward women.

> This form of analysis took us beyond the narrow and false boundaries that all too often needlessly restrict social researchers. Such boundaries often confine the inquiry only to violent individuals or to specific violent families and lead to the partialling [*sic*] out of those individuals or families from the wider social, economic and political world. We avoided this narrow approach by embedding our analysis of individual violent behavior in the wider social and cultural context. This was done by exploring the manner in which economic and social processes operate directly and indirectly to support patriarchal domination and the use of violence against wives. This method sharply contrasts with the bulk of social science research which attempts to abstract and isolate social problems and social processes from the wider social context in which they occur. (1979, ix–x)

As Linda Gordon argues in her important book *Heroes of Their Own Lives* (1988), "family violence has been historically and politically constructed" (3). Thus, a contextualized political and historical analysis must engage the concrete conditions that promote violence in the family, as well as changing definitions of what constitutes violence, what penalties are extracted, and what societal beliefs help structure gender relations. Moreover, feminist activists like Ann Jones (1994a and 1996) clearly identify the deep-structural nature of the ideological framing of much of this decontextualized research by simply asking what should be the obvious question. Rather than asking, "Why does she stay?" or "What kind of woman is the battered wife?" we should be asking questions about the perpetrator of this kind of violence, such as "Why does he do it?"

Yet as Dobash and Dobash (1979) have documented in shocking detail, the preponderance of research into "family violence" continues the historical legacy of studying the victim, "the wife-beater's wife," rather than the wife-beater and the social-political economic context that sustains and encourages male violence against women. Ann Jones even provides further evidence of the domination in the field of this kind of biased research, which even "male experts" have evaluated as virtually worthless to an understanding of wife abuse.

So adept have the experts been at studying women while hiding women's complaints, blaming women while silencing them, that two male "experts" who reviewed the heavy body of "standard literature" in the field in 1986 remarked: "The search for characteristics of women that contribute to their own victimization is futile. . . . It is sometimes forgotten that men's violence is men's behavior. . . . What is surprising is the enormous effort to explain male behavior by examining women. It is hoped [presumably by the authors] that future research will show more about the factors that promote violent male behavior and that stronger theory will be developed to explain it." (Jones 1994a, 153)

Yet highly prejudicial and reductive types of empirical studies continue to eclipse other more relevant, contextual analyses in much of the academic literature and popular media. Perhaps the widespread acceptance and support for truncated empirical research is due, in part, to the way in which the findings of these studies preserve and reinforce prevailing societal attitudes and beliefs about the stereotypical "nagging and dominating wife" who provokes and deserves her husband's beatings. And because it masquerades behind a guise of "objectivity," this literature can be used as "scientific" evidence of the legitimacy and credibility of biased ideological assumptions. However, the complete misrepresentation of such studies as "objective" and the manner in which problematic research is mediated by the researcher's conscious or unconscious preconceived notions is revealed in Dobash and Dobash's critique of one of the methodologies employed, "the multifactor approach," which is widely used in many of these empirical studies.

Investigators using this method seek to list or to discover various factors related to violence in the family. This inductive, abstract empiricism assumes an atheoretical and objective approach to social reality whose positivistic rationale is erroneous. These naturalists of the social sciences always begin with certain presuppositions regarding the phenomena about which they are collecting facts. One could not begin to collect facts without a theory and a method that enabled one to perceive those facts. Often these investigators are unaware of their own theories or prejudices though they become very apparent when the collected facts are presented. (Dobash and Dobash 1979, 24)

Antifeminist ideologues like Hoff Sommers and others extol the pretense of neutrality, in conjunction with the dominant share of funding afforded positivist noncontextual research and the academic qualifications of coordinators like Straus et al., as well as the sheer number of times the studies are cited. But in truth Hoff Sommers capitalizes on any empirical studies that advance her contention that gender feminists are misrepresenting and exaggerating the reality of violence against women (1994, 194) and that lend credibility to her inaccurate contentions. Moreover, Hoff Sommers fails to mention the criteria by which such funding is undertaken and disseminated. Ann Jones, on the other hand, provides some background in this account.

In 1978 the National Coalition Against Domestic Violence, a coalition of grass-roots women's groups struggling on shoestring budgets to shelter and provide services for battered women, recommended that federal research grants "be limited to those helping local groups meet particular programmatic needs." . . . [However] the substantial grants—from the National Institute of Mental Health, the Department of Justice, and other federal agencies—went instead to psychologists and sociologists, mostly men, with academic credentials and affiliations, who could be counted on to be "objective"—that is, to *not* take the side of women. (1994a, 153)

Indeed, betrayal feminists, like Hoff Sommers and Roiphe in particular, as well as other noncontextual thinkers and positivist researchers, depend upon so-called objective research to authenticate their opinions and attack other feminists. They would lead us to believe that legitimate empirical studies are immaculate and unsullied (as does so much of the popular media). Yet for those who are even rudimentarily literate in the field, the idea of a study that examines aspects of human relations as impersonal, objective, and value-free is clearly bogus.

"HOW TO LIE WITH STATISTICS"

Darrell Huff, a member of the American Statistical Association, compiled items sent to him by "a number of professional statisticians—who, believe me, deplore the misuse of statistics as heartily as anyone alive" as part of a classic 1954 text *How to Lie with Statistics*. Huff demonstrates in great detail the variety of dimensions in which empirical studies can be biased, ranging from the "sample" chosen, to the class, race, sex, and professionalism of the interviewers. He emphasizes especially the biases in relation to that of the sample interviewees and the formulation, setting, and composition of the interview questions. In addition, he calls for interrogation of the kinds of questions employed as well as the mediation of the study by the funding agency. "[T]he laboratory with something to prove for the sake of a theory, a reputation, or a fee" (1954, 123) provides examples of some of the factors that might bias research. Huff concludes, "You have pretty fair evidence to go on if you suspect that polls in general are biased in one specific direction" (1954, 26).

Huff goes on to say, "Actually, as we have seen, it is not necessary that a poll be rigged—that is, that the results be deliberately twisted in order to create a false impression. The tendency of the sample to be biased in this consistent direction can rig it automatically" (26). Moreover, in relation to much of the research in the area of violence against women, this pretense of objectivity is riddled with bias, which most certainly taints the findings of such surveys.

> Survey instruments characteristically used to conduct quantitative research on intimate violence have reproduced a bias toward nonfeminist interpretations of power and violence in relationships. The flaws in survey instruments that generate this bias are not limited to the content of interview questions. The most important barrier to adequate assessments of the extent and dimensions of intimate violence through surveys is the context of the interaction between interviewer and interviewee. (Brush 1993, 249)

Brian Easlea expresses his concern and condemnation of the notion of objective social scientific studies, especially in view of the consequences of such published research's results for "social intervention."

> Moreover, since the gathering of "social data" and the testing of social theories are themselves social activities of a "perturbing" kind we may in general conclude that a scientific investigation of one's own society necessarily implies social intervention either with intended or unintended social consequences—but consequences just the same. From the sending of questionnaires, through publication of results, to full blooded political action, social science is an activity in which the concept of the detached, non-interfering scientist is a fiction. Social life and development is a process in which the social scientist is himself a participant. The question therefore arises, how ought the social scientist to participate and with what social objectives[?] (1973, 152)

Yet social scientists like Straus and Gelles and most of those "qualified academics" who collect the big bucks from the established funding agencies purport to operate within a "value-free" paradigm. Straus and Gelles's "family systems" framework exemplifies what Easlea describes as a "value free" and "objective" paradigm, which is, in fact, "subjective" and thus "a passionate commitment based to a large extent on aesthetic preferences" (1973, 279, 280). Within this context, it is hardly surprising that Jones (and others) has found that the dominant research in the area of violence against women is hardly objective: "Gender bias oozes from the very methods of the academics: quantitative, statistical, 'objective,' and as distant as possible from the real experiences of real women" (Jones 1994a, 154).

Moreover, the implications of Straus's "objective" Conflict Tactics Scale, as employed within his limited framework, have had serious consequences for perpetuating misleading evidence concerning women's active responsibility and participation in battering relationships as well as so-called husband abuse. Basically, the Conflict Tactics Scale measures the frequency and type of confrontation initiated by the individuals in a relationship.[8]

> In the 1970s, while psychologists studied women's "helplessness" and passivity (instead of men's violence and aggression), sociologists tried to measure the exact

"magnitude" of "family" violence, spending money that might have gone to fund shelters and save lives. At the University of New Hampshire Family Violence Research Program, professors Murray Straus and Richard Gelles, assisted by Suzanne Steinmetz, devised a "Conflicts Tactics Scale" to score fights in violent "families" on a convenient numerical basis, regardless of context, intention, relative size of the contenders, or real damage done. The experts then conducted a large survey, and in 1977 pronounced the battle between the sexes a statistical draw. (Jones 1994a, 154)

In light of this, it isn't difficult to see how Suzanne Steinmetz drew upon the findings of this study (as well as other sources) to substantiate her claim that women, in fact, batter men and hence propagated the myth of "the battered husband syndrome" (Brush 1993, 242). And even though her methods and assumptions were seriously criticized, the "battered husband syndrome" has now become a part of our everyday popular lexicon and has been appropriated and exploited by a variety of antifeminist pundits and organizations. Indeed, Camille Paglia makes reference to "underreported husband-battering" in her polemic on women's responsibility in battering relations (Paglia 1994, 43).

The development and translation of the Conflict Tactics Scale is an apt practical example of Easlea's critique of "the ideology of 'value-free' social science [as] not only intellectually stultifying but also, given the direction of existing trends, exceedingly dangerous" (Easlea 1973, 322). Yet there is little, if any, publicity to correct Steinmetz's erroneous findings, which is particularly disturbing given that "The earliest critics claimed that Steinmetz distorted her research findings and fabricated her claim from improperly reported data" (Brush 1993, 242).

Indeed, Hoff Sommers fails to report, in her decontextualized heralding of findings by, or provoked by, Straus, Gelles, and Steinmetz, the highly contentious and questionable nature of the work and that these studies have been an object of considerable investigation and critique.

[P]ro-feminist academic researchers have engaged themselves year after year in doggedly deconstructing the shoddy studies based on the "logical positivism and abstract empiricism" of the Conflict Tactics Scale. (To cite examples of the Scale's failings, and of the general idiocy of trying to evaluate complex issues in simplistic statistical terms, on the Conflict Tactics Scale hitting your "partner" with a pillow counts the same as hitting him or her with a sledgehammer, and two slaps on the wrist count the same as two knife attacks.) (Jones 1994a, 154–55)

In an attempt to resolve the debate concerning the veracity of the battered husband syndrome once and for all, Lisa Brush, who was at the time a doctoral candidate in sociology and a family policy fellow with the Institute for Legal Studies at the University of Wisconsin-Madison, conducted her own study, which met with all the scientific criteria for a legitimate empirical investigation. Her paradigm, however, which she defines as a "feminist approach" makes no claims to being "neutral" or "value-free," but fits with the contextual antireductionist perspective advocated by radical social scientists like Easlea. Brush argues that:

> According to feminist critics . . . the measures of violence in Straus's CTS [Conflict Tactics Scale] are inadequate to the task of describing or analyzing intimate violence because they confound acts with outcomes and lump together settings and persons. A family systems approach, critics claim, overlooks important gendered variations in norms, legitimation, and above all, power. A man's striking a woman has different effects, consequences, and meanings than a woman's striking a man, these feminists hold, which the universalizing effect of the family systems approach obscures. In the family systems paradigm, the vital question of self-defense and the context of violent acts goes unexplored, women's actions are misinterpreted and misrepresented, and the dynamics of domestic violence is misunderstood. (Brush 1993, 241)

Due to the contextually more sophisticated and multileveled nature of Brush's methodology and perspective, she presents us with a far more credible explication of the perpetuation of violent acts by both men and women and disputes the existence of a "battered husband syndrome."

> The data analysis presented . . . showed that although NSFH [The National Survey of Families and Households][9] respondents confirmed that women were not any more pacific than men in the course of disagreements, women were more likely than men to report that they were injured in the course of disagreements with their partner. This result held even for those cases in which both men and women were violent. These findings empirically refute the "battered husband syndrome." At the same time, they demonstrate the importance of developing innovative methods of eliciting information about intimate violence from survey respondents. (Brush 1993, 247–48)

Although studies mediated by feminist frameworks, like Brush's, are proliferating betrayal feminists, like Hoff Sommers, as well as contemporary media culture, tend to neglect these analyses, which are far more dialectical and often at odds with the dominant conservative attitudes toward the battered woman. Indeed, there is an abundance of research that contextualizes women's violence and challenges the denial of critical feminist research promoted by the betrayal feminists and is apparent in the studies they choose to attack. Such feminist research provokes shifts in opinions about women's roles in violent relationships and also in legislative policy (which necessarily involves funding and employment) and infrastructural constraints. For, rather than promoting a model of equal culpability "for acts of violence in heterosexual couples, feminist researchers argue against the claim that men and women engage in equal amounts of violence" (Kurz 1993, 257).

> They argue that data proving such an equivalence of violence, particularly data based on the CTS, are flawed. The scale does not ask what acts were done in self-defense,

who initiated the violence, or who was injured. In their view, the validity of the scale is undermined because the continuum of violence in the scale is so broad that it fails to discriminate among very different kinds of violence. (Kurz 1993, 257–58)

Yet betrayal feminists continue to promote and reinforce what Phyllis Chesler identifies as a "psychological double standard" in regard to female recipients of abuse and continue to employ highly ideological subjective standards in their decision to cite so-called objective research and facts to substantiate their arguments. The deleterious consequences of such a mind-set are that:

Women are held to higher and different standards than men. People *expect* men to be violent; they are also carefully taught to deny or minimize male violence ("I don't believe any father would rape his own child") and to forgive violent men ("He's been under a lot of pressure," "He's willing to go into therapy"). On the other hand, people continue to *blame women* for male violence ("She must have liked rough sex if she stayed married to him," "She provoked him into beating her"). . . . Also, people *do not* expect and will not permit women to be violent—not even in self-defense. (In fact, most people consistently confuse female self-defense with female aggression.) In addition, people demand that women, but not men, walk a very narrow tightrope of acceptable behaviors—perfectly and with a smile. (Chesler 1994, 87)

Further, battered women feminist scholars, like Ann Jones and Lenore Walker, argue that the reification of the myth of the abused woman, of woman as the inscriber of her own destiny, lies in the conviction of those who have never been in this type of situation. While some believe that they would most certainly leave after the first assault, this attitude, which is so easy and logical in theory, is far more difficult and complicated in practice, according to researchers like Walker and Jones. In fact, the question "Why didn't she leave?" was the one most repeatedly asked in relation to Hedda Nussbaum. It is a question that instead of having a clear, precise answer—in true dialectical fashion—leads to higher levels of questions and an abundance of literature on the complexities of this life-threatening enigma. In the next section, I will discuss in detail the case of Hedda Nussbaum to further interrogate the issue of violence against women and the extent to which theories of the colonization of women and a critical and dialectical feminism can help address crucial issues confronting contemporary women.

THE STRANGE CASE OF HEDDA NUSSBAUM AND THE FEMINIST VICTIMIZATION DEBATE

The Hedda Nussbaum trial is important because it was pivotal in shaping theoretical and practical feminist thought and policy, as well as forensic psychology, in relation to issues of family violence. Furthermore, this controversial case proved particularly significant for feminist theory in that it provoked wide discussion, debate, and theorizing on the contextual relations associated with the situation of battered women, notions of victimization, and the nature of gender difference (Farganis 1994). It also generated debate over feminist understandings and definitions of the nature of victimization.

As we shall see, an examination of the bizarre and horrible case of the Steinberg-Nussbaum pathological relationship and some of the analyses it provoked makes visible the real need for critical and dialectical feminist analysis. Examination of feminist responses to the case reveals as well the erroneous assumptions inhabiting the betrayal feminists' party-line concerning the totalitarian nature of so-called victim feminism. Furthermore, the name Hedda Nussbaum has become so closely associated with the term *victim*, in relation to battered women within the field of family terrorism, that the two are often perceived as being synonymous. Thus, it provides a useful test case to engage key issues in interpreting family terrorism. Moreover, as Ann Jones reminds us, discussion of this case is consequential "precisely because so many have said and written so much about it" (Jones 1994a, 15). Finally, as an extreme case of woman abuse and child murder it throws into high relief the kinds of problems millions of women and children face at a variety of levels every day.

Curiously, the case against Joel Steinberg for the murder of his illegally adopted daughter, Lisa, would probably not have attained such infamy and prominence had it not been that it was the first televised trial in New York State (Boylan 1994 www.cjr.org). It was, in fact, broadcast during an eighteen-month experimental period to initiate and examine televised access to courtroom proceedings in New York. Thus, what has today become commonplace in the living rooms of America was a novel experience for New Yorkers who tuned in to view Hedda Nussbaum, testifying *live* on three New York network TV stations (preempting regularly scheduled programs) against her common-law husband, Joel Steinberg (*Newsweek*, Dec. 12, 1988, 56).

The case first came to public attention in November 1987, when Hedda Nussbaum and her partner, Joel Steinberg, were arrested for the murder of their six-year-old, illegally adopted daughter, Lisa Steinberg, in New York City. What made this now infamous couple so simultaneously abhorrent and fascinating was that they hardly fit the stereotypical profile of those associated with situations of "domestic violence." In contrast, Joel Steinberg and Hedda Nussbaum, on the surface, appeared to epitomize the general criteria of the 1980s yuppie lifestyle. Both white, Jewish, professionals—Joel a lawyer and Hedda a former Random House senior editor turned full-time mother—they lived with their six-year-old daughter, Lisa, and seventeen-month-old son, Mitchell, in a fashionable brownstone. Joel and Hedda lived on one of the best streets of the enviable upper middle-class neighborhood of Greenwich Village, "a part of New York City noted for its artists, writers, theatrical performers, bohemians, and well-to-do, white-collar professionals" (Farganis 1994, 98).

However, behind this facade was an aberrant and abusive reality that escalated into Lisa's death at the hands of her father. Indeed, Lisa was no stranger to her adopted father's pathological style of paradoxical physical and psychological abuse. "During the trial, a prosecution witness who once saw Steinberg hit Lisa recounted that the father told his daughter, 'Blink and smile'—and the little girl obediently complied" (Summers 1989, 54).

Lisa Steinberg died four days after her father attacked her—on that fateful November 1987 evening—so savagely that he knocked her unconscious. Instead of seeking medical attention, he and Nussbaum allowed their comatose daughter to lie for most of twelve hours on the bathroom floor before calling for help. Indeed, Steinberg forbade Hedda from seeking any assistance, and she complied with his orders, even though she was left alone with Lisa and Mitchell (who, it was later discovered, was also illegally adopted) while Joel went out for dinner with a bail bondsman friend (Brownmiller 1989, 336). Steinberg's attempts to revive Lisa on his return proved futile. Yet it was only later, when it appeared that Lisa had stopped breathing—some time after Joel and Hedda had engaged in their nightly ritual of free-basing cocaine—that Joel finally gave Hedda permission to call 911. Although Joel steadfastly asserted his innocence, it became immediately apparent to the paramedics and police, who arrived shortly after the emergency call was made, that this was a case of child abuse. Further investigation revealed that city agencies, as well as Lisa's school, had received complaints about possible abuse in the Nussbaum-Steinberg home, but no formal action had ever been taken to pursue or address these matters. Under the circumstances, it was not surprising that the police decided to pick up Hedda Nussbaum and Joel Steinberg, from what was described as a "filthy, stinking, pigsty," for questioning, only a few hours after Lisa had been taken to the hospital. Moreover, legal authorities arranged for New York Special Services for Children to take immediate custody of the horribly neglected Mitchell, who was discovered covered in urine and feces and tied to his playpen in the living room of the family's tiny one-bedroom apartment.

At the police station, Hedda—who suffered deformities from old and fresh injuries via what appeared to be long-term, consistent battering—and Steinberg were separated and questioned individually. Both were subsequently charged with "attempted murder, assault in the first degree, and endangering the welfare of a child" (*Newsweek*, Dec. 12, 1988). They were ultimately charged with murder after the hospital decided to unplug the brain-dead Lisa from her life-support system (Brownmiller 1989; Farganis 1994; Jones 1994a).

The New York district attorney's office eventually dropped all charges against Hedda Nussbaum—"on the grounds that she was physically and emotionally incapable either of harming Lisa or coming to her aid" (*Newsweek*, Dec. 12, 1988, 57). She was granted immunity in exchange for crucial testimony necessary for Joel's prosecution for the murder of their daughter. Indeed, her testimony was mandatory for Steinberg's conviction, as the case against him was purely circumstantial. And it was through the seven days of her testimony that the extensive, multileveled reign of terror perpetuated on Hedda and the children by Joel Steinberg was revealed—as well as the perverse and pathological nature of their relationship of violence. It was the immunity decision, fueled later by Nussbaum's ensuing testimony, that provoked contention, debate, and anger within a wide range of observers, including those within the feminist community. For as Brownmiller describes it, "Many of us old-warrior feminists who followed the case from the beginning thought that Nussbaum should have been standing trial as well, for reckless endangerment of a child, at least" (1989, 335).

Hedda's testimony hardly assisted in counteracting such assessments of her predicament and actions. On the contrary, both the form and content of her deposition transformed her into one of the most hated women in America. As Ann Jones describes it,

> Day after day in December 1988 that face came into our homes on our television sets, and there in the privacy of our living rooms, our kitchens, our bedrooms, Hedda Nussbaum stared at us. That face made some people weep. It made others want to destroy her. Especially women. Put her on trial, they said. Lock her up. Get rid of her. Just look at what she let him do to her. Look at what she let him do to her *child.* (1994a, 167–68)

Hence, even though Hedda Nussbaum was not indicted in the murder of Lisa Steinberg, she was, in a sense, put on trial not only for her role in the death of her adopted daughter but also for her responsibility for her own assault at the hands of her common-law husband. To be sure, some "advocates for battered women . . . saw Hedda Nussbaum as a victim: a woman so badly assaulted, psychologically and physically, that *decision* was beyond her" (Jones 1994a, 176). Moreover: "They were dismayed at the sudden wave of 'Hedda bashing.' Sympathizing with Nussbaum, Gloria Steinem tried to explain the disagreement among women: 'Either you allow yourself to realize that it could have been you or you're so invested in making sure it couldn't have been you that you reject the victim' " (Jones 1994a, 176).

Indeed, although no feminist has ever denied the question of Hedda Nussbaum's *moral* responsibility "to act for the good of her child," this dispute captures many of the differences within the feminist terrain on the nature of victimization, family terrorism, and free will (Jones 1994a, 176). However, it must be noted that neither side of this controversial issue has ever held a position that resembles that of the oversimplified version of "victim feminism" posited by betrayal feminists. This distorted perversion of the real complexities of the debates provoked by the notion of victimization, as Ann Jones reminds us, is just one of

> an alarming set of claims, often articulated by young, educated women like Katie Roiphe and Naomi Wolf, suggesting a growing impatience with feminist issues. These authors maintain that many women are fantasizing their victimhood, or imposing it on themselves. The fact is, they say, public policies and revamped per-

sonal norms have created a society with a level playing field for both men and women. Consequently, individual women today should possess the wherewithal to just say no to men who have the gall to threaten them. (*New York Times*, March 20, 1994)

This popular mythical depiction of so many women's everyday experience of violence is hardly espoused by any feminist, regardless of her position in contestations regarding victimization. To comprehend the complicated nature of the arguments generated by these matters, however, necessitates further inquiry into the details of this bizarre and aberrant case, as disclosed, primarily, through Nussbaum's public account. Although I am in no way claming universal significance in a highly specific case, there are structural patterns in the case that assist in explaining and comprehending the contemporary perceptions and treatment of battered women.

Before engaging in further analysis, it is important to note that some activists have rejected the use of the term *family violence* for the same reasons some have renounced the *domestic violence* label. As Marian Meyers explains it:

> The terms *family violence* and *domestic violence* will not be used to denote battering because these terms obscure the relationship between gender and power by failing to identify the perpetuators and victims. In fact, in 95% of the cases of domestic or family violence, the victims are women and the aggressors are men. (Meyers 1997, 7)

In fact, Meyers's assessment of the term *family violence* is correct within the context of male violence against women. However, Meyers is falling prey—like too many other feminists and other researchers—to the same kind of disregard and failure to recognize the realities of the widespread, global nature of emotional, physical, and sexual violence that is perpetuated against children and the elderly by both men and women every day.[10] Hence, I would argue that the term *family violence* is appropriate for delineating and making apparent the dominant-subordinate pathological relations that take place in unequal family power relationships, although I prefer the term *family terrorism*, which I delineate in the next chapter.

JOEL AND HEDDA

It was 1975 when the attractive, shy Hedda Nussbaum met and fell head over heels in love with the charismatic, good-looking criminal attorney Joel Steinberg and about one year later that she moved into his one-bedroom Greenwich Village brownstone apartment. Steinberg, in fact, was involved in numerous nefarious activities, in addition to his somewhat unorthodox legal practice, which allegedly included questionable involvement with child adoptions as well as illicit drugs—

primarily with what had become the drug of choice for the fashionable 1970s and 1980s elite—cocaine. In fact, the majority of his clients "were reputedly involved in organized crime" (Walker 1989, 149). Indeed, Hedda and Joel were chronic abusers of drugs like cocaine and later became devotees of one of the most expensive, addictive, and highly dangerous derivatives of cocaine use: free-basing (*Court T.V.*, Dec. 7, 1994; *Newsweek*, Dec 12, 1988; Brownmiller 1989).

Augmenting their joint drug habit was a shared obsession with nontraditional therapy, and it was only a matter of time before Hedda took the place of Joel's ex-girlfriend in his Reichian therapy group (*Court T.V.*, Dec. 7, 1994). Added to this deadly combination were nightly "debriefing," role-playing, sex, and S & M fantasies. In these criticism-therapy sessions the ever-pacing Steinberg acted as all-knowing clairvoyant guru-advisor to the worshipful Nussbaum, who dutifully sat at the foot of his bed, treating his counsel as gospel. Here you have a perfect recipe for pathological psychological manipulation. According to Nussbaum, Steinberg—who Brownmiller (1989) describes as a "psychopathic charmer"— was "playing a calculated game of mind control," bombarding her with "mixed signals" and paradoxical injunctions (*Newsweek*, Dec. 12, 1988, 60). Psychologists later likened Steinberg's tactics to "brainwashing techniques" (*Court TV*, Dec. 7, 1994). The effectiveness of Steinberg's pseudotherapeutic technique was largely due to his sophisticated employment of contradictory messages. On the one hand, he coached Nussbaum and forced her to assert herself at work and to demand numerous raises, which resulted in her becoming the highest paid editor in her department at Random House. Yet he negated these feats by taking credit for the accomplishments himself and continually reminding her that she owed all her success to him. He also showered her with faint praise for her intellectual abilities, as, within Steinberg's warped, arrogant worldview, his own brilliance demanded that he be paired with a woman of lesser, but extraordinary abilities. As Susan Schechter, who has worked with battered women for many years and served as the program coordinator at Boston Children's Hospital for AWAKE (Advocacy for Women and Kids in Emergency), explains it:

> Steinberg did a kind of therapy with her every night. He had her make lists of all the things she wasn't doing right. He actually ate away at her psychological self. That's very typical. She said that he was very helpful in her career, that he encouraged her to get promotions and raises. But on the other hand, he beat her so brutally, so frequently, that she lost her job. (1989, 62)

Steinberg's infrequent gestures of support, however, were gradually overshadowed by his physical and emotional regime of debilitating disparagement, persecution, and assault. This is a typical technique of many batterers in their bid for asserting and maintaining the pathological system of control and dependency that mediates so many abusive relationships.

> [T]he Amnesty International chart of coercive methods . . . will confirm that Joel Steinberg's "help" was textbook brainwashing. *Isolation, monopolization, induced*

debility, threats, occasional indulgences, demonstrating omnipotence, degradation, enforcing trivial demands—Steinberg did it all. Certainly a Greenwich Village apartment seems nothing like a jungle prison camp, but equivalent effects can be produced in any place where a diligent controller can hold his victim in relative isolation—in a religious cult, for example, or a brothel, or a family. Typically the effects of brainwashing are capitulation, compliance, dependence upon the interrogator, anxiety, and despair. On Hedda Nussbaum, the effects were predictable and grim. (Jones 1994a, 184)

Steinberg gradually supplemented this program of psychological abuse with one of the most horrific escalating regimes of physical torment on record. In fact, Steinberg, unlike the majority of male batterers of women, would best be described as a sadist who has incorporated techniques of the classical torturer. Many believe that he learned these techniques during his past and somewhat mysterious background with the U.S. armed services.

Over a seven-year period Steinberg's assaults on Nussbaum resulted in such injuries as a ruptured spleen, broken knee, and numerous broken ribs. He had "choked her hard enough to damage her vocal cords, burned her body with a propane torch, hit her hands, feet, and sexual organs with a broomstick, urinated on her, forced her to sleep while handcuffed to a chinning bar, pulled her hair out and poked his fingers in her eyes. Nussbaum said she was also forced to take cold baths (both as punishment and to reduce the swelling) and often slept in the bathtub or on the floor" (*Newsweek*, Dec. 12, 1988, 61). He had also beaten her repeatedly with a metal exercise bar, knocked out many of her teeth, and broken her nose on so many occasions that it was described as "caved in." He hit her head against walls, filing cabinets, and an assortment of other objects. And he gave her so many black eyes, split lips, and various other cuts and bruises—which couldn't be hidden by makeup or clothing—that she was eventually fired from her Random House position because of the consequential chronic absenteeism provoked by shame or incapacitation (Jones 1994a, 170–71). Hedda was also forbidden to eat any of the food in the apartment and was forced to scrounge for food in the neighborhood dumpsters.

She should have died. All the specialists and advocates called in to the case after Nussbaum and Steinberg were arrested on November 2, 1987, said they'd never seen a woman so badly battered yet still alive. A doctor from New York University Medical Center who examined Nussbaum "from head to toe" on November 3, 1987, described the forty-five-year-old woman to the jury as anemic, debilitated, malnourished, wasted, limping, and hunchbacked from osteoporosis. He found old and new lacerations on her scalp, chunks of hair torn out from the right side of her head, an old ulceration and a new fracture on her nose, a black eye, lacerated upper lip, three- or four-month old fractures on both cheekbones, a scar on the abdomen, bruises on the abdomen and back, eight fractured right ribs, seven fractured left ribs, a very large new bruise on the right hip with many scarred areas around it, old abrasions of

Chapter 3

the left leg, and two deep, three-inch-wide ulcers on the right leg, which was infected, partly gangrenous and red and swollen from foot to knee. The ulcerated lesions on Nussbaum's lower right leg were "potentially fatal" injuries, the doctor said, which if untreated could have led to blood poisoning and cardiovascular collapse. (Jones 1994a, 168–69)

Unlike most batterers, Steinberg never apologized to Hedda for any of the abuse he inflicted upon her. Nor did he demonstrate any sign of remorse or guilt for his actions. Rather, he either justified his torturous practices as being "for her own good" or denied responsibility and attributed the injuries to others or to herself. "Steinberg used to say to her, 'Just look at what you've done to yourself!' " (Jones 1994a, 197). Indeed, this kind of behavior is consistent with that of what is defined as a sadistic personality, complete with requisite sociopathic character. Such a pathological person is incapable of feeling any semblance of empathy or, as in Steinberg's case, an inability to even feign any degree of responsibility or self-recrimination. In this sense, Steinberg falls into what some experts define as the most dangerous category of batterer, that characterized as "lethal batterers" (Jones 1994a, 184).[11]

"He always warned me just before he hit me," she said. He listed one by one the offenses for which he was about to beat her. She testified, "That was the time I was most afraid of him." (Jones 1994a, 188)

There were, however, periodic "honeymoon" periods between beatings, and during one of those periods, in May 1981, Joel Steinberg brought home Baby Girl Launders, a child for which Steinberg had been paid $500.00 by the baby's mother to place for adoption. Instead, Steinberg kept the baby, renaming her Lisa. Although, according to Nussbaum, Steinberg stopped his physical abuse for six months after Lisa joined the family, it was only a matter of time before his escalating brutality was directed at his daughter as well as his partner. He also continued in his multidimensional assaults on Hedda, tearing up freelance work she brought home, assigning her multiple self-degrading writing assignments and ripping up and destroying her clothing. He also monitored all her phone calls and banished her friends and family from the apartment, guaranteeing that she be totally housebound. She did, however, work as a paralegal for Joel, who had moved his somewhat unorthodox law practice into the apartment.

One of the strangest dimensions of their partnership, which intensified with the escalation of Joel and Hedda's cocaine free-basing habit, corresponds with the pathological therapeutic dimensions of their relationship. Although the details are unclear, it seems that throughout the years of Steinberg's manipulative pseudotherapy, which was usually combined with various forms of substance abuse, Steinberg managed to convince Nussbaum of his godlike, paranormal, extrasensory, supernatural healing powers. He also cultivated the existence of a secret, omnipresent hypnotic cult. Steinberg convinced Nussbaum that this cult had somehow gained control of her and that she, in turn

> possessed awesome power of hypnosis, powers so great, so special, so terrifying that she was the one person in the world who could hypnotize *him*. He was susceptible to her, he explained, because she was the one person with whom he let down his defenses. Under his mesmerizing influence she came to believe that her parents and sister and several of Steinberg's former clients and friends were secret members of the same hypnotic cult. This central delusion, insidious and cocaine-induced, was the glue that bonded their folie a deux. (Brownmiller 1989, 341–42)

In fact, this absurd notion obsessed both Steinberg and Nussbaum, and an ever-increasing paranoia enslaved them (a common deleterious side effect of free-basing cocaine).[12] Joel, it seems, fell into his own trap regarding the powers of this cult. Thus, he conveniently used it to rationalize his many problems, identify supposed enemies, and to absolve himself of all responsibility for the beatings and torture he inflicted upon his family. Moreover, Joel became convinced that "Lisa and baby Mitchell were also infected by the cult," which was revealed through the children's "staring" at him (Brownmiller 1989, 344). "[Joel and Hedda] had incorporated the fearful watching of two desperate children into a delusional fantasy that began as a game" (Brownmiller 1989, 344).

It is within this psychopathological context that the tragic death of Lisa Steinberg can be interpreted. For the neglected, battered, terrorized, and abused six-year-old Lisa Steinberg was finally murdered by Joel for "staring."

> Steinberg came into the bathroom holding Lisa in his outstretched arms. "She was lying in his arms, limp," Nussbaum said. "And I said, 'What happened?' He said, 'What's the difference what happened? This is your child. Hasn't this gone far enough?' " Nussbaum later explained that Steinberg said he was angry at Lisa for staring at him. "He said, 'I knocked her down and she didn't want to get up again. This staring business had gotten to be too much.' " Steinberg put Lisa on the bathroom floor and got ready to go out.
> While Nussbaum attempted to revive her daughter, Steinberg told Nussbaum to "relax, go with her. Stay in harmony with her." "He was always talking like that," Nussbaum awkwardly explained. "He always wanted us to be on the same wavelength." Then Steinberg left for dinner, promising to take care of Lisa when he got back. "Don't worry, just let her sleep," Nussbaum said Steinberg told her. "I will get her up when I get back." (*Newsweek*, Dec. 12, 1988, 57–58)

Even given the conditions of the living hell that typified Hedda and the children's everyday existence, her testimony, especially in regard to her feelings about Joel, nevertheless, was both astonishing and appalling. The word *golem* is a Yiddish term that roughly translates to mean "a lifeless figure" or a "shapeless mass without a soul" (Rosten 1968, 137), and it is a term that helps to capture the essence of Hedda Nussbaum's behavior, demeanor, and appearance at the trial.

In fact, even before the trial, assistant district attorney John McCusker described Hedda's behavior at the time of her arrest as characterized by a "total zombie-like quality." Moreover, Joseph Petrizzo, the child welfare worker who had come to pick up Mitchell, the youngest child, could not help but notice serious problems in the family. He observed that Hedda, who "was a mass of black and blue marks" and had an obscenely swollen face, "looked a bit dazed and confused . . . she just seemed out of it" and said nothing when her second child was taken away (Jones 1994a, 173). And it was in this "zombie-like" state that Hedda took the stand and gave her testimony. Susan Brownmiller (1989) observed that Hedda's eyes were dead and her body stiff (334).

> When she took the stand herself, Nussbaum spoke like a woman who had forgotten how. The monotony of her voice, the lack of emotional timbre, the "flat affect" marked her as a severely traumatized woman, afraid to reveal anything in her speech and manner for fear it might be, as always, wrong. That was only to be expected, but Nussbaum kept lapsing into silence. (Jones 1994a, 173)

Indeed, the analog dimension of her verbal communication was horrifyingly monotonous, as the same dead voice, devoid of emotion, passion, anger, or remorse was employed to describe everything from the litany of torture inflicted upon her by Joel Steinberg, to the death of her daughter, Lisa. More unbelievable and outrageous, however, was what she said about Steinberg.

> Advocates for battered women who plied the press corps with earnest position papers expected to hear Hedda Nussbaum talk about physical fear and terror, about a life with no options. Instead Hedda talked about love, cocaine, and [Joel as] an Old Testament God who was omnipotent, cruel, stern, seemingly capricious in his punishments, but a miracle worker who was also just. (Brownmiller 1989, 335)

It was a surreal experience, to hear testimonials of unconditional love and devotion for Steinberg, emitted from a mouth that had had to be surgically reconstructed because of the brutality of Joel's unrelenting assaults upon her. Yet Hedda demonstrated no anger or hatred for her abuser and instead justified his beatings claiming, "he said he was trying to help me, or he said I'd been lying to him, that I wasn't behaving in a manner acceptable to him" (cited in Brownmiller 1989, 341). She believed, it was reported, that Joel was beating her for her own good (*Court TV*, Dec. 7, 1994). And shockingly, she did not perceive herself as a battered woman, treating each beating, instead, as an isolated event. "I always thought each one was the last. I loved Joel so much. I always felt there was much more good between us than not" (Hedda Nussbaum, cited in Jones 1994a, 185). Her identity was so pathologically entwined with her godlike perceptions of Joel that she deemed him to be Pygmalion and she the statue coming to life under his touch and influence (*Court TV*, Dec. 7, 1994).

Ann Jones describes the horrified reaction to Hedda's unexpected testimony, especially in regard to her explanation for her failure to come to the aid of her dying daughter.

And who knew that when she spoke she would say unspeakable things? She said she had worshipped Steinberg as "God." She said he had the power to heal. She said he was a wonderful man. She said he had left her alone with the unconscious Lisa for three hours, and during that time she hadn't called 911 or the pediatrician who lived in the neighborhood because she "trusted" Steinberg; he had said that *he* would get Lisa up and heal her, and she didn't want to show "disloyalty" to *him*. She said that when Steinberg returned she prepared cocaine for him and smoked a little herself, and then for hours worried about Lisa as she half-listened to Steinberg talk. She said that in effect she had let Lisa die. And she said, weeping, that she didn't know why. (1994a, 175)

Within this context, it is no wonder that so much hostility was directed at Hedda. Nor is it surprising that so many vehemently argued about the culpability of Nussbaum in regard to Lisa's death, which lead, in turn, to serious questions and arguments concerning the credibility and legitimacy of the so-called battered wife syndrome. The complexities involved in these debates are seminal in that they provide for a better indication of the paradoxical and diverse issues mediating any understanding and employment of victimization. And since the Nussbaum case "was considered a courtroom text on the battered wife syndrome," it is appropriate that this contentious and enigmatic phenomenon be examined within this context (*New York Times*, Oct. 27, 1994).

VICTIMIZATION AND THE LOVE/HATE DOUBLE BIND

It is important to note that Hedda Nussbaum's case is an extremity, particularly in relation to her overpowering obsession with Joel, which even eight years later, had yet to dissipate (*Court TV*, Dec. 7, 1994). Her attitude, however, and those of other severely damaged people who share this characteristic (which includes similar kinds of extreme cases of women and child abuse) makes more sense when recontextualized within the wider framework of torture or terrorism. This kind of behavior, in fact, has been described by some psychiatric experts as similar to the kinds of emotional and physical debilitation experienced by prisoners and hostages after having had extreme forms of mental and physical torture imposed upon them. Indeed, one psychiatric expert, testifying for Hedda in her November 1994 hearing, characterized Nussbaum as a classic example of the *Stockholm syndrome*. This term refers to hostages in a bank in Stockholm who became intensely bonded with their captors, during and after their release. It is important to recognize, however, that most battered women grow to hate their abusers, although, for the sake of their own safety, they don't often articulate it, while others are trapped in a psychopathological love/hate double bind. Susan Schechter provides some insight into this paradoxical situation.

Women love their partners, but for many battered women this changes over time. Typically, once a woman realizes she's living with a truly violent person, a lot of the love turns to hate. And what she loves, by the way, is not the abuse, but the good moments, the times when he isn't violent. She wants the relationship without the violence, and he often promises her that she will have it again. (1989, 62)

Further, Lenore E. Walker, considered a leading expert in the area of battered women, points out, "Battered women are not blind; most of them understand that there is something seriously wrong with the men who alternately hurt and nurture them" (1989, 70). Although some women, like Nussbaum, appear to be enamored with their batterers, this aspect of the case is not a key aspect of the underlying pattern of her situation that many feminists are concerned with in their attempts to analyze and relate this case to other cases of battered women. Yet, it is a dimension of the paradoxical position in which battered women and abused children—unlike practically any other kind of victimized people—find themselves. In fact, the situation of the abused woman is the ultimate concrete, material reality of living a "double bind." As Reinhild Traitler-Espiritu so astutely describes it:

Violence against woman's body is often the merging point, the terrain where caring and brutality meet and where men are unable to keep the two messages, the call to care for life and the command to destroy it, apart. (1996, 78)

And, it is in this sense that the pathological relations of male abuse of women should be examined within a wider critical feminist systemic framework. We need both analyses of how men use violence to control women and analyses of how women have managed to exert power in extreme situations. This is all the more impressive because this exertion of power, resistance, and agency emanates from such disadvantaged positions. Indeed such analysis, which characterizes the best feminist research, does not, as Hoff Sommers, Paglia, and other feminist impersonators claim, endorse a "victim feminism." The historian Linda Gordon, for instance, who studies family violence from a contextual perspective, describes her research within the kind of multiperspectival and critical feminist approach that I am advocating in my studies. Gordon writes:

There has been a tendency in telling the histories of oppressed peoples, whether women, the poor, or blacks, to turn survivors into heroes, to romanticize forbearance. I have not been tempted to do this, because in family-violence studies, many who did not survive were equally brave, including the alcoholic, the delinquent, the depressed. Few of the victims succeeded in full escape; few were without some moment of complicity or resignation that lessened their resistance, at least temporarily. And many who were victims were also oppressors. (Gordon 1988, book-jacket frontispiece)

The abundance of research and interrogation of the battery of women and family terrorism, however, takes place at the erroneous level of psychologizing and personalizing these relations within a decontextualized notion of "dysfunctional families." Such analyses put particular emphasis on the outlandish and absurd investigation and so-called analysis of the victims of abuse, rather than on the abuser or the systemic conditions that mediate and perpetuate this kind of behavior. Marian Meyers (1997) argues that this kind of reductionist perspective, in fact, naturalizes "the relationship of sexist violence to male supremacy. What can be called anti-woman violence because it is directed *specifically against women* by men appears to be not simply common and everyday but 'just the way things are,' part of the natural and correct order of the universe" (26). She goes on to demonstrate how this kind of misogynist bigotry infiltrates and mediates the kinds of individualistic, decontextualized, bifurcated research that dominates the field. Such perspectives consequently serve as one of the greatest barriers to productive examinations and subsequent changes in the deleterious relations of family terrorism and crimes of violence against women and children.

> Even sociologists and psychologists who study or attempt to "cure" battering tend to see it not as the practice of male domination and control but as the result of family dysfunction. Traditional sociological approaches are concerned with patterns of relationship within families or between couples as well as with the culture, norms and values guiding behavior. From this perspective, violence is seen as a response by both sexes to structural and situational stimuli. (Meyers 1997, 26)

It is in this sense that it becomes apparent and necessary that an attempt be made to assess the general sense of revulsion, rather than pity, that Nussbaum elicited. As Ann Jones puts it, "As a rule, when we contemplate the victimization of our fellow human beings, we have the least sympathy for the worst case. Psychologists know that this is just another common defense by which we distance ourselves from disaster, but it's curious and disturbing nonetheless, violating at once the laws of logic and the leanings of the heart" (1994a, 180). This notion of "distancing" is particularly relevant to our perceptions about a diversity of disenfranchised, marginalized, sick, homeless, indigent, refugee, immigrant, elderly, mentally challenged, differently abled and incarcerated members of what is often deemed to be the societal underclass. And it is especially applicable to popular beliefs about women like Hedda Nussbaum.

Jones goes on to describe the manner in which we quantify and distinguish between abused women in binary terms. Women who manage to flee or those who save their children from abuse are awarded the status of heroic or "good" battered women, while those who stay or don't protect their children from their partners' assaults are perceived as the "bad" ones, or as collaborators in their own misery. In Jones's analysis, "Illogical though it may be, *the greater the abuse, the less our sympathy for the sufferer.* We are inspired by those who gallantly pass through hardship, but we despise those who succumb. We admire those who triumph over adversity, but we condemn the full-blown victim" (Jones 1994a, 181).

Jones's insightful analysis brings to light a deep-rooted ideological prejudice that lies in our social unconscious—and, when seriously recognized and questioned, assists in understanding and answering many of the questions related to battered women and the more general terrain of victimization. Ann Jones employs this type of analysis to explain a dimension of the hostility directed toward Nussbaum. "Thus, for many complex reasons, many who followed the Steinberg case—in the jury box, in the press rows, in the papers, on television— came to see Hedda Nussbaum as a 'willing' victim, which is to say, really not a victim at all. And by focusing on the victim, they managed to lose sight of the criminal, and the crime" (Jones 1994a, 181).

However, this notion of "a willing victim" neatly blocks the types of dialectical investigation necessary for an active comprehension of the highly complex, contextually multileveled reality of the situation of battered women and for the potential for any serious social change. Moreover, it also provokes a binary either-or mythical appraisal of the situation, which, in turn, promotes and maintains the artificial, ideological, division between the subjective and the objective domains. Such a reductionist perception, I might add, is classically reflected in the feminist impersonators' pop philosophy. Witness, for example, Camille Paglia's ruminations on the topic, which so aptly reflect, reinforce, and exploit dominant assumptions on woman-battering relationships and thus speak to her popularity with establishment media culture.

> Here is the crux of the relationship, which has to be defined as sadomasochistic on *both* sides. His pleading reactivates the maternal in her. She forgives him. Never is he more open, vulnerable, and intimate than when he begs for a second chance—"I'll never do it again." His tenderness and affection enamor her. *She is addicted to the apology.* She is overwhelmed by sensory ecstasy, by the heightened passions of rage and frenzy yielding to the melting reunion of boy and mother, who nestles her son against her bosom. As in the self-flagellation of medieval Catholicism, physical pain may produce spiritual exaltation. The battered woman stays because she thinks she sees the truth and because, secretly, she knows she is victorious. (1994, 44)[13]

Although Paglia's scenario is completely at odds with much current literature in the field, especially the psychological domain specializing in these matters— which rejected the masochistic model of the battered woman decades ago—her analysis is so appealing precisely because it presents a bifurcated subjective/objective sense of credibility to this dynamic (Walker 1989, 36).[14] For we have—at the subjective level—the "willing victim" who finds fulfillment in a dysfunctional sadomasochistic relationship, which, supposedly, has been documented in the "objective," scientific literature, as it has most certainly been reified in multiple forms of media culture. Indeed, this ideological myth has been widely employed to explain the nature of wife abuse. Moreover, the relationship has become subjectified and personalized, which reduces the complexity of wife battering to the domain of individual preference and the dimension of the private and negates any societal environmental influence in these matters. Hence, it makes the battered woman abused by men responsible for her situation, labeling her depraved and thus exonerating all other women who do not share her predilections.

In fact, this subjectivized viewpoint absolves social institutions from taking serious action in these matters because "the problem is her fault and the solution her responsibility" (Jones 1994a, 139). This psychologizing of the problem, as Jones notes, reduces and decontextualizes the phenomenon to one of "personal psychology instead of material conditions of peoples lives" (1994b, 62). Yet in another of Paglia's unsubstantiated denouncements, she once again exploits the sexualizing and psychologizing of familiy violence to perpetuate the common stereotype of the equal culpability notion that is so prevalent in popular discussions of the abuse of women.

> There [is] rarely much psychological inquiry into the sticky complexities of sexual attraction and conflict that implicate *both* partners in any long-running private drama. . . . The batterer, like the serial adulterer, is an infantile personality who is fixated on the mother archetype in his wife. He demands her undivided attention, the narcotic of her quiet consolation. . . . The more he misbehaves the more she feels she needs him. She finds his adolescent rambunctiousness both daunting and endearing—and, it has to be said, sexually exciting. (Paglia 1994, 43)

Paglia continues to employ her peculiar version of fractured Freudianism and pop-psychology to frame her deterministic and damning picture of sick codependency for which the woman bears the decided responsibility.

> What leads up to the first blow is always the same: provoked or not, she has pushed his buttons of dependency. Once again, he faces his insignificance in women's eyes. He has dwindled back to boyhood, where women ruled him. To recover his adult masculinity, he lashes out at her with his fists. He savors her pain and fear, but her refusal to defend herself takes the fight out of him. He is sickened, desperate, apologetic. (Paglia 1994, 44)

Jones characterizes and contextualizes this position, which she demonstrates is a depiction conventionally perpetuated by mass media, as one that is biased by the batterers' perspective as well as being an insidious form of blaming the victim.

> "The two are locked in a sick battle that binds—and reassures—even as it divides." This is hogwash! Where do they get this shit? From talking to batterers who say, "I

hit her and then she deliberately defied me until I had to hit her again." They would not get this story from a woman.

This is a deliberate misinterpretation of what some women might say; battered women will sometimes say that they knew a beating was coming so they tried to provoke him at a certain time when they thought they could control it. . . . It's not "locked in a sick battle," it's a last-ditch effort to try to maintain some kind of control over a situation that you can't escape from. And some women are so conditioned to think they did something wrong to "cause" an attack that they report it that way. What everyone . . . forgets is that provocation is not a crime. Battering is. (1994b, 61)

This is especially reinforced by the naming of these acts of violence as "domestic," which, as Jones points out, makes it appear less threatening or "tamer than the real thing" (1994a, 1). Further, the implications of this problematic labeling are that this form of violence is different or of a "special category" that is not as serious as the real thing (Jones 1994a, 56). In this sense, it is treated as "a kind of violence that women volunteer for, or inspire, or provoke" (Jones 1994a, 56). This victim blaming is the illogical response to a binary, one-dimensional, individualized, and hence reductionist worldview. "In the United States, 'domestic violence' is addressed in terms of the personal psychology of individual victims and (far less often) perpetuators. 'Domestic violence' is a 'social' problem only in the sense that it affects an aggregate of those supposedly aberrant individuals" (Jones 1994a, 211).

In the next chapter, I will take a closer look at familial violence in the context of what I call "family terrorism." I argue that the concept of family terrorism provides a contextualized and concrete framework to do research into violence against women and children that focuses on gender relations, specific socio-political, economic, and ideological mediators of family violence, and the particular facts of each case, while providing systematic concepts that help illuminate the phenomenon as a whole.

NOTES

1. Faludi adds: "When simply asked if they consider themselves feminists, 51 percent of women say yes; when told that a feminist is 'someone who supports political, economic, and social equality for women,' the proportion jumps to 71 percent" (1996b, 28). Baumgarten and Richards add that "according to a 1998 *Time*/CNN poll, more than 50 percent of women between eighteen and thirty-four say they are simpatico with feminist values but do not necessarily call themselves feminists" (2000, 83). Ironically, however, many contemporary young women are rejecting the feminist label due to the influence of postfeminist and media demonization of the term. On the other hand, the neglect of issues of race and class by sectors of mainstream feminism have kept some women of color from employing the term. As Sista II Sista (a collective of young women of color) explain it: "In this country, what has become mainstream feminism—the struggle for social, political,

and economic equality for women—hasn't been women struggling for all women. It lacks a class and race analysis. . . . It isn't just about the discourse, it's about what issues you work on. I don't see major welfare rights or major anti-sweatshop or women worker movements on the feminist agenda. Until feminists are adamantly and passionately fighting against these issues that affect women of color and poor women, who are the most disenfranchised in this system, we can't call ourselves feminists." Cited in *Ms.* (February–March 2001, 50).

2. According to 1998 National Violence against Women Survey "approximately 1.5 million women and 834,700 men are raped and/or physically assaulted by an intimate partner annually in the United States" (www.ncjrs.org/txtfiles/172837.txt). Of course, as I note throughout my studies, certain statistics and empirical research can be questioned, and this is particularly the case concerning rape and violence against women. The main difficulties are not, as Roiphe, Hoff Sommers, and other antifeminists argue, alleged feminist inflation of statistics. Rather, as James McBride argues,

> The difficulty in obtaining consensus on the numbers of victims is in part empirical and in part definitional. The shame and fear that haunts the everyday life of domestic abuse victims prevents many from seeking the assistance they need to extricate themselves from the situation. And when they do receive medical treatment, some victims mask the true cause of their condition. (McBride 1995, 12)

3. Hoff Sommers's chapter on "Rape Research" in *Who Stole Feminism?* incorporates extensive citations and discussions from the work of Roiphe as well as Paglia, presenting them as experts in the field. And Paglia, as Faludi points out, who has no proficiency in the area of rape research, was the only "feminist" a reporter for *Newsweek* could find to agree with Roiphe's assessment (Faludi 1995, 37). Moreover, Faludi points out that "Roiphe and others 'prove' their cases by recycling the same anecdotes of false accusations; they all quote the same 'expert' who disparages reports of high rape rates. And they never interview any real rape victims" (1993, 61). Moreover, Hoff Sommers fails to engage any of the major feminist literature on rape and violence against women, such as the many sources that I am drawing on, including Dobash and Dobash 1979, Walker 1989, Gordon 1988, and Jones 1994a and 1996.

4. FAIR describes itself as "a national media watch group offering well-documented criticism in an effort to correct bias and imbalance. FAIR focuses public awareness on the narrow corporate ownership of the press, the media's allegiance to official agendas and their insensitivity to women, labor, minorities, and other public interest constituencies. The group seeks to invigorate the First Amendment by advocating for greater media pluralism and the inclusion of public interest voices in national debates" (*EXTRA!* Special Issue, 1992, n.p.).

5. Wolf goes on to comment that "The researchers at Old Dominion University issued a letter explaining that their sample was small but it did show a pattern of an increase in violence, and offering their support to the FAIR spokespeople. FAIR says their letter to *The Washington Post* claiming that Ringle never spoke to the group's main office and that he took quotes out of context went unpublished. Finally, the *American Journalism Review* concluded that FAIR was 'hardly faultless' in using the 40 percent figure in a document; but also that, while Ringle was right about the lack of solid data, he 'does appear to have twisted and used quotes selectively to support his thesis.' "

"The story here," says Jim Nourekian of FAIR, "is not the excesses of Sheila Kuehl.

The story is that when that much attention is being given to a [women's] issue, it provokes a response from reporters [like Ringle]. *The coverage of domestic violence we got was on back pages, but those papers which reprinted Ringle's story ran it as front-page news"* (Wolf 1993, 100; emphasis mine).

Interestingly, although Hoff Sommers takes Wolf to task for her "victim feminism" throughout *Who Stole Feminism?* she forgives Wolf for her sins after the publication of *Fire with Fire,* which I presented as part of the antifeminist feminism syndrome in chapter 2 (see Hoff Sommers 1994, 244–45). Yet Hoff Sommers seems not to have read Wolf's position on the Super Bowl issue, which undermines her own dogmatic assertions.

For additional studies that provide a wide range of documentation of increased violence against women on Super Bowl Sunday and during the Gulf War, see James McBride (1995, 4ff), who provides an analytical explanation of how "blood sports" help encourage violence against women. However, McBride is perfectly aware that there are problems with many statistical and empirical studies of violence against women, that there is no necessary correlation between the Super Bowl and increased violence, and that there are indeed many explanations of why violence toward women might increase during the Super Bowl period (1995, 1ff). Moreover, McBride polemicizes against all one-sided approaches to violence against women and offers multiperspectival interpretations, ones that I develop myself in the course of my studies.

6. Ironically, part of Hoff Sommers's defense of Gelles and Straus is in response to what she alleges is feminist enmity toward their work. She claims Gelles's and Straus's work "fell out of favor" with feminists in part because they were men (1994, 194). However, what she fails to mention is that Straus and Gelles worked with Susan Steinmetz on a number of their studies, including the highly contentious CTS. Hence, once again we are privy to Hoff Sommers's one-dimensionalized, invented man-hating myth regarding so-called gender feminists and the manner in which she is constantly manipulating material to fit her often illegitimate claims.

7. It is important to note that Dobash and Dobash's 1979 critique of the employment of a general systems theoretical model for understanding wife abuse appears to stem from their identification of how this model is often applied in its purest, mathematical quantitative sense to such empirical studies. However, within a transdisciplinary perspective, general systems theory has been of assistance to the ongoing development of what has been labeled "a communicational approach" (which is often associated with the Palo Alto School of Communications). In this sense, general systems theory can be translated in a dialectical fashion that is quite unlike the deterministic, mechanized form attacked by Dobash and Dobash.

8. Yet the CTS continues to be employed in contemporary studies such as the National Violence Against Women Survey, which "used a modified version of the conflict tactic scale" (U.S. Department of Justice 1998, www.ojp.usdoj.gov/vawo). As Kurz explains it,

[T]he Conflict Tactics Scale (CTS) [is] an instrument that asks one member of a couple, drawn from a random sample of married people composed one half of men and one half of women, to fill out a form indicating if or how many times he or she performed specific actions during the previous 12 months. . . . This survey instrument asks about conflicts between husbands and wives in the previous year and measures conflict resolution on a continuum from nonviolent tactics (calm discussion) to the most violent tactics (use of a knife or gun). (1993, 254)

9. Lisa Brush employed the National Survey of Families and Households for her study, which "was funded by a grant . . . from the Center for Population Research at the National Institute of Child Health and Human Development" (Brush 1993, 240).

10. As Farganis notes: "In their work on family violence, Wini Breines and Linda Gordon emphasize the need to see violence as a form of power and therefore, the need to involve the state in what some regard as an invitation to state regulation of private affairs." In addition, this perspective demands "that the class and race dimensions of gendered lives be taken into account" (1994, 97).

Norman Denzin provides us with a revealing picture of the prevalence of child abuse in the United States: "Child and juvenile crime is a fact of life that continues to escalate in American society in urban, rural, and suburban settings. In this context every home in America is a scene of family violence—not typically perpetrated by children—at least once a year. How surprising can child violence figures be when we learn that kids in 60 percent of American homes confront child abuse yearly, including sexual abuse, hitting, and battering—not to mention emotional violence" (Denzin, cited in Steinberg and Kincheloe 1997, 21).

11. A *Newsweek* (Jul. 4, 1994, 23) report notes:

Indiana University psychologist Amy Holtzworth-Munroe divides abusers into three behavioral types. The majority of men who hit their wives do so infrequently and their violence doesn't escalate. They look ordinary, and they're most likely to feel remorse after an attack. "When they use violence, it reflects some lack of communication skills, combined with a dependence on the wife," she says. A second group of men are intensely jealous of their wives and fear abandonment. Most likely, they grew up with psychological and sexual abuse. Like those in the first group, these men's dependence on their wives is as important as their need to control them—if she even talks to another man, "he thinks she's leaving or sleeping around," says Holtzworth-Munroe. The smallest—and most dangerous—group encompasses men with an antisocial personality disorder. Their battering fits into a larger pattern of violence and getting in trouble with the law. Neil S. Jacobson, a marital therapist at the University of Washington, likens such men to serial murderers. Rather than becoming more agitated during an attack, he says, they become calmer, their heart rates drop. "They're like cobras. They're just like criminals who beat up anybody else when they're not getting what they want." Men who batter share something else: they deny what they've done, minimize their attacks and always blame the victims.

12. Dr. Michael Allen, an assistant professor of psychiatry and assistant director of the Psychiatric Emergency and Admitting Services at Bellevue Hospital, who had examined Hedda Nussbaum after her arrest explained to Susan Brownmiller that "Cocaine causes people to be hypervigilant. . . . Extraneous events take on a frightening significance. As they become more paranoid, it's typical for these people to believe others are staring at them and even to react to people as if they were" (Brownmiller 1989, 346).

13. Paglia's ludicrous claim that battered women are addicted to aspects of an abusive relationship is not grounded in any empirical or family violence studies and, once again, seems to be employed to ingratiate herself with those in positions of power who espouse the masochistic mentality of victim bashing and publicize her comments. Indeed, Lenore E. Walker who is far more knowledgeable in the field, refutes this notion. "[C]ontrary to myth, a battered woman, once out of the battering relationship, is unlikely to become

involved with another batterer. If they become involved again at all, these women usually do so with gentle, nonviolent people. . . . This phenomenon has . . . confirmed my belief that battered women, including battered women who kill their abusers, are by no means 'addicted' to violent situations, and are neither masochistic nor sadistic. On the contrary: once free of abuse and terror, their lives can be very good indeed" (1989, 7).

14. Paglia's stance appears to originate in a study that was more than thirty years old at the time of her writing and that has been widely critiqued and rejected within not only the feminist terrain but especially within the areas of forensic psychology that specialize in these matters. For a scholar who claims to be on the "cutting edge," her lack of literacy in the area is a poor reflection of her rudimentary research skills.

In 1964, one of the first U.S. studies of battered women, conducted by three men and significantly entitled "The Wife-Beater's Wife: A Study of Family Interaction," studied women in Framingham, Massachusetts, who had charged their husbands with assault, and found the women "castrating," "aggressive," "masculine," "frigid," "indecisive," "passive," and "masochistic." What's more, the authors concluded, the husband's assaultive behavior served "to fill a wife's need even though she protested it." . . . The neo-Freudian psychiatric researchers who studied the wife-beater's wife found her "deviance" deep within her own distressingly "masculine" psyche, feminine only in its profound "masochism." Thus they redefined a universal crime as a personal psychological aberration. They blamed the wife-beater's wife not simply for falling victim to battering but for *causing* battering and then lying about it afterward. Without the wife-beater's wife there would be no wife beating. The reasoning is indeed so smooth it almost sounds rational (Jones 1994a, 138–39). Jones goes on to demonstrate how the study has been criticized and refuted by countervailing evidence.

4

Family Terrorism

The ideological nature of the language commonly employed to describe the battery of women neutralizes and incorrectly frames the reality of this violent crime. Euphemisms such as *conjugal violence, spousal abuse, intimate partner violence, marital disputes, stormy relationships,* or *crimes of passion* suggest that both partners are equally responsible for the violence, even though according to most studies the overwhelming majority of perpetrators are men (Tjaden and Thoennes 2000, iii, 56).[1] I, therefore, suggest the term *family terrorism* to describe the context of male violence against women and the assault of children (especially sexual abuse and incest) as well as elderly abuse. Although women and children certainly commit violent acts, it is the structural position of patriarchal violence and escalating poverty, many feminists and antiviolence activists argue, that creates a terroristic situation in which the weaker members of the family or community are subjected to constant threats of violence and brutality.

It is in this sense that in regard to child abuse, women are all too often culpable, and recontextualizing these kinds of violent relations is not intended to excuse or deemphasize women's role in them. Empirical studies and family violence research have, in fact, revealed shocking revelations concerning the high rates of child abuse and murder. These include a Carnegie report that claims that "one in three victims of physical abuse is an infant less than a year old," and that the children most at risk are those who constitute part of the one-quarter of children who are born into poverty. The studies also include a text by Richard Firstman and Jamie Talan entitled *The Death of Innocents,* which reports that many cases of child abuse have, for years, been misdiagnosed as SIDS (Sudden Infant Death Syndrome), "a mysterious malady which is blamed for 3,200 infant deaths each year in the United States alone" (*New York Times,* Sept. 11, 1997).

The book recounts numerous cases of suspicious deaths and injuries that have not been investigated because doctors have mistakenly classified abuse cases as possible

SIDS or near-miss SIDS. It suggests that a misguided medical theory and misleading scientific articles some years ago led to misclassifications that may have continued to the present. (*New York Times*, Sept. 11, 1997)

Mike A. Males provides us with an overview of family terrorism in the United States:

"Rape in America is a tragedy of youth," the National Victim Center reported in 1992. Of their sample of 4,000 adult women, one in eight had been raped, 62 percent of these prior to age 18. A *Los Angeles Times* survey of 2,600 adults nationwide found 27 percent of women and 16 percent of men had been sexually abused in childhood. The average age at the time of victimization was nine for victims, 30 for abusers. Half of the abusers were "someone in authority." (Males 1996, 17).

Indeed, the dramatic dimensions of abuse and violence—especially the kinds directed against women, children, and the elderly—have reached epidemic proportions. This claim is supported by the first international conference on the sexual exploitation of children, held in Stockholm in 1996. The conference identified the rapidly growing "business of child prostitution and trafficking" as "a multibillion dollar a year industry" (*New York Times*, Aug. 26, 1996).[2] Further, the Amnesty International, *Children's Report for the 2000 Campaign to Stamp Out Torture* provides us with a shocking pronouncement on the global state of family terrorism, specifically in regard to violence against children:

Violence against children is endemic: children are tortured by the police or security forces; detained in appalling conditions; beaten or sexually abused by parents, teachers or employers; maimed, killed or turned into killers by war.

Some are victims many times over, first of the chronic poverty and discrimination that renders them vulnerable to torture and ill-treatment, then to the injustice and impunity that allows it to continue unpunished. (www.stoptorture.org)

The systemic nature of family violence is further established by the escalating rate of violence against the elderly.

The National Elder Abuse Incidence Study (NEAIS) found that an estimated total of 550 thousand elderly persons experienced abuse, neglect and/or self-neglect in domestic settings in 1996. . . . The NEAIS estimated that for each new incident of elder abuse, neglect, and/or self neglect reported in 1996, four or five incidents went unreported. Almost 62% of the substantiated reports were incidents of maltreatment by other persons, while 38% were self-neglect incidents. The most common types of elder abuse, in order of frequency, are: neglect, emotional/psychological abuse, financial/material exploitation, and physical abuse. The majority of victims are among the oldest elders (80 years old and over) and are more likely to be women. Abusers are more likely to be male and family members, especially adult children. (Soto-Aqino, Congressional Research Service 1999, 2)

Disparities of wealth, inflation, annihilation of social services and pension plans have and will contribute to the lack of adequate care and quality of life of senior citizens. Indeed, many of the deplorable conditions and the kinds of family terrorism that define too many of the lives of elderly people is only the tip of the iceberg; especially given that the U.S. census discovered an "extraordinary burst in longevity" of seniors. In 2000 there were 68,000 citizens who were 100-years-old, double the number documented in 1990 and medical researchers are expecting a 71 percent increase in a decade (*ABC News*, July 30, 2001).

Many critical feminists and human rights activists would argue that forms of family terrorism are representative of the patriarchal, hierarchical nature of violence, which underscores local and global social, political, and economic relations. Moreover, the abuse of the elderly, in particular demonstrates that family terrorism is hardly limited to the private realm, especially given the role of private and public living institutions and hospitals. Hence, my use of the term "family terrorism" is related, in part, to definitions of patriarchal families as well as a far more expansive, semiotic notion of the "family"—both are mediated by ideas concerning the public and private domains (see chapter 5).

I have accordingly developed the expression "family terrorism" to provoke a dialectical shift in addressing issues of violence against women, children, and the elderly that is far more extensive and interrelated to social, political, and economic dimensions (which necessarily include relations of gender, race, ethnicity, class and sexuality) than conventional thinking about what violence or abuse of women and children usually signifies. The concept of family terrorism thus provides a critique of the problematic nature of such limited ideological descriptions as "domestic violence," or its latest incarnation "intimate partner abuse"—which even further neutralizes and reduces the real complexity of the relationships it is allegedly delineating. As Ann Jones explains it:

"Domestic violence" is one of those gray phrases, beloved of bureaucracy, designed to give people a way of talking about a topic without seeing what's really going on. Like "repatriation" or "ethnic cleansing," it's a euphemistic abstraction that keeps us at a dispassionate distance, far removed from the repugnant spectacle of human beings in pain. . . . Even feminist advocates for women, who called their cause "the battered women's movement," eventually succumbed; they adopted "domestic violence" in their fundraising proposals, so as not to offend men controlling the purse strings by suggesting that men were in any way to blame for this "social problem." So well does the phrase "domestic violence" obscure the real events behind it that when a Domestic Violence Act (to provide money for battered women's services) was first proposed to Congress in 1978, many thought it was a bill to combat political terrorism within the United States. (Jones 1994a, 81–82)

According to bell hooks "domestic violence" has been used to cover up the severity and systematic nature of family terrorism. She argues that it is "a 'soft' term which suggests it emerges in an intimate context that is private and somehow less threatening, less brutal, than the violence that takes place outside the home" (2000b, 62). hooks continues:

> This is not so, since more women are beaten and murdered in the home than on the outside. Also most people tend to see domestic violence between adults as separate and distinct from violence against children when it is not. Often children suffer abuse as they attempt to protect a mother who is being attacked by a male companion or husband, or they are emotionally damaged by witnessing violence and abuse. (2000b, 62)

Ann Jones points out that it was during the U.S. Carter administration (1976–1980) that discourse such as "wife beating," was replaced with highly neutral "professional vocabularies" such as "spouse abuse," "conjugal violence," "marital aggression," and of course "domestic violence" (1994a, 82). At this time, "a great renaming took place, a renaming that veiled once again the sexism a grass-roots women's movement had worked to uncover" (Jones 1994a, 82). The term "partner abuse" or "intimate partner violence" (which is widely used in contemporary studies) further neutralizes violent relations in terms of both gender and sexuality. For example, "The National Violence Against Women (NVAW) Survey on the Extent, Nature, and Consequences of *Intimate Partner Violence*," was co-sponsored by the National Institute of Justice and the Centers for Disease Control and Prevention (Tjaden and Thoennes 2000).

Consequently, I employ the term "family terrorism" to address violence in the family in a more multidimensional and realistic manner, in which the abuse and neglect of women, children, and the elderly is emphasized. Moreover, this term draws on work of critical antiviolence feminists like Linda Gordon who sees family violence as "a political issue" (Gordon 1988, 5). She is concerned with the abuse and neglect of children and discusses this within a contextual framework that includes the roles of women in terrorizing and/or neglecting their children. This, of course, includes traditional, "alternative" and/or single mother families. Central to her analysis are the mediating effects of class and money in relations of violence within the family.

In addition, I find bell hooks's employment of the term "patriarchal violence" especially appropriate. As she explains it: "The term 'patriarchal violence' is useful because unlike the more accepted phrase 'domestic violence' it continually reminds the listener that violence in the home is connected to sexism and sexist thinking, to male domination" (2000b, 61–62). It is within this context that the abuse of children and the elderly, as well as the escalating nature of global violence against women and children should be understood as a systemic process. Indeed, hooks points out that even a "a mother who might never be violent but who teaches her children, especially her sons, that violence is an acceptable means of exerting social control, is still in collusion with patriarchal violence." She clarifies the relationship of patriarchal violence to parental violence and women's role as collaborator and/or colonizer in this relationship: "Clearly most women do not use violence to dominate men (even though small numbers of women batter the men in their lives) but lots of women believe that a person in authority has the right to use force to maintain authority" (hooks 2000b, 64). Moreover,

> since women remain the primary caretakers of children, the facts confirm the reality that given a hierarchichal system in a culture of domination which empowers females (like the parent-child relationship) all too often they use coercive force to maintain dominance. In a culture of domination everyone is socialized to see violence as an acceptable means of social control. Dominant parties maintain power by the threat (acted upon or not) that abusive punishment, physical or psychological, will be used whenever the hierarchical structures in place are threatened, whether that be in male-female relationships, or parent and child bonds." (hooks 2000b, 64)

Indeed, it is within this context that subjectivist misperceptions of wife abuse as the fault of individual women are problematic. For women especially, finding flaws in the battered woman's character allows them to say, "This could never happen to me." Within this subjectivist perspective, then, only certain women will be battered or will themselves exert violence, and that will be purely as a result of some personal defect—a "fact" backed up by numerous objective studies that demonstrate that battered women share a deficiency in certain kinds of traits. Once again, then, we are blinded by the decontextualized separation of subjectivity from objectivity.

William B. Helmreich, "a professor of sociology at the City College of New York and an expert in group responses to public events," describes the public's fascination and disgust with Hedda Nussbaum in terms of this type of mind-set in that "she crossed the line. . . . That's frightening. But at another level, it's reassuring because we know that we didn't cross that line. The formula is neat: not 'There but for the grace of God go I,' but 'There, thank God, goes someone who is most decidedly not me' " (cited in Jones 1994a, 174).

This type of subjective rationalization has deleterious consequences for the victims and survivors of wife abuse and for the kinds of contextual, dialectical, multidimensional analyses that are necessary for both understanding and changing a cancerous situation whose epidemic proportions have only recently been acknowledged. Indeed, it is hard to fathom that the two to four million U.S. women battered every year all share some kind of psychological or genetic deviancy, or kinky perversity, that provokes or justifies their own abuse.

Hence, feminists like Judith Lewis Herman argue that what happened to Hedda Nussbaum could happen to any of us, in that "under extreme duress anyone can be 'broken' " (cited in Jones 1994a, 174). And indeed, this is a perspective shared by many feminists and social scientists in the field, because it situates the problem within the more social public domain. The implications of this type of epistemological perspective toward the issue of family terrorism, as Jones points out, is a terrifying prospect in that "survivors of severe trauma—combat soldiers, prisoners of war, rape victims, disaster victims, hostages, battered women—*universally* attribute their survival largely to good luck" (1994a, 174). Thus, the act of viewing the battered woman (or any marginalized people, in fact) as "other" and deeming her responsible for her own abusive situation is, in fact, an act of collective denial, as

> who wants to believe that our well-being hinges upon chance? . . . [W]e search the *victim* for those peculiarities of psyche and circumstance that made the life give way, or, worse, impelled the victim to step across the line herself, deliberate and heedless. Herman says that we try "to account for the victim's behavior by seeking flaws in her personality or moral character" because, having no knowledge of terror and coercion, we presume that in similar circumstances we "would show greater courage and resistance than the victim." (Jones 1994a, 174)

It is within this context that the pejorative connotation of the term *victim* and the consequent successful exploitation of it by the betrayal feminists discloses its harmful implications.

"WHY DOESN'T SHE LEAVE?" PERPETUATING MYTHS ABOUT BATTERED WOMEN

What is often unknown, or has somehow been buried, in Hedda Nussbaum's case is that she did, in fact, try to leave on a number of occasions and she did ask for help. As Jones describes it, "What was extraordinary about the case . . . is the fact that not a single person responded to Nussbaum's efforts to get away from Steinberg. Not her family or emergency-room doctors or social workers or psychiatrists or police or neighbors. Literally, no one" (*Montreal Gazette*, Mar. 19, 1994).

In fact, the case of Hedda Nussbaum is a representative example of how battered women do indeed attempt to leave or ask for help through both overt and covert actions. It also dramatizes the enormous deficiencies in the system that make it so difficult for them to escape, and provides the tendency to blame themselves for their situation. Andrea Dworkin confirms this dilemma through her devastating account, drawn from her own experience and inspired by what she angrily perceived as a lack of understanding for Hedda Nussbaum's plight. Dworkin's testament is, in fact, an indictment against the erroneous ideological nature of the question, "Why doesn't she leave?" And in this sense, it is worth quoting at length as an indication of the confusing, hostile environment facing the contemporary battered woman and the diversity of real issues that must be addressed in response to this deceptively simple question.

Battery is a forced descent into hell and you don't get by in hell by moral goodness. You disintegrate. You don't survive as a discrete personality with a sense of right and wrong. You live in a world of pain, in isolation, on the verge of death, in terror; and when you get numb enough not to care whether you live or die you are experiencing the only grace God is going to send your way. Drugs help. . . .

Your neighbors hear you screaming. They do nothing. The next day they look through you. . . . Your neighbors, friends, and family see the bruises and injuries—and do nothing. They will not intercede. They send you back. They say it's your fault or you like it or they deny it is happening. Your family believes you belong with your husband.

If you scream and no one helps and no one acknowledges it and people look right through you, you begin to feel you don't exist. If you existed and you screamed, someone would help you. If you existed and were visibly injured, someone would help you. If you existed and asked for help in escaping, someone would help you.

When you go to the doctor or to the hospital because you are injured and they don't listen or help you or they give you tranquilizers or threaten to commit you because they say you are disoriented, paranoid, you begin to believe that he can hurt you as much as he wants and no one will help you. When the police refuse to help you, you begin to believe that he can hurt you or kill you and it will not matter because you do not exist. . . .

Eventually I waited to die. I wanted to die. I hoped the next beating would kill me. . . . When he hurt other people, I didn't help them. Nussbaum's guilt is not foreign to me. (Dworkin 1993, 237–38)

Dworkin, writing from the perspective of one who's been there, raises a number of significant issues directly related to dominant beliefs concerning battered women and victimization. Perhaps most importantly, she reveals how societal attitudes and institutions insidiously prevent abused women and children from demanding and being afforded the protection they so urgently need and deserve. Indeed, we are all too commonly bombarded with the message that these women fail to inform others of their predicament and choose to stay in these relationships. According to the American Academy of Family Physicians: "Many barriers impede the recognition of problems with violence in patients and their family. Several myths about family violence exist: the misconception that victims are poor, inner-city women and children, the belief that violence is rare or does not occur in families that seem normal, the feeling that family violence is a private matter, and the notion that victims are in some way responsible" (2000, www.aafp.org/policy/issues/v-violenceposition.html). Yet as Linda Gordon writes:

[I]n this society of great inequality, interventions against family violence have been and continue to be discriminatory. Class privilege brings with it immunity from discovery and/or intervention. Not only have poor, working-class, immigrant, and black people been discriminated against, but so too have women, despite the feminist influence in stimulating anti-family-violence intervention. The disrespect and victim-blaming of many professionals towards clients was the worst, because they were proffered by those defined as "helping." Loss of control was a debilitating experience for many clients, including those who may have gained some material aid. Often the main beneficiaries of professionals' intervention hated them most, because in wrestling with them one rarely gets what one really wants but, rather, is asked to submit to another's interpretation of one's needs. (1988, 298–99)

And indeed, the disgust and revulsion for the battered, abused, and often raped woman—which operates, primarily, at a kind of collective unconscious level—is further intensified by the dimensions of "otherness" that characterize her societal status. As numerous critical feminists and revolutionary black feminists, in particular, have demonstrated and documented, race, ethnicity, and class bigotry magnify and compound the kinds of blaming-the-victim mentality that permeate so many public social agencies and institutions. Nikol G. Alexander and Drucilla Cornell discuss this kind of scapegoating attitude in relation to blacks in the United States. "Fantasies about what it means to be black allows government institutions, as well as white citizens, to rationalize behavior that is in fact based on unconscious fears expressed in projected identifications. One tragic result of this for our body politic is scapegoating" (1997, 86).

Moreover, in reality, gender, race, ethnicity, and class relations (as well as sexuality and physical abilities) are intertwined and cannot be separated and disconnected, as numerous vulgar or reformist feminists have maintained within erroneous perspectives regarding violence against women (for example liberal feminists like ex-NOW member Tammy Bruce, who came out publicly after the O. J. Simpson trial with a position that privileged gender over race and class in relation to "domestic violence"). For as Tania Das Gupta reminds us, "categories of gender and race [cannot] be separated in order to achieve so-called 'definitional clarity.' . . . [R]ace, class and gender relations are made even more complex because they are further mediated and organized by the state" (1991, 5).

Indeed, this notion of recognizing the disparities of experience and privilege, in accordance with race, class, sexuality, and ethnic or cultural differences, cannot be effaced when addressing the experiences of the multiplicities of different types of women. This is especially so when one is examining relations of violence perpetuated against women and children and the kinds of public and private support and empathy for the victims of male battery and abuse that can be expected.

> There is much evidence substantiating the reality that race and class identity creates differences in quality of life, social status, and lifestyle that take precedence over the common experience women share—differences which are rarely transcended. The motives of materially privileged, educated, white women with a variety of career and lifestyle options available to them must be questioned when they insist that "suffering cannot be measured." (hooks 1984, 4)

Marian Meyers provides a useful representative overview of some of the leading black feminists' perspective on matters of race, gender, and violence that elucidates and clarifies much about widespread contemporary victim-blaming attitudes. In Meyers's words, "Gender, race, and class are interwoven in ways that draw on common stereotypes, with sex the 'main theme associated with poverty and with blackness.' The very term *black women* is overlaid with popular notions about just who black women are socially, politically, and economically" (1997, 31).

Indeed, feminists like Esmeralda Thornhill have argued that the category of "women" does not encompass, within much of the dominant ideological code, the large majority of marginalized women. Her argument, as Das Gupta (1991) puts it, demonstrates that:

Black women were forced through historical circumstances to adopt non-traditional roles. "Black women had to be nullified as Women," often with the complicity of white women, through such barbarous acts as beating, floggings, and various forms of sexual exploitation. In response to these experiences, black women had to "toughen up fast" and had to "assume a masculine role" in order to survive. In turn, white racists redefined this reality to negatively stereotype black women as being aggressive, Amazonian and, alternatively, either asexual or "sexually loose." (5)

Patricia Williams further expands on how this reactionary stereotype affects underlying dominant perceptions concerning the rape of black women. She astutely and accurately describes this ideological practice of masculinization of black women "[in] the sense that black women are figured more as 'stand-ins' for men, sort of reverse drag queens, women pretending to be women but more male than men: bare breasted, sweat-glistened, plough-pulling, sole supporters of their families. . . . As historian Debra Gray White and psychologist Jessica Daniels have suggested in their studies of stereotypes of black women, how can such a one be raped?" (Williams 1997, 285).

Paradoxically, however, an opposite form of stereotype also permeates the public discourse, further perpetuating a kind of bigotry that seems specifically reserved for black women, and other marginalized women who share—to various degrees—their experience and background. Moreover, as Williams points out race and class are often misrepresented as synonymous in that:

The figure of "the" poor single mother in today's policy debates is always a black teenager, a younger version of the picture Clarence Thomas painted of his sister: addicted to those HUGE welfare cheques; given over to the life of lust and laziness to which her "pathological" dependence has presumably so accustomed her; bearing profligate (rather than prodigal) children, an over-ripe fruit of a Tattooed Harlot, spilling a profusion of Bad Seeds into an overtaxed world, a model of hard-hearted female calculation rather than maternal deference, a creature in whom willfulness and agency are categories of the irrational. (Williams 1997, 289–90)

bell hooks points out that this kind of mass misrepresentation of black women helps to lead poor and working class people "to blame their economic plight on black people or people of color" (2000a, 117). Yet, in fact, as hooks argues, it is white folk that are disproportionately poor—"the vast majority of the poor continue to be white. The hidden face of poverty in the United States is the untold stories of millions of poor white people" (2000a, 117). Mass media, however, tend to escalate and naturalize these stereotypes, so it is important to reject scapegoating based on race, class, region, or age.

Audre Lorde addresses contradictory myths about women of color in terms of rationalizing victim blaming, especially in the case of black women and the violence perpetuated against them.

> One tool of the Great-American-Double-Think is to blame the victim for victimization: Black people are said to invite lynching by not knowing our place; Black women are said to invite rape and murder and abuse by not being submissive enough, or by being too seductive. (Lorde 1984, 61)

Patricia Hill Collins accurately describes the dominant ideological distinction between the white and black woman, illustrating how

> racial and class oppression are sexualized in the image of black womanhood. . . . White women may be depicted as objects, she states, whereas black women are depicted as animals. Thus black women who are raped are twice victimized—first by the actual rape. . . . But they are victimized again by family members, community residents, and social institutions such as criminal justice systems, which somehow believe that rape victims are responsible for their own victimization. (1990, 178–79)

This is also the case, as Emma D. LaRocque points out, with Aboriginal women in regard to sexual abuse and situations of the battery of women and family terrorism (1995, 111). Patricia Hill Collins goes on to demonstrate the stigmatization of black women in pornography, citing Alice Walker, "where white women are depicted in pornography as 'objects,' black women are depicted as animals. Where white women are depicted as human bodies, if not beings, black women are depicted as shit" (1998, 92).

Angela Davis also concurs that this ideological myth that reduces black people to the level of animals and makes them responsible for their own colonial status and repressive experiences is prevalent. Framing these scapegoating techniques within a contextual, metacritical perspective that recognizes the "interconnectedness of the race, gender and class oppression that characterize the society" she argues that

> the myth of the black woman as "chronically promiscuous" is inseparable from the myth of the black man as rapist, for if black men are invested with animal-like sexual urges, black women likewise are invested with bestiality. The result, Davis says, is that because black women are viewed as "loose women" and whores, they are not considered legitimate victims of sexual violence. (Meyers 1997, 31)

In her many works on the intersection of gender, race, and class oppression (1981, 1985, 1990), Davis illustrates the effort to conceptualize sexual violence against African American women as part of a system of oppression in which sexual violence has been central to the economic and political subordination of African Americans overall.

Audre Lorde (1984) manages to explicitly and eloquently capture the essence of this deplorable ideological scapegoating practice in terms that accurately describe this process as an expression of either-or, bifurcated logic.

> Much of Western European history conditions us to see human differences in simplistic opposition to each other: dominant/subordinate, good/bad, up/down, superior/inferior. In a society where the good is defined in terms of profit rather than in terms of human need, there must always be some group of people who, through systematized oppression, can be made to feel surplus, to occupy the place of the dehumanized inferior. Within this society, that group is made up of Black and Third World people, working-class people, older people, and women. (114)

Moreover, it bears repeating that we cannot underestimate the role of poverty in igniting the flames of violence and family terrorism that plague the nations throughout the world. And the connection between the inhuman environments engendered by the hopelessness of poverty and violence and family terrorism are too often ignored and deemphasized. Neither can we ignore the fact that a disproportionate number of people of color, the majority of which are women and children, find themselves trapped within this largely inescapable domain.

> It must be noted that the vast majority of poor people in the United States are women and children. In 1993, 14.7 million women ages eighteen and over were officially classified as poor; *these women constituted 37.4 percent of people living in poverty.* In the same year, 15.7 million children under the age of eighteen officially lived below the poverty line; *these children constituted 40 percent of all poor people in the United States. Therefore, women and children in 1993 made up over three-quarters (77.4 percent) of all Americans living in poverty.*
>
> Analyzing the poverty rate by race, we see that in 1993 blacks (33.1 percent of whom lived in poverty) and Hispanics (30.6 percent) had poverty rates three times that of whites (9.9 percent). The poverty rate of children demonstrates this disturbing phenomenon even more dramatically. . . . [I]n 1993, 22.7 percent of all children under the age of eighteen lived in poverty. [This revealed] a disproportionate representation of black and Hispanic children. (Sidel 1996, 70; emphasis mine)

Immanuel Wallerstein (1990) argues that it is, in fact, an ideological process of scapegoating—which finds its basis in sexism and racism—that reinforces, naturalizes, and sometimes attempts to disguise the inequities of poverty within a victim-blaming perspective. Hence, "those who are worse off, therefore those who are paid less, are in this position because they merit it. The existence of unequal incomes thus becomes not an instance of racism-sexism but rather of the universal standard of rewarding efficiency. Those who have less have less because they have earned less" (46). Wallerstein concludes:

> racism and sexism complement this universalizing theorem very well. Racism and sexism, when institutionalized, create a high correlation between low group status and low income. Thus, those at the lower end of the scale are easily identifiable by what may then be termed cultural criteria. . . . Culture now becomes the explanation of the cause. Blacks and women are paid less because there is something, if not in their biology, at least in their "culture," which teaches them values which conflict with the universal work ethos. (1990, 46)

Patricia Williams (1997) further reveals another of the myriad costs of poverty for battered and sexually abused women and children as well as the deleterious and depressing realities facing women who leave their abusers.

> Concern about bottom-line economic survival is not unrelated to issues of physical health and emotional well-being as the romantic lore of the solidly middle class might make it out to be. In an era when health benefits are so outrageously expensive even for the healthy well-to-do, when shelters are so limited, and when psychological services of all sorts are being wiped out, including counseling for batterers as well as for the battered, the fear of being out in the cold and literally homeless cannot be deemed a casual one. (287)

Moreover, Williams goes on to demonstrate how the victim-blaming mythology especially affects and justifies the relations of poverty and isolation that define the existence of all too many battered women and children:

> The degree to which battered women of all classes fall into poverty at greater scales and seek welfare in disproportionately large numbers is too often seen as their own irrationality—the choice of a bad man, the choice to be poor—rather than as part of a quite predictable chain of cause and effect. Battering inflicts trauma. Trauma paralyzes. It is the very logic of battery to exact debilitating social and economic cost; it is the rationality of the batterer to control his victim by making her as socially isolated and economically dependent as possible. (287)

Within this context, the oppressive treatment of battered women by many social agencies is hardly surprising, especially given the way family terrorism is treated by the mass media. Marian Meyers's textual analytic study of the media sadly confirms critical feminists' analyses of the classist and racist dimensions involved in the prevalent misogynist reality of blaming the victims for the escalating abuse and violence against women and children.

> This study found that all women who are the victims of violence—regardless of race or class—are represented within the news media as potentially to blame for their own victimization. . . . This does not mean that race and class are irrelevant to the

portrayal of women in the news. As the quantitative part of this study indicated, crimes against white women with money are more likely to be considered newsworthy than crimes against black women without money. . . . Within this framework, racial and male supremacist ideologies converge to establish blame for black female victims beyond what is generally assigned to white women. (1997, 65–66)

Meyers's findings also supported "Geraldine Finn's (1989–1990) study of news coverage of 'domestic terrorism' [that] concluded that the State and the media collude to exonerate male perpetrators. She states that the inequalities of social relations 'encourage and condone' violence against women and children" (1997, 29). The condoning, promotion, and provocation of male violence against women within the mass media, she argues, takes place within a larger frame that addresses family terrorism and sexual abuse in a psychologized and individualized, decontextualized manner.

> By presenting stories of violence against women as separate discrete incidents, the news also reinforces the idea that this violence is a matter of isolated pathology or deviance, related only to the particular circumstances of those involved and unconnected to the larger structure of patriarchal domination and control. This mirage of individual pathology denies the social roots of violence against women and relieves the larger society of any obligation to end it. (Meyers 1997, 68)

It is hardly surprising, in this light, that social agencies, support organizations, and public institutions have adopted policies and exhibit behaviors that reflect dominant race, class, and sexual biases and prejudices toward battered and abused women. Eisenstadt (1999) points out that "only in the past 20 years have state and federal officials dealt with domestic violence through the justice system, with punishment and incarceration." She also notes only in the recent past have medical associations and government institutions begun to deal with the problem, however inadequately. No doubt some progress is being made. According to the American Medical Association: "Most states have improved the legal remedies available to battered women, and a number of state health departments have developed protocols for health care providers." Furthermore, the Joint Commission on Accreditation of Healthcare Organizations (JCAHO) "has required that all accredited hospitals implement policies and procedures in their emergency departments and ambulatory care facilities for identifying and referring patients as victims of abuse. The standards require educational programs for hospital staff in domestic violence, as well as elder abuse, child abuse, and sexual assault" (2001, www.ama-assn.org/ama/pub).

Nonetheless, there are still serious problems concerning the treatment of abused women by the medical establishment. As F. Steven Land, M.D., notes in the *American Family Physician*: "We all know that it is a well documented fact that 90 percent of America's physicians are not even asking the question" of domestic abuse (Nov. 1, 2000). Moreover, in "a recent study of women seeking emergency care, the prevalence of ongoing domestic violence was found to be 12%. Sadly, only 2.6% of these patients were screened for domestic violence" (*Journals and American Medical News*, Feb. 29, 2000). Further, despite the large number of battered women seeking medical care for problems of battering, it has been estimated that health care professionals correctly diagnose only one in 35 cases" (American Academy of Family Physicians, 2000, www.aafp.org).

Hence, the majority of physicians continue to actively avoid questioning the patient as to the cause of her injuries, accepting instead often-transparent evasions (Jones 1994a, 146). As the protagonist, Paula Spencer, reveals in Roddy Doyle's fictional account of one woman's experience with abuse, " 'I'd tell them everything if they asked,' she says of the emergency room staff who never question her repeat visits, or who chalk them up to her drinking or clumsiness or bad luck. She knows that she's invisible to them; they never see her as a whole, only the particular afflicted part—leg, arm, breast, head—she presents for their ministrations" (cited in Mary Gordon, *The New York Times Book Review*, Apr. 28, 1996, 7).

Doyle's title, *The Woman Who Walked into Doors* (1996), aptly represents the kinds of translucent excuses often employed by battered women to explain their injuries. Even common sense would seem to dictate that an active interventionist policy on the part of the medical profession would assist in alleviating the widespread violence against women and children. As the American Academy of Family Physicians warns:

> Family violence will affect at least one-third of the patients cared for by family physicians, and the impact of family violence may become evident in the one-on-one relationship of the family physician and the patient. It is imperative that physicians become aware of the prevalence of violence in all sectors of society and be alert for its effects in their encounters with virtually every patient. (2000, www.aafp.org)

Widespread lack of empathy for battered women directly relates to the misdirected but widely acceptable sense of disgust reserved for these kinds of so-called victims, which, as has been previously demonstrated, have been so maliciously stereotyped within popular culture, especially by the collaborationist feminists. And, as so many battered women can attest to, even though various U.S. surgeons general have recommended that the AMA develop policies for intervention and action in cases of assaults against women, there have been no concrete, concerted efforts to do so. And there is still no policy directing caregivers to report these crimes. Indeed, studies confirm the perceptions of battered women—based on their experiences with the medical profession—that echo those expressed by Hedda Nussbaum, Andrea Dworkin, and the protagonist in *The Woman Who Walked into Doors*. As Ann Jones notes,

[One study affirms that a medical practitioner's] "[f]ailure to acknowledge the woman's abusive experience is often psychologically damaging in itself." And another stresses that "disconfirmation of abuse by a care giver is an important factor in the development of subsequent psychopathology." In other words, the way doctors and nurses and counselors treat battered women—as though nothing happened—drives them *crazy*. (Jones 1994a, 148)

Jones expands on the logical consequences of these types of bigoted attitudes, which most certainly mediate the actions of those in the social services and "helping professions." "Privately, they may fear and despise the battered woman for being the victim she is. They grow impatient with her and angry that she presents herself to them, wanting something from them, wanting *help*. Why doesn't she help herself? (If she were anyone else, with any other kind of problem, they would see that asking for help *is* a way to help one-self). . . . Sometimes they say: why don't you just leave?" (Jones 1994a, 149).[3]

Once again we are faced with this ideologically biased question. A question, which so many feminist experts in the field have pointed out, that is most inappropriate, given the actual circumstances of violence against women and children. Indeed far more appropriate and reasonable questions include, "Why does he beat her?" or "What can we do to prevent this?" or, as Donna Miller, the executive director of Hiatus House, a battered women's shelter in Windsor, Ontario, reformulates it, "How do they gain the strength to leave?" (*The Weekend Windsor Star*, Mar. 30, 1991, E1). A far more pertinent and revealing question would be why this question is asked at all, as it deflects from the real source of the problem—the abuser—and perpetuates a blaming-the-victim mentality. Jones, in fact, exposes the ideological nature of this question, which she suggests is not a question at all.

It doesn't call for an answer; it makes a judgment. It mystifies. It transforms an immense social problem into a personal transaction, and at the same time pins responsibility squarely on the victim. It obliterates both the terrible magnitude of violence against women and the great achievements of the movement against it. (Jones 1994a, 130–31)

At another level, there are some adequate responses to this question that assist in our assessment of the multileveled, contextual nature of the problem. As Lenore Walker states, "To understand [why some women don't leave], we must understand something of the socialization process of little girls in our society, the process that teaches girls to grow into women who accept the temper tantrums of men without allowing it to diminish their love for them, until it is too late" (1989, 70). Further:

This process does not affect only those women who are abused physically but impacts on all women who endure the psychological abuse of men, too. In our culture, women are usually trained to believe that men are invariably "imperfect," that they must put up with any and every imperfection in the men they love, in order to get any love in return. . . . Like most women socialized in our culture, as well as in other cultures, the battered woman is trained to make excuses for a man's imperfections, even at the risk of her own physical well-being. And, equally crippling to her, she is trained to blame herself for some of his worst behavior. If she were a good enough wife, goes her internal line of reasoning, she could make him stop beating her; he would not have to hurt her. (Walker 1989, 70)

Angela Caputi, a professor of American Studies at the University of New Mexico, expands upon the pathological nature of women's socialization in this regard. "Women are trained to think that we can save these men, that they can change. . . . That mythology, she notes, is on full display in 'Beauty and the Beast': the monster smashing furniture will turn into a prince if only the woman he's trapped will love them. Many abusers can be charming—and abused women often fall for their softer side" (*Newsweek*, Jul. 4, 1994).

Such psychological analysis, however, must be contextualized within the real economic consequences that constrain so many abused women and children. Hence, the reality of family terrorism must be recontextualized within a dialectical framework, where the multiple ideological values and beliefs that provoke and reinforce this pathology can be examined and subsequently changed and the determinate social conditions can be analyzed.

"SEPARATION ASSAULT" AND THE FAILURE OF PUBLIC INSTITUTIONS

Perhaps one of the most revealing responses to the query as to "why women don't leave" is that women *do* in fact leave, or attempt to leave, these relationships, and many are killed by their abusers as a result. The problem is so daunting that the term *separation assault* was coined to describe the prevalence of this situation. Martha R. Mahoney, the law professor who created the label, employs it "to describe the 'varied violent and coercive moves' a batterer makes when a woman tries to leave him" (Jones 1994a, 150). Unfortunately, the question of why women don't leave is often framed by the either-or, deterministic philosophy that punctuates dominant perceptions of victimization as a situation of choice. In Lenore Walker's analysis, she points out that it is assumed that if the women would leave, "then the battering would stop. Years of research have proved that assumption to be untrue; the abuse often escalates at the point of separation and battered women are in greater danger of dying then" (1989, 47). Disputing the myth that it is relatively easy to leave an abuser, Walker highlights the real risks involved in such a decision:

The increased terror experienced by the battered woman during separation, divorce, and child custody proceedings is based undeniably in reality. Separation creates a period of unprecedented danger in battering situations, a danger not often recognized by others. The batterer would often rather kill, or die himself, than separate from the battered woman; he is always more terrified of abandonment than of violence. . . . The battered woman perceives that he will do anything to keep her from leaving him. Her fear for her life, and for the lives of her children and other family members and friends, is likewise based on undeniable truth that, if she does not know consciously she will certainly intuit. Life hangs in the balance: hers, his, everyone's. (1989, 65–66)

Margaret Byrne, the director of the Illinois Clemency Project for Battered Women, who is familiar with these kinds of cases, explains that it is all too common for a husband to threaten to hunt down his partner and kill her when she initiates steps to leave him: "Severing ties signals the abuser that he's no longer in control and he responds in the only way he knows how—by escalating the violence. . . . 'It's this male sense of entitlement—"If I can't have her, no one can,'" says University of Illinois sociologist Pauline Bart" (*Newsweek*, Jul. 4, 1994). And Tjaden and Thoennes indicate that "the termination of a relationship poses an increased risk or escalation of intimate partner abuse . . . interviews with men who have killed their wives indicate that either threats of separation by their partner or actual separation are most often the precipatating events that lead to murder" (2000, 37).

And not only are these not idle threats, but they often intensify rather than abate over time. Although some experts tag the first two years after a breakup as the most dangerous, others feel this is a highly conservative estimation. They state that there is no way of assessing a statute of limitations on the harassment and death threats and attempted murders by those who are inordinately obsessed (*Newsweek*, Jul. 4, 1994). Moreover, a study published in 1989 in *Law and Society Review* by Angela Browne, a psychologist, and Kirk Williams, a sociologist, found that most of the women killed in twenty-five states were killed after they had separated from or divorced their partners, according to homicide statistics compiled by the Centers for Disease Control in Atlanta, Georgia (cited in Walker 1989, 65). Moreover:

If a battered woman chooses to leave her mate, she may be signing her own death warrant. At Harvard University's Children's Hospital, where violent families are being counseled, a psychiatric social worker explained, "The man feels vulnerable and that vulnerability infuriates him. He feels a mounting frustration similar to what an angry parent feels when trying to discipline an increasingly 'defiant' child. All the man can understand is that his wife is 'disobeying' him. It becomes a power struggle. If she manages to escape, revenge becomes his motive, and the ultimate revenge for some of these men is to kill." (Stephenson 1995, 229)

Hence, another answer to why women stay in a battering situation directly relates to the torturous materiality of "separation assault." As Martha R. Mahoney describes it:

> *Separation assault* is the attack on the woman's body and volition in which her partner seeks to prevent her from leaving, retaliate for separation, or force her to return. It aims at overbearing her will as to where and with whom she will live, and coercing her in order to enforce connection in a relationship. It is an attempt to gain, retain, or regain power in a relationship, or to punish the woman for ending the relationship. It often takes place over time. As Mahoney points out, the battered woman whom we think of as "staying" with a batterer, or returning to him, is usually a woman held captive by the force of separation assault. And as we have seen time and time again, when a woman perseveres in her struggle to get free, the grand finale of separation assault is often her own death. (Jones 1994a, 150)

However, dominant myths deny the rationale of a woman who claims she is afraid to leave an abusive situation for fear of her ultimate death or that of her loved ones. For media culture and prominent speakers and public figures have led us to believe that there are societal safeguards designed to assist and protect any woman who decides to leave her abuser. And it is this very phantasmagoria that underlies the question of why women remain with men that brutalize them.

> The danger today is that we overestimate society's changes. Implicit in the question, "Why doesn't she leave" is the assumption that social supports are already in place to help the woman who walks out: a shelter in every town, a cop on every beat eager to make that mandatory arrest, a judge in every courtroom passing out well-enforced restraining orders and packing batterers off to jail and effective reeducation programs, medical services, legal services, social services, child care, child support, affordable housing, convenient public transportation, a decent job free of sexual harassment, a living wage. (Jones 1994a, 204)

Yet the collaborationist pseudofeminist feminists, in particular, choose to exploit this myth to attack "victimization" and "infirmity feminism" (as Paglia calls it) "with its bedlam of bellyachers" (*Toronto Star*, Nov. 8, 1994). Such a MacGuffin underscores the oversimplified yet seductive and appealing nature of blaming the victims. In fact, existing social institutions and services are ill prepared to meet the demands necessary to adequately address the diversity of problems associated with battered women and children. For example, in the United States, there are only about one thousand shelters for abused women and children, and federal and state funding for these shelters are short term and minimal (Jones 1994a, 229). Consequently, as June Stephenson documents, in the mid 1990s 40 percent of women who were seeking help at shelters were turned away (Stephenson 1995, 234). Indeed, it would appear that society takes far more seriously the rights of animals than those of women and children, given that there are three times as many animal shelters in the United States than there are shelters for battered women and their children (Devitt and Downey 1992, 14). The National Resource Center on Domestic Violence, however, reported that there were approximately 1900 domestic shelter programs in the United States. This (inadequate!) increase perhaps reflects the positive effect that feminist activists had in the 1990s in publicizing and addressing the problems of domestic violence. It is disheartening, however, that Hoff Sommers and her Independent Women's Forum are attacking rape crisis centers as "feminist centers," the Bush administration has closed down the White House Office on Women, and federal funding for domestic violence shelters is threatened (see chapter 1). Moreover, shelters for the homeless can hardly be considered an option, given the dangers posed by them for women and children, especially, of sexual abuse, attacks, and even murder.

Even the idea of shelters demonstrates the regressive attitudes toward dealing with wife abuse, for as Jones points out "shelters are kind of reverse jails for women" (1994a, 59). It seems to be common sense that the perpetrator of the crime should be arrested and legally evicted from the home, but in reality, it is usually the victim who is punished. In a just social order, the battered would be able to stay in their homes and batterers would be incarcerated. Yet within the established society, shelters for abused women and children are necessary to provide sanctuaries to protect people from violence. Even in shelters, however, women are not safe and a far greater effort on the part of the legal system and the police to protect women from male violence is necessary. Indeed, as the National Center for Victims of Crime explains it: "The realities of restraining orders are that they are not always effective. They are not always enforced, and it is sometimes difficult to catch a person in the process of breaking the order—which is a requirement in many jurisdictions before the police can enforce the order" (www.ncvc.org, 1997). In fact, the American Bar Association study found that 60 percent of the women with temporary restraining orders reported the order was violated within the year it was issued" (Tjaden and Thoennes 2000, 54).

The bias against women in family terrorism situations exists in part because violence against women is not considered to be a real crime. In addition, as Jones contends, the battered woman provides a necessary service for the maintenance of our current sociopolitical economic system as we know it. Still, the fact remains that relatively modest support exists for the realization of systemic policies and legislation that would radically decrease or alleviate this crucial problem.

In the aggregate, battered women are to sexism what the poor are to capitalism—always with us. They are a source of cheap labor and sexual service to those with the power to buy and control them, a "problem" for the righteous to lament, a topic to provide employment for academic researchers, a sponge to soak up the surplus violence of men, a conduit to carry off the political energy of other women who must care for them, an example of what awaits all women who don't behave as prescribed, and a pariah group to amplify by contrast our good opinion of ourselves. And for all their social utility, they remain largely, and conveniently, invisible . . . the battered woman is a scapegoat. Man vents his violence upon her and blames her for it. And so do we. How else can we explain this curious fact: that when a man commits an act of unspeakable violence, public blame falls upon the woman who failed to prevent it? . . . This, then, is what battered women are for. Like prostitutes (who commonly are battered women themselves), battered women serve to drain away excess male violence and assaultive sexuality. (Jones 1994a, 205, 207–8)

Jones's angry analysis might appear, to some, as too reminiscent of the paranoia that provokes so many conspiracy theories. However, one cannot help but ponder her appraisal, given the wretched paucity of support provided the battered women by the criminal justice system as well as the more general failure to deal with this societal pathology in an equitable and appropriate fashion. Moreover, one cannot help but reflect on her seething indictment, given that it would be fiscally expedient, in the long term, given the enormous costs to the system (i.e., homelessness, drug abuse, alcoholism, relational criminal activities, foster care, medical care, social assistance, shelters, hospitalization, special education, and institutions) to adequately address violence against women and children and as a societal, rather than individual, problem and crime. Indeed, family terrorism involves one of the "single largest causes of injury to women in the U.S." but also, according to the March of Dimes, it is "a major cause of birth defects in the U.S." (Sheffield 1995, 432).

In any discussion of the relationship of police in situations of family terrorism, two prominent myths continue to be tediously employed. The public has been duped into believing that incidents of so-called domestic violence are considered to be the most ominous and perilous duties of police work. In reality, however, robberies, burglaries, and drug-related crimes pose the greatest threat to police safety. This particular urban legend, as Jones suggests, developed partially because of FBI statistics on police casualties that lumped "domestic disturbance" calls under the more general category of "disturbance" calls, which includes "far more dangerous street and barroom brawls and 'man-with-a-gun' calls" (Jones 1994a, 140). When you append these misleading statements that reflect "old policemen's tales about particularly explosive domestic situations," with the actual breakdown and description of police involvement in these situations, it becomes apparent that the majority of " 'domestic disturbance' calls involve 'minor assaults' which pose a danger to the victim, but little or none to the police." (Jones 1994a, 140). And even if it were the case that the majority of these calls posed danger to the police, Jones persuasively and logically argues, "it's a peculiar logic that excuses cops from duty just when the trouble starts and leaves it up to women to deal single-handedly with men too dangerous for armed police to handle! . . . That in itself tells you how much we value women, how much we blame women for their predicaments, and how easily we abandon them" (Jones 1994a, 140).

The second of these myths involves the so-called failure of battered women to press charges against their abusers. Whereas there is some dimension of truth to this claim, it still qualifies as an ideological myth because of the omission of related imperative contextual information, especially those statistics and documentation that implicate the police in racist, sexist, and classist behaviors. Moreover, such a situation often dissuades poor women or women of color from calling for police assistance (Jones 1994a; Meyers 1997, 100).[4] Indeed, what should be a relatively straightforward area of criminal justice behavior and legislated punishment is in reality a quagmire of inconsistent laws that vary from state to state, and psychologized/subjectivist attitudes. While family violence against women and children should be treated like any other situation of felony assault, in situations of men assaulting their partners, charges vary—if they are made at all—when the police are involved.

There is as of yet no federal law regarding wife abuse in either the United States or Canada. Instead, it is the locality that defines if the assault is treated as a misdemeanor or a felony, or if the person assaulted is responsible for placing charges.[5] As Jones points out, this confusion and lack of clear legislation or action reifies and justifies some police complaints regarding women who fail to press charges after the police have arrested the abuser (Jones 1994a, 57). Yet, paradoxically, research demonstrates "that given the slightest help with complicated legal procedures, women follow through with remarkable tenacity" (Jones 1994a, 143). Moreover, in cases where women were killed by their partners, "police statistics show that 85 to 90 percent [of these women] had sought police protection—and half had done so on at least five separate occasions" (Devitt and Downey 1992, 15). These are statistics that would seem to demonstrate how much (or how little) support "women who leave" can actually count on from the criminal justice system.

Realistically speaking, it is remarkable that so many women do pursue charges against their abusers, especially in light of their proximity and relationship to the transgressor. In fact, common sense would seem to dictate that the battered woman is hardly in a position to have arrested the man who has assaulted her (and perhaps her children) and threatens to continue to do so. Moreover, shifting the burden of responsibility on her shoulders allows the abuser to further blame her, rather than the police (or the system), for his predicament with the law, and hence would seem the best provocation for further beatings and torture upon his release. From a contextual perspective it appears absolutely ludicrous to expect the abused to, essentially, punish her abuser for a crime that, if perpetrated against a stranger, would be perceived as a criminal activity that would prompt immediate police intervention and the arrest of the aggressor on felony charges.

Only relatively recently have certain U.S. states and municipalities instituted mandatory arrest statutes, which force the police to treat battered wives as crime victims and legally obliged the police—and not the assaulted woman—to sign the complaint against the assailant, arrest him, and let the state enforce its own laws against him. When these policies were implemented, U.S. studies found that there were "dramatic decreases in domestic assault and homicide" (Jones 1994a, 141). In this regard, even a "Police Foundation working paper concluded as early as 1983 that: 'It is clear that the recidivism measure is lowest when police make arrests' " (*Time*, Sept. 5, 1983, 22). Yet, it appears that many police officers resent these kinds of pro-arrest policies and often return to their "traditional 'discretionary' methods" or have adopted a shocking, but predictable, behavior toward this legislation (*Time*, Sept. 5, 1983, 22).

> In fact, hard-hitting mandatory arrest laws have generated new problems for battered women. "[E]very state that has instituted mandatory arrest has seen a backlash against women, with more women being arrested," said Joan Zorza, the author of a 1994 study of the problem by the National Center on Women and Family Law.
>
> Some women's advocates blame poor police training and negative social attitudes toward women [and] . . . say the rising arrest rate for women shows a backlash among officers who resent being stripped of their discretion by mandatory arrest laws. Zorza cited a study of the Boston police that showed just seven officers made half of the department's arrests of women in domestic violence cases. (*Austin American-Statesman*, Apr. 28, 1996)

The lack of appropriate societal literacy in the horrendous reality of wife assault and general cavalier attitudes toward this crime are further evidenced in that "Some experts say male abusers are manipulating the new laws. They cite the Sacramento man who scratched a scab on his ear to make it bleed. Then he called the police and had his wife arrested. A California man went into the back yard and hit himself on the head with a brick. Police were hauling his wife off to jail when neighbors ran out and said they saw the man injure himself" (*Austin American-Statesman*, Apr. 28, 1996). Indeed that these kinds of reports are afforded any credence speaks volumes for the manner in which the reality of family terrorism is negated and trivialized—and all too often transformed into a kind of sick joke. Yet police collaboration in these kinds of backlash attempts of some men to abuse their wives or partners in what constitutes a new dimension of assault and shame is hardly astonishing, given what Lenore Walker has discovered about the general worldview and underlying mentality and attitudes of many members of law enforcement agencies: "Until recently, police rarely provided battered women with effective or adequate protection. Most police officers seem to feel that what goes on between husband and wife is outside the realm of public law and order. Many men join the paramilitary police force to meet their own macho needs for power and control; these men may side with the batterer, certain that the battered woman must have done something to deserve the abuse" (1989, 53).

However, to scapegoat the police is an inappropriate and noncontextual reading of the matter. Indeed, family terrorism must be perceived within a more holistic, multileveled dialectical framework, and, as Jones emphasizes, one should see the problem as being one of a systemic nature: "The real culprit is the prosecutor. If the prosecutor's office is not going to follow through by prosecuting even without the woman's help—they can use 911 tapes, hospital records, proof of previous battery—why should the police arrest anybody? So we have to insist that the whole system work as a *system*" (Jones 1994a, 57).

In addition, many abused and battered women fail to contact the police due to excesses in regards to mandatory arrest—in which the "primary aggressor" is supposed to be arrested, but often both partners are arrested due to "dual arrest" policies. This practice often discourages future complaints and punishes abused women by arresting them. As Tjaden and Thoennes note in their U.S. Department of Justice Report:

> Most intimate partner victimization is not reported to the police. Approximately one-fifth of all rapes, one-quarter of all physical assaults and one-half of all stalkings perpetrated against female respondents by intimates were reported to the police. . . . The majority of victims who did not report their victimization to the police thought the police would not or could not do anything on their behalf. These findings suggest that most victims of intimate partner violence do not consider the justice system an appropriate vehicle for resolving conflicts with intimates. (2000, v)

Yet, many prosecutors have demonstrated that it is possible to convict wife batterers in cases where the abused woman has recanted her charges due to an understandable terror of threats of reprisal—which are all so common in these types of cases (*New York Times*, Jun. 9, 1996, 4E). Often testimony is difficult to obtain because of various real or imaginary issues that tend to plague long-term recipients of chronic physical or psychological abuse. As Maggie Pasquale, the deputy bureau chief of the Family Violence and Child Abuse Bureau in the Manhattan District Attorney's office, contextualizes this recurrent problem, "A great number of the domestic violence victims decide for various reasons—emotional or financial, pressure from the family—not to testify against the abuser" (*New York Times*, Jun. 9, 1996, 4E).

However, in the first case of its kind, prosecutors in New York City decided to go ahead with a case against a man who "over a period of eight years . . . struck his wife, stabbed her, twisted a string around her neck so tight it left scars, put a gun to her head, burned her buttocks with an iron, and routinely threatened to kill her," despite his wife's later decision to retract her accusations. They addressed her retraction by calling an expert witness on so-called battered women's syndrome to testify for the prosecution (*New York Times*, Jun. 9, 1996, 4E).

> The expert, Karla Digirolamo, former director of the New York State Office for the Prevention of Domestic Violence, not only told jurors why some women become reluctant to take on abusive husbands, but she also explained why many battered women return to their abusers. In effect, the prosecutors used the witness to contradict Ms. Brown, victim and erstwhile complainant. The gambit turned out to be a

smart one: The jury found Mr. Ellis guilty of assault. On May 30, Manhattan Supreme Court Justice Charles Tejada, calling Mr. Ellis "cowardly," handed him the maximum sentence of up to 10 years. The prosecutors vowed to use experts on battered women again. (*New York Times*, Jun. 9, 1996, 4E)

The O.J. Simpson trials in the mid-1990s publicized the problems of wife-battering and led to more proactive approaches by prosecutors. However, the Simpson case also dramatized the prejudice of courts toward males in that Simpson was awarded the custody of his children, even though he was found guilty of the murder of his wife in a California civil court. There were also calls following the Simpson case for district attorneys to get tougher on domestic violence. As Gloria Alred commented: "Clearly, it is time for D.A. offices around the country to stop treating most cases of spousal abuse as misdemeanors. . . . Where there are allegations of spousal abuse or abuse of a person in a dating relationship, and there are allegations of serious injury, the D.A. as a matter of public policy, should always file felony charges" (*Ms.*, July/August 1996, 25).

Some cities have implemented specialized "domestic violence courts" involving judicial training in matters of family terrorism, which some suggest were provoked by the critical public response to the Simpson case. Yet the failure of many prosecutors to adequately deal with the abuse of women appears to go hand-in-hand with another integral and most potent systemic component—the judge who wields enough authority to make a substantial difference toward impeding much of family terrorism. Indeed, the judge is able to remove batterers from their homes, while offering adequate protection to the victims and potential victims of his abuse, legislating serious jail time, especially for repeat offenders, as well as sentencing batterers to combined "sanctions and rehabilitation." These penalties can "include finding the offender guilty, ordering him to make restitution, limiting his visitation privileges, or sending him to jail" (Jones 1994a, 216–17). Yet, this is hardly the norm regarding judicial treatment of men who terrorize their female partners. Often the judicial establishment, too, tends to react to this outrage by turning away, and ignoring or denying its seriousness and reality. Any decisive remedial handling of the abuse of women was so negligent that

in 1986, then-governor Michael Dukakis had to assemble a task force to investigate the state judiciary's lack of compliance with a domestic abuse prevention law on the books since 1978. From judges in both New York and Illinois who have ruled that a man cannot be considered an unfit parent merely because he has murdered the mother of his children, to a judge in Georgia who "ridiculed" a severely battered woman (who was later murdered by her estranged husband) and "led the courtroom in laughter as the woman left," [Ann] Jones['s] strongest examples of institutional neglect come from the judicial arena. (*The San Francisco Chronicle*, Jul. 3, 1994)

Ironically, as Phyllis Chesler points out, many of the same judges who bend over backward to dismiss and often empathize with male abusers, reserve their harshest judgment and rage for women, especially those women who kill an abusive husband or lover: "battered women who kill in self-defense account for about half of all women who kill. Even here, men and women are not 'equal.' (Non-battered) men kill their female domestic partners three to four times more often than (battered) women kill their domestic partners/aggressors. Battered women who kill in self-defense rarely 'get off' and, to date, are rarely granted clemency; most are given long or even life sentences" (1994, 91).

Given the collective repugnance for the battered women's plight, especially within the ideological framework of "why doesn't she leave?" and the associated tendency to blame her or treat her as "a willing victim," one would think that the woman who kills her abuser in self-defense would be afforded a certain degree of respect, forgiveness, and leniency. Yet, the harsh reality of the inequity that seems to haunt contemporary women in a multitude of dimensions is particularly evident here. Judicial punishment for women accused of spousal abuse is more severe than it is for men found guilty of generally more heinous crimes (in that most of these women who murder their partners do so in self-defense). As Michael Dowd, the director of the Pace University Battered Women's Justice Center documented, "the average sentence in the U.S. for a woman who kills her mate is 15 to 20 years [while] for a man [it is] 2 to 6 [years] (*Time*, Jan. 18, 1993, 38).

Yet, despite this mountain of documentation, studies, testimonies, and credible expert critiques of the delinquency of the various aspects of the system that fail to adequately address what many feminists, government agencies and other groups have labeled an escalating plague, betrayal feminists are sacrificing their sisters and placing them in extreme danger in order to buttress their MacGuffin-ism of "victim feminism." "[Y]oung, educated women like Katie Roiphe and Naomi Wolf [suggest] a growing impatience with feminist issues. These authors maintain that many women are fantasizing their victimhood, or imposing it on themselves. The fact is, they say, public policies and revamped personal norms have created a society with a level playing field for both men and women. Consequently, individual women today should possess the wherewithal to just say no to men who have the gall to threaten them" (*New York Times*, Mar. 20, 1994).

It is heartbreaking that many women will blame themselves when the system fails them, due in part to the popularity, persuasiveness, and influence of the collaborationist feminists in shaping public opinion. This is especially sad because many of the women who are victims of family terrorism have not had the same opportunities as the betrayal feminists to become literate in the relevant issues. Moreover, the sound advice and empowering, antidefeatist, constructive proposals for substantial change in regard to contemporary systemic treatment of the abuse of women and family terrorism advanced by knowledgeable critical feminist activists like Ann Jones are ignored in public forums like the media. Hence, more constructive feminist positions get neutralized or twisted by the seductive lies, entrenched within the betrayal feminists' attacks on that most effective of decoys, the MacGuffin of a grand victim feminist conspiracy.

> [Ann Jones] conveys an intelligent analysis of violence and victimhood. And she offers a well-conceived, if visionary, blueprint for social and institutional change: women must have the resources to support themselves and their children, while the staffs of agencies that respond to domestic violence must become more sophisticated about its causes and consequences, and prepared to intervene jointly and effectively. Such reforms would, as she puts it, protect the right of women "to be free from bodily harm." (*New York Times*, Mar. 20, 1994)

Of course, the above proposal is only an indication of a far more detailed program for concrete changes in contemporary procedures regarding family terrorism, which is hardly exclusive to Jones. However, these kinds of solid, progressive, pragmatic, well-researched, recommendations are rarely publicized or generally known. This is owing in part to the backlash against feminism, of which the betrayal feminists are the most clever and visible proponents (see chapters 2 and 3). Indeed, antifeminist feminists collaborate with other reactionary factions to perpetuate the myth that feminists are completely out of touch with concrete reality. They distort or ignore real politically empowering platforms (and programs) in favor of the generic accusation that feminists expend their creativity on defeatist abstractions reflective of a self-pitying, weak, and destructive mindset.

Yet, it might prove useful to recall that issues of family terrorism are relatively recent concerns of public discussion and debate. As Nancy Fraser reminds us:

> Until about fifteen years ago, the term "wife battering" did not exist. When spoken of publicly at all, this phenomenon was called "wife beating" and was often treated comically, as in "Have you stopped beating your wife yet?" Linguistically, it was classed with the disciplining of children and servants as a "domestic"—as opposed to a "political"—matter. Then, feminist activists renamed the practice with a term drawn from criminal law and created a new kind of public discourse. They claimed the battery was not a personal, domestic problem but a systemic, political one: its etiology was not to be traced to individual women's or men's emotional problems but, rather, to the ways these problems refracted pervasive social relations of male dominance and female subordination. (1989, 175)

POVERTY, SCAPEGOATING THE POOR, AND BLAMING THE VICTIM

It is imperative that relations of family terrorism and violence against women and children be contextually situated within a concrete, material framework that defines, mediates, and provokes the epidemic of misdirected violence and murder. This includes material determinants such as class, poverty, and race, as well as gender and a wide array of psychological and social conditions. Many studies of violence against women and children, however, neglect or downplay the role of poverty and class that are important determinants of family terrorism. For example, a study by the U.S. Centers for Disease Control, in Atlanta, Georgia, found that

> family and intimate assaults represented 20% of the homicide reports filed in Atlanta in 1984. . . . The CDC concluded that fatal and nonfatal victimization rates for African Americans and other minorities were three times the rate of those of whites. In addition, just over a quarter (27.3%) of Atlanta's 394,017 residents live in poverty, according to the 1990 federal census. Of the 102,364 below the poverty level, 88,718 (86.7%) are black and 11,239 (11%) are white. (Meyers 1997, 5)

Indeed, Meyers (and many other scholars and activists) emphasize the crucial role of poverty in provoking all kinds of violent relations, especially those I'm describing as acts of family terrorism. And it bears repeating that it is within this context that the flaws of many dominant researchers in the field of family violence are once again made glaringly apparent. In fact, much of the underlying argument of this text addresses the failure of many vulgar feminist (and antifeminist) writers to engage the issue of "class." Economic relations, however, not only prove seminal to a dialectical understanding of the conditions of women but also play a fundamental role in analyzing and discerning the complexities involved in gender violence and family terrorism. As Nancy Fraser so aptly prophesied:

> What some writers are calling the "coming welfare wars" will be largely wars about, even against, women. Because women constitute the overwhelming majority of social-welfare program recipients and employees, women and women's needs will be the principal stakes in the battles over social spending likely to dominate national politics in the coming period. Moreover, the welfare wars will not be limited to the tenure of Reagan or even Reaganism. On the contrary, they will be protracted, both in time and space. (Fraser 1989, 144)

Fraser also argues that "the fiscal crisis of the welfare state coincides everywhere with a second long-term, structural tendency: *the feminization of poverty*" (Fraser 1989, 144). In light of the growing number of single-mother households and the growing percentages of women and children living at poverty levels, it is scandalous that so many reformist feminists (what Eisenstein calls "mainstream equal rights feminism") and feminist impersonators ignore the reality of class in myriad problems, including violence against women and children (Eisenstein 1996, 113). In fact, as hooks asserts: "Most American citizens do not acknowledge the reality of class difference, of class exploitation, and they continue to believe that this is a classless society" (2000a, 156). However, many who recognize class equate it solely with economic dimensions. But as Rita May Brown contextually explains it: "Class is much more than Marx's definition of relation-ship to the means of production. Class involved your behavior, your basic assumptions, how you are taught to behave, what you expect from yourself and from others, your concept of future, how you understand problems and solve them, how you think, feel, act" (cited in hooks 2000b, 39).

Certain hegemonic social groups, however, wage war against both oppressed class and gender groups. Under the Bush administration, the escalating power of the new right and antifeminism is already leading to a disregard of women, the poor, and the oppressed on both a global and local level. One of the Bush admin-istration's first actions was to call for cutting off aid for birth control and prenatal counseling for women in developing countries, throwing red ideological meat to his salivating antiabortion fanatics. The Bush administration also closed the White House Women's Office of Initiatives and Outreach, signaling an intention to undo the progress made for women during the Clinton period. The office had encouraged all women, regardless of party affiliation, to participate in govern-ment and had encouraged programs that would benefit women.

Revealing what "compassionate conservatism" and his pledge to "leave no child behind" meant in practice, Bush cut child care grants by $200 million, reduced spending on programs dealing with child abuse by $15.7 million, planned to eliminate the $20 million provided by Congress for improved child care and edu-cation for preschool children, and planned "to cut to the bone a $235 million program to train pediatricians and doctors at the nation's children's hospitals" (see www.salon.com/mwt/feature/2001/03/23/childcuts/index.html). On a hard right free fall, the Bush administration also dropped testing for salmonella in ground beef in school lunch programs, eliminating a program "that caught five million pounds of meat that had salmonella in it last year," and allowed schools to use irradiated beef that many believed to be dangerous (*New York Times*, Apr. 5, 2001).

For some decades now, there has been a demonization of the poor, single, teenaged mother (predominantly portrayed as a woman of color) and the war against youth that scapegoats the young for what are largely adult male induced phenomena (e.g., rape, family violence, etc.). Mike Males demonstrates this "vic-tim blaming mentality" through his documentation of a discussion that took place on the Senate floor in 1994, which established "the 'dreadful facts' that the 'men' involved in 'teenage pregnancy' are 'considerably older' and are 'often abu-sive, exploitative, or overpowering.'" However, "the discussion on the Senate floor revealed the continuing, extraordinary reluctance of top Washington policy makers to discuss the role of adult men, and sexual abuse, in 'teenage' mother-hood" (Males 1996, 98). He goes on to further reveal that the conventional beliefs of the collective public, concerning the "drain" and "laziness" of the wel-fare single mother, is also a well-worn myth and that in reality, legitimate statis-tics confirm that the equating of teen mothers with welfare dependency is a serious misnomer, several congressional studies show. Half of all adolescent mothers do not receive AFDC. Of course [of] those who do, 40 percent are off AFDC within one year, and 70 percent within four years, of giving birth. The average teen mother on AFDC, despite being poorer before becoming pregnant than the average adult mother, stays on the welfare rolls only one year longer than the average mother who gives birth in her 20's. Those who are on AFDC received a whopping $376 per family, $133 per individual, per month in 1994. This is what the screaming over the "social costs of teen mother-hood" is all about. (1996, 82)[6]

Males's indictment against the media, political establishment, and some feminists, in regard to the general lack of outrage and public and academic disclosures about poverty and violence against women and children, provides further ammunition against the misrepresentation of feminist positions toward family terrorism propagated by the escalating legions of feminist impersonators. Todd Gitlin reveals further dimensions of how "blaming the victim" is combined with upholding the myth of the "American Dream" and deservedness of those who "have" by exposing how this "staggering inequality . . . has come to be accepted as normal in a country where the average chief executive officer in a large corporation *collects 149 times the pay of the average factory worker*" (Gitlin 1995, 225–26).

During the past decade, both Democrats and Republicans have cut back welfare state assistance and poverty programs. The Bush administration claims welfare programs encourage out-of-wedlock births and social ills and plans to promote marriage and fatherhood as an antidote to social problems (*The Washington Post*, April 15, 2001, A1). On the whole, conservatives blame 1960s radicalism and Great Society programs and a culture of permissiveness for the breakup of the family, escalating crime, and other social troubles.

Ruth Sidel also provides an explanation for the popular pastime of "blaming the victim" and scapegoating the poor for escalating social problems:

One of the functions of designating certain people as enemies is the bringing together of the rest of society. For the first time in over half a century the United States does not have significant external enemies. The relentless rhetoric against poor single mothers has provided an enemy against whom politicians and conservative ideologues can rally and against whom they can mobilize public opinion and the voting electorate. (Sidel 1996, xviii)

Although it is at times tedious to read listings of statistics, it often proves necessary, given the context of research that pertains to dialectical shifts in the kinds of theory and activism necessary to promote innovative forms of scholarly investigations and political practice. It is with this in mind that some of the findings of Ruth Sidel (1996), an advocate and expert on social policy and sociology of the poor, and Mike Males, a long-term activist and social ecologist, become relevant. Although these findings should be (and are being) updated, they are relevant as indicators of these pathological realities. In fact, Sidel documents the associations of poverty with women, the disenfranchised, the marginalized, and people of color, demonstrating how empirical research, properly contextualized, can advance a progressive political agenda.

Males and Sidel both accurately pinpoint the genuine culprit for escalating local and global violence on a spiraling vortex of economic, class, gender, and racial disparities. Males proposes solutions to "reduce child, teen, and young-family poverty" (1996, 275):

> It is the front from which the worst adult and adolescent destructions arise, an environment whose survival rules demand skills inimical (and understandably so) to larger society. It is not simply poverty, but America's enormous income disparities (the largest of any industrial nation, a 1995 Organization for Economic Cooperation and Development study found) which are most concentrated in high-income high poverty states such as California and New York, that lead to social detachment and violence. Reducing poverty and income disparity is an achievable, and elsewhere achieved, goal. (1996, 275)

Addressing these problems as systemic, Males notes, will require "massive redistribution of wealth away from a variety of affluent elder personal and corporate interests back to young families and the schools, universities, and transitional services upon which they depend" (1996, 275). It will also require reversing the tendency to scapegoat the young and poor and perceiving that poverty, violence, and family terrorism are directly related. Such perspectives provide alternatives to the kinds of liberalism and antifeminism that continue to decontextualize abuse, attempting to convince themselves, the populace, and the funding agencies that battery and abuse cross all class and race "lines." Indeed, even though the elite and rich are certainly not immune to wife abuse and family terrorism, economic privilege is often "the difference that makes the difference." For affluence obviously allows for a less-alienating form of employment for men who tend to bring their frustrations home, and offers women some possibilities for escape from abuse. Yet as Males points out:

> In the U.S. of the 1990s, 16 million children and teens live in poverty. Some 350,000 young are confirmed victims of violence and sexual abuses inflicted by caretakers (mostly parents) every year. Given such conditions, teenage violence is not surprising; it is just like the adult violence from which it stems. In 1993, teenagers experienced three murders and 40 violent crime arrests per 1,000 teens living below federal poverty guidelines—the same rate as among similarly impoverished adults in their 20's and 30's. (1996, 6)

In this study, I have attempted to show that in the last twenty years, mainstream and vulgar feminist approaches have not adequately conceptualized the issue of male violence against women and children and family terrorism. They have tended toward personalizing, domesticating, and psychologizing the problem, when not simply blatantly ignoring it, minimizing it, or explaining it away. Even worse, as I demonstrated in my studies, a cadre of antifeminist (pseudo)-feminists have blamed the victim, or denied the extent of the problem, using their influence in the media and public sphere to denounce those feminists and activists who are trying to address the problem. They have also contributed to depoliticizing and personalizing a highly charged and important political issue. Thus, against these tendencies, I have attempted to demonstrate the enormity of the problem, to criticize those who would deny it, and to suggest the inadequacies of some mainstream and academic approaches to the issue, while proposedly alternative ways of conceptualizing the problem and supporting activist attempts to deal with the issue politically. Consequently, in my concluding chapter I would like to make some further remarks delineating my own approach, while bringing together some of the major themes that I have adumbrated in this study.

NOTES

1. The Academy of Family Physicians concludes that from two to four million women are abused by intimate partners each year. Of these, 2,000 to 4,000 die of their injuries (www.aafp.org/policy/issues/v-violenceposition.html). Other estimates are even higher. It is impossible to know exactly how many women are abused each year because so many cases go unreported. Hence, statistics must only be employed as approximate representations and not absolute facts, as I argue in chapter 3. One of the offensive dimensions of Hoff Sommers and the Independent Women's Forum is that they cite highly questionable statistics as the "facts" about date rape, violence against women, and so on, always dramatically undercutting research by feminist scholars, as well as official government agencies, to make it appear that feminists are hysterics who exaggerate violence against women. Despite the preponderance of statistics in a wide range of studies documenting the enormity of male domestic violence against women, the mass media perpetuate the lie that women are equally culpable. Kristen Golden criticizes the "misleading coverage [that] perpetuates myths about women provoking men's anger and abuse. Witness headlines like 18-YEAR-OLD KILLED BECAUSE SHE DATED OTHER MEN, POLICE SAY. Out of 1,000 newspaper articles I recently read covering domestic violent deaths, only one headline got it right: WIFE BEATER CONVICTED OF MURDER" (Golden 1994).

2. The ECPAT, an international advocacy organization in Thailand estimates that one million children are child prostitutes in Asia (see *Ms.*, Mar./Apr., 1997, 15–16 and first discussion in chapter 5 of this text). Bob Herbert provides us with a glimpse into this unimaginable, but inescapable, hellish reality of too many of the world's children:

> It is possible but not easy to imagine lives more hideous than those of the generations of children who are fed like cheap fuel into Thailand's flourishing sex industry. In some Thai villages, girls are dragged out of school as early as sixth grade and taken to the brothels of Bangkok and other centers of the sex trade. . . . The demand for the young girls seems limitless. Each year tens of thousands of sex tourists from Ger-

many alone visit Thailand, according to the international children's advocacy group Terre des Hommes . . . you can actually buy a virgin girl for $200.00. (*New York Times*, 1996, A15)

3. Jodean Nicolette and Jim Nuovo note that: "Faced with the prevalence of domestic violence, physicians have struggled to understand and characterize violence between partners and to develop and implement effective interventions that include prevention. For many reasons, most of these interventions have focused on treating the victims of domestic violence, rather than on treating the perpetrator." They also argue one "important reason why therapy is focused on the victim, rather than on the perpetrator, is the possible internalization by health care providers of the social acceptance of the victimization of women" (*American Family Physician*, December 1999, www.aafp.org/afp/991201).

4. Commenting on the long history of documented and acknowledged racist attitudes and behaviors of U.S. police and officials, David K. Shipler argues, "Of the country's institutions, police departments are probably furthest behind in addressing racism in their ranks" (*New York Times*, Feb. 7, 1997). Included in his overview of this legacy of racism is the outrageous extent to which it was entrenched within the Los Angeles Police Department, where, according to "the Christopher Commission, which investigated the Rodney King beating in 1991, officers felt so comfortable in their bigotry that they typed racist computer messages to one another apparently confident that they would not face punishment" (*New York Times*, Feb. 7, 1997).

5. There are federal guidelines in the cases of "Noncitizen Victims of Family Violence" that address the growing escalation of "battered alien spouses" (most of whom are women) and children of U.S. citizens and lawful permanent residents; see "Immigration: Non Citizen Victims of Family Violence Report," *Congressional Research Service*, August 7, 2001, 1). Unfortunately, it provides no recourse for the multiplicities of women and children residing in the United States without immigration papers, who are exploited and terrorized on a daily basis. A recent ruling did allow, however, asylum for victims of family terrorism in which a Mexican woman was allowed to stay in the U.S. when a court ruled that she would be abused by her father if she was returned home to Mexico (*Los Angeles Times*, March 22, 2001: A3 and A22).

6. Males also argues that

The demeaning images of pregnant teenagers manufactured by supposedly child-centered Washington policy makers and lobbies betray a particularly vicious opportunism. Privileged official declaimers have proven too squeamish to face *even in* concept the childhood rapes and sexual abuses endured by most pregnant and parenting teens. "Rapes in America is a tragedy of youth," the National Victim Center reported in 1992. Of their sample of 4,000 adult women, one in eight had been raped, 62 percent of these prior to age 18. A *Los Angeles Times* survey of 2,600 adults nationwide found 27 percent of women and 16 percent of men had been sexually abused in childhood. The average age at the time of victimization was nine for victims, 30 for abusers. Half of the abusers were "someone in authority." . . . Two-thirds of pregnant and parenting teens in a mostly white Washington state sample had been sexually abused or raped. . . . Childhood sexual abuse was the single biggest predictor of teenage pregnancy over the past 40 years, a 1995 paper by University of Chicago sociologists found from their survey of 3,400 American adults. (1996, 17–18)

In 1996, the Aid to Families with Dependent Children (AFDC) program was replaced by the Personal Responsibility and Work Opportunity Reconciliation Act (PRWORA). This bill replaced the Federal statute that governed the AFDC program with a block grant that states can use to provide cash and services to low-income families with children, largely free of federal requirements on state program rules. The results, so far, have not been encouraging. Although many have been taken off of welfare rolls, poverty has increased. See "Wisconsin Welfare Reform a Mixed Bag, Study Shows: Though the number of people on the rolls has dropped, most are still living in poverty," *Los Angeles Times*, April 12, 2001, A31 and "Study Finds Widening of Gap Between Rich, Poor," *Los Angeles Times*, Oct. 20, 2000.

5

Colonization, Dialectics, and Borderland Feminisms

In this concluding chapter, I will be especially concerned with how colonization theory and transformative Borderland feminisms prove valuable for helping us to understand and consequently redress many of the tortured experiences of women and children trapped within the pathological rapids of what I call "family terrorism." After discussing some key issues of colonization theory and its applicability to the situation of women, I will provide an analysis of basic concepts of dialectical theory and how it offers a productive epistemological framework for analyzing the condition of women.

I argue that colonization theory, dialectics, and what some are calling "borderland feminisms" provide concepts for addressing concerns set out in previous chapters, involving the brutalization of women, children, and the elderly. Against the truncated empiricism of certain versions of academic feminisms and rejecting the dualisms and reductionism of antifeminism, I stress the importance of perceiving the world in a dialectical fashion through the teachings of a number of radical critics of colonization, racism, globalization, and violence against women and children. It is hardly surprising that many of these scholars are associated with revolutionary forms of feminism that are concerned with and embrace "difference" and "otherness." Many of these critical feminists inscribe aspects of their analyses with notions associated with colonization theory, which address issues within the "borderlands" and "intersections" of race, ethnicity, sexuality, and class as well as gender. My argument is that these types of considerations are translatable and highly relevant to the process of the domination of women, especially in theorizing male violence against women and children and the dynamics of family terrorism within both local and global contexts.

Returning to the theme of colonization, which was highly popular in the post-1960s era but has been neglected within many feminist discussions in recent years, allows for comprehensive and critical perspectives on violence against women and children in what I call "family terrorism" (chapter 4). To be sure, theorizing the domination and oppression of women is a highly controversial aspect of feminist theory, which has provoked a number of serious debates. Yet, that there is no homogenous, universally agreed-upon set of parameters that define feminism does not mean that it is merely a splintered terrain characterized by battling vanguard groups. However, we cannot deny that there is a dimension of feminism that has fallen prey to the divide-and-conquer tactic characteristic of the colonizing strategy. It is hardly surprising, then, that contemporary pseudo-feminist writers who employ reductionist, deterministic, and nondialectical models subscribe to the same kinds of problematical essentialist individualist and empiricist ideologies that were characteristic of some versions of early liberal feminism.

Within this context, a more expansive investigation of either-or oppositions within both a historical and materialist theoretical framework is presented as the pathological nature of a critique of binary logic. Such analysis also helps to demonstrate how a reductive logic is undercut by the dialectical both/and multidimensional vision espoused by a critical feminist approach. This approach requires both historical contextualization of categories and the ability to think about the commonalities of women through concepts of gender to preserve difference. Sandra Harding provides an illuminating analysis of the importance of gender for feminist theory and the need to think through difference as well:

> [A]s a symbol system, gender difference is the most ancient, most universal, and most powerful origin of many morally valued conceptualizations of everything in the world around us. . . . As far back in history as we can see, we have organized our social and natural worlds in terms of gender meanings within which historically specific *racial, class, and cultural institutions and meanings have been constructed*. Once we begin to theorize gender—to define gender as an analytic category within which humans think about and organize their social activity rather than as a natural consequence of sex difference, or even merely as a social variable assigned to individual people in different ways from culture to culture—we can begin to appreciate the extent to which gender meanings have suffused our belief systems, institutions, and even such apparently gender-free phenomena as our architecture and urban planning. (1986, 17)

Harding thus makes it clear that she is not privileging gender over other dimensions of difference, otherness, and marginalities, a charge that was often directed at second wave radical and socialist feminists in particular for their failure to link gender to race and class. The productive dimensions of dialectical and critical feminisms are also revealed through such notions as "contradictions," "paradoxes," and the embrace and recognition of "difference" and "otherness," which are relations that tend to both unify and divide dialectical feminist schools. Indeed, the ability to understand the distinction between "oppositions" and "contradictions" can assist in an understanding that this division, unlike that provoked within and by nondialectical feminist research, is an urgent and useful characteristic of dialectical thought. Sandra Bartky provides an eloquent articulation of this notion:

> To say that feminist consciousness is the experience in a certain way of certain contradictions in the social order is to say that the feminist apprehends certain features of social reality as intolerable, as to be rejected in behalf of a transforming project for the future. What Sartre would call her "transcendence," her project of negation and transformation, makes possible what are specifically feminist ways of apprehending contradictions in the social order. (1990, 14)

Hence, whereas "oppositions" merely denote contrasts like "black" or "white," "contradictions" involve forms of oppression, conflicts, and struggle often within a hierarchical framework that includes the economic and political marginalization of peoples of color and the ways that their oppression is in contradiction to the ideologies of democracy, equality, and social justice. Bartky goes on to provide us with further insight into how recognizing contradictions generates insight and struggle:

> Feminists are no more aware of different things than other people; they are aware of the same things differently. Feminist consciousness, it might be ventured, turns a "fact" into a "contradiction"; often, features of social reality are first apprehended *as* contradictory, as in conflict with one another, or as disturbingly out of phase with one another, from the vantage point of a radical project of transformation. (1990, 14–15)

Indeed, the failure to take into account the dialectical role of contradiction in feminist thought and praxis can undermine feminisms as an emancipatory system of coalition and alliance politics and can block many from investigating and applying its multidimensional progressive potential. For as critical feminists remind us, a failure to grasp dialectical notions—such as mutualities and conflicts, commonalities and differences, and the espousal of reductive and essentialist binary oppositional logics—has permeated much of the discourse within the complex and intricate terrain of "violence against women" and "family terrorism." For instance, one of the most heated debates within feminism in recent years has been over whether pornography promotes violence against women and whether it is sexually liberating or demeaning for women. Positions have tended to solidify into pro- or antiporn, thus often occluding contextual analyses and the contradictory nature of the phenomenon. Nancy Fraser exposes the deficiencies and inadequacies of this kind of polemical reductionism.

> "After years of debating this issue back and forth, no account that equates the whole of pornography with misogyny is defensible. . . . But the same is true of a wholesale

equation of pornography with sexual liberation," she cautions. "We need to recognize that pornography is a complex issue with many strands, and the key to sorting them out is to avoid inflammatory and moralistic rhetoric." (cited in Lord 1997, 40)[1]

In contrast to reductive and one-sided approaches to violence against women and children, many revolutionary woman-of-color theorists and activists, and Borderland/transformative feminists, have addressed issues of violence against women and children in a contextual, dialectical fashion, often since the early days of the second wave. Hence, it is important to avoid being seduced by bifurcated logic, for, as Fraser reminds us, "ideology loves dichotomies," especially false ones. "Hence [it] follows that critical theorists need to problematize gender-associated binary oppositions lest their theories succumb to the disease they aim to diagnose" (1989, 8).

In this chapter, I will use critical feminisms to develop critiques of essentialism and binary discourse, and to show how dialectical feminist epistemologies and theoretical concepts aid in addressing and struggling against violence against women and children. One must, however, view the work of dialectical and critical feminism as being epistemologically and theoretically "in progress," as it involves multiplicities of theories and practices that are continually developing and expanding. Indeed, as with any evolving dialectical theory, it is impossible to find a "contemporary metatheoretical statement" to explain this perspective (Wilder 1978, 19). Furthermore, to trace the development of a transdisciplinary manner of "seeing" poses problems in itself, in that:

> The differentiation of a new paradigm . . . does not happen suddenly at an identifiable moment. It is, therefore, difficult to say that any given part of the unfolding of the new vision was due to one rather than another of the workers in the field. (Bateson 1976, xi)

Bateson's insights are an apt description of the current state of critical and dialectical feminism, as this type of approach is transdisciplinary and multiperspectival, transcending conventional boundaries, imposed upon disciplines, and beginning to set up a theoretical vocabulary and syntax for explaining real concrete relations. Such a transdisciplinary project "is not dependent on any particular science or discipline for its representative metaphors, nor on any specific jargon for its models of information and transformation, relationship and change" (Wilden 1980, xix). Thus, an emergent critical feminist approach cannot solely rely on feminist writings but rather draws on texts from other discourses and traditions to advance its project. As Vron Ware reminds us, "There is a search going on for new reference points, new concepts with which to describe exciting and visionary futures for all those who have been marginalized by the dominating structures of race, class and gender" (1992, 243).

In the next section, I will suggest how the notion of colonization can be appropriated and transformed by critical feminism to address patriarchal violence against women and children. Although a number of feminist theorists have abandoned traditional colonization theory, due in part to the manner in which it was universalized and essentialized by some of the early second-wave radical and socialist feminists, I will examine some ways that theories of colonization can be useful in analyzing relations of family terrorism, note limitations of these kinds of approaches, and stress the need for supplementation by the perspective of a critical transformative feminism.

COLONIZATION, WOMEN, AND DIALECTICS

> It is hard to find an enemy
> who has outposts in your head
>
> Sally Kempton, American journalist

> The oppression of women knows no ethnic or racial boundaries, but that does not mean it is identical within these boundaries.
>
> Audre Lorde, *Sister Outsider*

When Robin Morgan formally proposed the analogy between women and a colonized people in 1967, she was accused of "going too far" (Morgan 1992, 161). Morgan's viewpoints on these matters are probably most typically associated with essentialized perspectives.[2] Indeed, it is unfortunate that aspects of her early radical separatism tended to distort and draw attention away from the utilitarian, emancipatory, and dialectical significance of making these kinds of connections within a framework of colonization. As she explains it (1992), to apply colonization to an entire gender—encompassing almost half of the world's population—bordered on the unthinkable.

Yet over the last few decades, we have witnessed a reemergence of the concept of colonization in the writing of a number of scholars. Those who deploy the concept often define their scholarship as "radical/revolutionary," "Marxian," "Borderland," or "transformative" feminism, and frequently engage the subaltern or postcolonialist debates. Although there is not a general label or classification by which these types of writings could be identified, there is most certainly a "pattern which connects" a diversity of feminist research, from a variety of arenas of thought.

Hence, a number of critical feminists have found the metaphor and dynamics of colonization appropriate for explaining the situation of oppressed people. However, to begin to consider the validity of the claim that different women are colonized often in multiple ways appears to necessitate the development or articulation of an epistemological shift in a number of the modes in which conditions of women have been traditionally studied. As Mary O'Brien explains, "In fact, the need to develop a theoretical basis for a feminism which can transform the world is an increasingly recognized need in the women's movement. The difficulty is knowing where to start. We cannot philosophize out of thin air" (1981, 4).

In light of O'Brien's advice, many feminists adopted the premise that women were a colonized people. However, as emphasized throughout this text, the essentialization of women as a universalized category neutralizes the multidimensionality of the materiality of "difference," which necessarily includes relations of class, ethnicity, sexuality, race, age, and physical abilities, to describe a few. Largely because of the white, upper middle-class, ideological bias of many feminists, the notion of analyzing a diversity of women's relations within a paradigm that embraced colonization theory became largely discredited. This theme, however, has been taken up among critical feminists and others who have been employing the real complexities of colonization to subordinated conditions for decades. Many of these are women of color who interrogate the borderlands between race, gender, class, and sexuality, and are acutely aware of the border between oppressors and oppressed and the global and systemic nature of domination.[3] However, their revolutionary applications of notions of colonization have received little of the notice and credibility afforded to more popular feminist theorists, especially within the academic domain where much of contemporary feminist theory is encouraged and rewarded.

The idea of associating a diversity of women's conditions with the process of colonization, in turn, leads to general investigations into dimensions of the construction of diverse women's different and shared realities. It also helps produce analyses of the multileveled nature of colonization as well as investigation into the dialectical both/and epistemology that would best frame this inquiry. As Denis Goulet notes, "To think dialectically is to decree the obsolescence of cherished concepts which explain even one's recent past. One of the marks of a true dialectician, however, is the ability to 'move beyond' the past without repudiating it in the name of new levels of critical consciousness presently enjoyed" (Goulet 1973, vii).

Simply put, to think dialectically, each level of research—as it relates to women and colonization—leads to higher levels of *questions* not only about the nature of the process of colonization but also about the contextual epistemology necessary for beginning to understand the complexities of specific conditions of oppression, injustice, and domination. In this sense, embracing a dialectical epistemology liberates the researcher to reach higher levels of inquiry into a more complex system and to relate them to practice. This approach engages multiple dimensions of the colonization process and proves useful to understanding many of the underlying patterns that construct oppressive and, especially, violent material conditions of women's different and shared experiences.[4]

It is hardly surprising that much of colonization research was conducted by—

and is primarily about—men, and thus includes implicitly—and in some cases, explicitly—a misogynist subtext. These revolutionary male writers, nevertheless, present powerful statements on the position of colonized peoples and the modes in which the roles of the colonized are reinforced by both the colonizer and the colonizer's constraining hegemonic code. Thus, rather than ignoring these works because of the outstanding "hole" of gender in their analyses, a dialectical approach encourages us to "work by identifying the male bias in established approaches. These must be examined from the perspective of women and the implications for the field of incorporating the perspectives and interest of women followed through" (Smith 1987, 16).

The writings of Frantz Fanon, Paulo Freire, Albert Memmi, and Jean-Paul Sartre, in particular, lend themselves to a translation that identifies and explains the different and often multiple forms of colonization of women. Sandra Lee Bartky makes this eloquently clear in an essay that documents the revelatory effects of Frantz Fanon's treatise on her own feminist philosophy. "Without wanting in any way to diminish the oppressive and stifling realities of black experience that Fanon reveals, let me say that I, a white woman, recognize myself too, not only in my 'shameful livery of white incomprehension,' but as myself the victim of a 'psychic alienation' similar to the one Fanon has described" (1990, 22).

Fanon was especially concerned with both the theoretical and practical dimensions of dialectics as an empowering process of decolonization in which the "colonized Self" can be liberated from the "tyrannical Other" and hence achieve "freedom" as well as "authentic individuality" (Caute 1970, 34). However, as critical feminists like bell hooks remind us, we cannot ignore the androcentric and often misogynistic postures of these writers, which are reflected and reinforced in their various pedagogies and texts. Rather than overlooking earlier colonization theorists because of their patriarchal bias, she counsels feminist activists to not occlude such inherent contradictions, but to learn from "the message content," while, at the same time, recognizing that this deeply embedded sexism "diminishes without negating the value of the works" (1984, 40).

Thus, while recognizing the male bias of many colonization theorists, one can translate some of their explanations of specific relations of colonized peoples to the multiple situation of women and children. (It is interesting to note that all but Sartre are writing from the perspective of the colonized, and all but Sartre are men of color.) As bell hooks reminds us:

> Unfortunately, it is not merely the politically naive who demonstrate a lack of awareness that forms of oppression are inter-related. Often brilliant political thinkers have had such blind spots. Men like Frantz Fanon, Albert Memmi, Paulo Freire, and Aime Cesaire, whose works teach us much about the nature of colonization, racism, classism, and revolutionary struggle often ignore issues of sexist oppression in their own writing. They speak against oppression but then define liberation in terms that suggest it is only oppressed men who need freedom. (1984, 39)[5]

There are a number of analyses of the colonization of critical feminists that complement and translate from these primary texts and thus contribute to a deeper understanding of family terrorism. To begin with, feminists who use colonization theory make it clear that the term *colonization* is often misused or incomplete. The oversimplified connotation of the concept, related to strict economic imperialism, or, as the *O.E.D.* defines it, "Of, belonging to a colony," is hardly an accurate description of the realities of this complex and multileveled system. As Sartre reminds us, the colonialist system is a form in motion (1968), of a historically specific and evolving form of domination, subordination, and collaboration.

What is made apparent is that "violence" is the "heart and soul" of colonization. Moreover, much of this violence is never consciously recognized or is often masked by terms such as *oppression* and *exploitation* (to name two). In other words, one often finds euphemisms for what is, in actuality, colonization. As Paulo Freire explains it:

> Any situation in which "A" objectively exploits "B" or hinders his pursuit of self-affirmation as a responsible person is one of oppression. Such a situation in itself constitutes violence, even when sweetened by false generosity, because it interferes with man's ontological and historical vocation to be fully human. With the establishment of a relationship of oppression, violence has *already* begun. (1972, 40–41)

Indeed, the recognition of this common thread of violence woven throughout this polymorphic process called colonization radically reframes our perception. As Tony Wilden notes, "We have watched the violence of the world economic system being directed at group after group on this tiny planet—violence physical, logical and psychological; political, ecological, and social. . . . [Yet] relatively little of this violence . . . is aimed at male WASPS like me" (1980, 35). Yet, whenever any group, race, or class is oppressed, women are involved. Women are unique in the sense that they are part of every people who have been forced into subordinate positions. Further investigation will almost always reveal that within oppressed groups, women suffer a double or multiple oppression. They are not only being oppressed by "dominant others," exploiting the particular race, class, or group to which they belong; they are also being oppressed by the violence directed at them by other members of their own class, race, ethnicity, or group—that is, males. These women might seem to constitute what Sheila Rowbotham calls "a colony within a colony" (1974, 206) or what Michele Wallace has described, in relation to black women in particular, as "the 'Other' of the 'Other' of both black men and white women, who are 'Other' themselves" (1990, 148). Colonized violence is brilliantly portrayed in the writings of Alice Walker. Throughout her Pulitzer Prize–winning novel *The Color Purple*, we are witness to its reality. Consider how Walker's protagonist, Celie, describes her husband's response to the news that she is leaving him:

He laugh. Who you think you is? he say. You can't curse nobody. Look at you. You black, you poor, you ugly, you a woman. Goddam, he say, you nothing at all. (1982, 213)

In fact, the complexities of colonization are hardly an abstract theoretical process. Indeed, its essential and practical consequences are regularly evoked by a number of contemporary radical activist scholars. Joy James, for example, argues that the "high infant and maternity rates and falling life expectancy rates" of African-descended women workers in the United States, "reflect the devastation of colonized life." In this sense she is identifying how the "double shift—of unpaid domestic labor and wage labor—has turned into a triple shift for a growing number of class women," which provokes "multiple exposures to overwork, ill health, and physical and psychological exhaustion" (James 1996, 116). She further identifies the shocking practical realities of this dimension of colonization in which the "number of women holding two or more jobs quintupled from 1970 to 1990, from 636,000 to 3.1 million" (James 1996, 116).

Further evidence of the colonized nature of much of the violence and subordination that defines both unique and shared conditions of women's multiple situation is revealed through examination of Fanon's and others' description of the theory and praxis of this process. Theories of colonization also provide perspectives to critique the dominant myths and treatments of the universalized stereotype of women, prevalent in divergent patriarchal cultures and societies, which covers over differences and specificities. Briefly put, contrary to the dominant ideology people are not born with a "colonized mentality." Colonial characteristics are not inherent, they are learned. False histories, false role models, and false expressions of a people's creative potential, together with socially imposed constraints that perpetuate these false belief systems, keep the colonized in their place. For the colonial is colonized historically, socially, politically, economically, and personally. The colonizer, through the use of "tokens" and the aid of "collaborators," ensures that the colonized remain in a state of "false" or "imaginary" consciousness. In other words, the colonized are taught to believe the dominant ideological myths about their collective being, act accordingly, and often collaborate in their own oppression.

Living under such a complex set of oppressive constraints, it is only natural the colonized define themselves by what they are not. The nonwhite, in white society, finds an existence mediated by the white code, just as the nonmale, in male society, finds an existence mediated by the patriarchal code. Western society is, of course, dominated by the white code, and most, if not all, societies today are dominated by patriarchal and capitalist forms. Under patriarchal capitalism then, it is quite "normal" for the woman to find her life mediated by what she is not. She is not male, and concurrently, often not represented within socially defined relations of power. She is the *colonisé*. Although this is also the case for marginalized men, they are still afforded power over women and children, while women are, as Simone de Beauvoir argued, the second sex. Although women as well as men are afforded power over children and the elderly, in cases of abuse, she is both colonized and colonizer. In fact, she is often a collaborator (see chapters 1–3).

Earlier feminist theory stressed that there appears to be a shared code among most patriarchal systems, delineating the separation and division of the "private" and "public" spheres, or "domestic/familial" and "governmental/sociopolitical" dimensions of given societies.[6] Moreover, there also are certain common assumptions regarding the characterization of these two spheres as hierarchically unequal. The public and the private domain are usually concurrently defined in gendered terms, in which one of these domains—usually the male and public sphere—is dominant over, and considered superior to, the other female and private sphere. Moreover, it is in this sense that those societal members associated with the dominant realm are afforded the more privileged status and the qualities of that society that are best described as the most credible or "normal," or "good." Accordingly, behaviors and traits connected with the subordinate female terrain will be deemed as Other, alien or deviant in some manner, in that the identity of members associated with the private and domestic female sphere is defined as secondary and inferior relative to the "norm." (This relationship is also described, within certain theories of colonization, as "master/slave," "dominant and subordinate Others.")

Furthermore, the gendered nature of the private/public split does not necessarily entail that all men will be relegated to the public/male domains and all women to the private/female dimensions. Indeed, historical and anthropological examinations of these societal splits demonstrate that often, anatomical gendered differences do not guarantee association or status within the realm most closely related to one's sex. For, in fact, male children and male slaves, as well as male members of some (or all, dependent upon the society) marginalized groups are often restricted to, or associated with, the subordinated/female or inferior realm. Hence, violent relations, in particular male violence directed against women, seem to be, at least in part, mediated by these hierarchical gendered divisions. Joan Smith argues that a patriarchal code in Western society nurtures and encourages "a deep seated hatred of women" and is responsible for serial murderers like Peter Sutcliffe, the Yorkshire Ripper of the late 1970s (Smith 1989, xvii). As she puts it:

> The discrimination and denigration and violence that women suffer are not historical accidents but linked manifestations of this hatred; I inhabit a culture which is not simply sexist but *occasionally lethal* for women. Misogyny wears many guises, reveals itself in different forms which are dictated by class, wealth, education, race, religion, and other factors, but its chief characteristic is its pervasiveness. . . . Nor is woman-hating found only in the male half of the human race. We are all exposed to the prevailing ideology of our culture, and some women learn early that they can prosper

by aping the misogyny of men; these are the women who win provisional favour by denigrating other women, by playing on male prejudices, and by acting the "man's woman." (Smith 1989, xvii)

Moreover, James McBride argues that male abuse against women is encouraged by societally sanctioned relationships or institutions, which demand and encourage large groups of men to work or train closely together in a highly rigid and segregated environment, governed by a complex—and often secretive— patriarchal code of behaviors. He identifies, for example, "blood sports" and "the rhetoric of combat" as two of these institutions (McBride 1995, xv, 35).[7] This notion, in fact, would seem to contribute to helping to understand the well-documented prevalence of violence against women by members of the military and sport industries—as well as in numerous university fraternities. McBride describes this code of behavior as the "symbolic and imaginary dimensions" of what he calls "the masculinist psychic economy" (1995, xvi). He goes on to argue that these codes frequently "screen an underlying dynamic of which the group may or may not be aware" (1995, xvi). Documenting the misogynist dimension to military socialization, he shows how a gendered hierarchy helps to explain the relationship between male violence against women and organized sports and war.

In the context of war, battering, and football, misogynist violence—either figuratively or literally expressed—reflects a particular configuration of the male psyche in which these social practices embody a culturally constructed psychological need to abuse women for the sake of a male identity recognizable to the homosocial community. Although the rules of war, like the rules of the game, do not specifically describe the enemy as woman, the discursive construction of the opponent as female bears witness to its prevalence in the male imaginary. (McBride 1995, xvi)

Indeed, analyses of masculinity and militarism are central to many critical feminist approaches. As bell hooks points out: "Early on in feminist thinking activists often failed to liken male violence against women to imperialist militarism. The linkage was often not made because those who were against male violence were accepting and even supportive of militarism. As long as sexist thinking socializes boys to be 'killers,' whether in imaginary good guy, bad guy fights or as soldiers in imperialism to maintain coercive power over nations, patriarchal violence against women and children will continue" (hooks 2000b, 65). Enloe argues as well: "Through wartime mobilization, postwar demobilization, and peace-time preparedness maneuvers, sexuality and militarism have been intertwined. They have been constructed and reconstructed together, usually with the help of deliberate policy decisions" (2000, 51). Moreover, many transformative feminists discuss militarization in relation to family terrorism. For example, "Guatemalan indigenous women have reported that domestic violence increased during the long years of civil war in their country" (Enloe 1993, 127).

The terrorization and objectification of women, many argue, is in fact an integral aspect of the construction of masculinity which is so fundamental to relations of colonization and military conquest. Mamma notes: "The harsh realities of conquest in Africa included widespread violation and degradation of African women. Where there was resistance, rape and sexual abuse, were inflicted on women and the same treatment was meted out to the wives, mothers, daughters, and sisters of men who were suspected of being members of resistant movements simply to humiliate them" (Mamma, 1997, 51).

Furthermore, Otherness is often a central dimension of the terrorization of different women in civil wars and other regional conflicts: "Women are frequently singled out for torture in *armed conflicts* because of their role as educators and as symbols of the community. Tutsi women in the 1994 genocide in Rwanda, and Muslim, Serb, Croat and ethnic Albanian women in the former Yugoslavia, were tortured because they were women of a particular ethnic, national or religious group" (Amnesty International News Release, 2000, www.web.amnesty. org). Thus, Eisenstein argues that

> war rape is sexualized violence that seeks to terrorize, destroy, and humiliate a people through its women . . . genocidal rape has its own horrors. It takes place in isolated rape camps, with strict orders from above to either force the woman's exile or her death. Rape is repeatedly performed as torture; it is used to forcibly impregnate; it is even used to exterminate. Women in the camps are raped repetitively, some as many as thirty times a day for as long as three consecutive months. They are kept hungry, they are beaten and gang-raped, their breasts are cutoff, and stomachs split open. (1996, 59)

Consequently, this kind of research of male violence against women and girls, family terrorism and colonization are a major component of transformative global feminisms. For, as Enloe points out, militarism is hardly the exclusive domain for patriarchal violence, and is, in fact, metaphorical in that critical transnational feminists are committed to talking "openly about men's violence against women—not just the violence wielded by the enemy's or foreigner's military men, but the violence perpetrated by civilian and military men of all communities" (Enloe 2000, 149).

Borderland/transformational feminists like Audre Lorde argue that the number of levels of violence imposed upon women is related to particular class, race, ethnic, and a variety of other determinants. Hence, when drawing upon the concept of colonization, we must be sure that we articulate dimensions of race, class, sexuality, culture, and other relations, which are crucial factors in constituting collective and individual women's concrete experiences of oppression. Moreover, we should heed the warnings of Homi K. Bhabha regarding an oversimplified analogy of colonization, which basically places all men in the role of colonizer and all women as the colonized. Such a binary opposition is a very undialectical translation and reduction of relations of multiple complexities. Bhabha alerts us to what he describes as "an imperialist cross-referencing that denies the meton-ymy of the colonial moment" (cited in Donaldson 1992, 6). Indeed, he argues that such a reductionist approach to colonization blinds us to the realities that necessarily include not only relations of gender, but also of race, class, sexuality, ethnicity, and ableness. Hence, gender is not always the fundamental characteris-tic of the colonized person. Moreover, there are occasions in which woman and the colonized can be both colonizer and colonized within different contexts. For as Bhabha puts it, "Recuperating the experience of the 'Other' as a signifier of women's experience, it actually functions as a 'narrative ruse' whose search for 'cultural commensurability' ethnocentrically elides the colonized's ambivalent, hybrid knowledges" (Donaldson 1992, 6).

Indeed, it is the problematic, overessentialized, and often rigid definitions of complex processes like colonization that have obstructed or negated some of the more productive translations of colonization theory as an integral aspect of dia-lectical theory and praxis. A more multiperspectival approach, for instance, would involve the reconfiguration of the notion of female gender as *not* a synonym for biological females and would address interconnections of things like gender, race, class, and sexual oppression. If, for instance, we treat "femininity" as a social con-struction and an "index," it illuminates the ideological construction and misuse of the term (i.e., such as the feminization of marginalized men, or calling men terms like *pussies*). This concept of index is a very useful term drawn from semi-otic theory, which defines it "as a sign that is connected to its *object*, either casu-ally or existentially" (O'Sullivan et al. 1983, 113). In fact, stereotypical characteristics of "femininity" are often attributed to those marginalized men who are typically described as "weak," "passive," "irrational," and the like.

Within this context, Frantz Fanon's examination of the relationship between the colonized person of color and the white, male colonizer bears reconsideration. Ato Sekyi-Otu (1996) insightfully proposes that:

> There *are* gendered inflections and nuances in the nature of a racially subjugated people's existential and affective relations with their masters. These inflections and nuances are recognizably derivative of generic structures of gender hierarchy, com-municative and affective restraints, compulsions, rules—to say nothing of their accompanying symbols and myths—with which the historical world is littered. (214)

However, rather than falling prey to the evils of vulgar essentialism or univer-salization, Sekyi-Otu is employing a metacritical both/and perspective that embodies notions of "sameness" and similarities of experiences as well as "differ-ence." Hill Collins describes this dialectical process as "intersectionality"[8]:

> Moving beyond difference (with its assumed question, difference from what?) to the conceptual terrain of intersectionality creates new conceptual space. By jettisoning the implicit assumption of a normative center needed for both oppositional differ-ence and reconstructive postmodern tolerance for difference, intersectionality pro-

vides a conceptual framework for studying the complexities within historically constructed groups as well as those characterizing relationships among such groups. (1998, 152)

Vulgar essentialist approaches, by contrast, would negate the existence and recognition of the contextually shifting complexity of interrelated levels of cultural and political identity. It is within this context that Sekyi-Otu's position on the pathological nature of colonized relationships becomes significant. "That peculiarity [a peculiar pathology of desire within the colonial context] resides in the fact that in the face of the white person all colonized subjects, men and women, are, so to speak, 'feminized' " (Sekyi-Otu 1996, 215).

Indeed, this reaffirmation of the ideological distortion of "femininity" and all the unconscious ambivalence and suspect baggage associated with the label links with the previous discussion on the delegitimization of male homosexuality as a feminized construct. As McBride argues, feminization is one of the underlying bases of violent relationships that pervade patriarchal cultures. "Within the masculinist psychic economy, a 'true' woman is veritably produced via domination. 'Real' men control 'real' women—those who are cultural female by virtue of their biology and/or behavior. . . . As a sign of domination in an androcentric social order, battering as praxis produces 'women.' The physical abuse of women, children, and even other men establishes both the 'femininity' (the weakness and submissiveness) of the victim and the 'masculinity' (dominance) of the batterer" (1995, 26–27).

McBride also notes that "This construction of gender countenances two cultural taboos—females who 'resist their natures,' that is, act 'mannishly,' and males who assume 'unnatural' roles, that is act effeminately" (1995, 26–27). His multiperspectival analysis also helps explain why gay bashers attack gay men to affirm their own masculinity.[9] And in addressing the battery of children within family terrorism as a dimension of colonization, McBride explains how women can perpetuate violence against children. As he notes:

> Sometimes children are literally caught between the batterer and the female partner and suffer "collateral damage"; sometimes they are directed targets of the batterer's anger. Physical beatings of children may occur in nearly 50 percent of the homes where a batterer resides; sexual abuse has been reported to be in as many as 30 percent of these homes. Most often, the child's tormentor is the batterer himself, but in some cases the child is beaten by the batterer's victim—the child's mother or stepmother. Many women find it difficult to sustain calm with the children when they are under such duress from their male partners. They strike out at their own children, either believing it legitimate as a result of acquiescing to their own fate or as a release from the terror that has become such a part of their daily existence. (1995, 10)

Moreover, many women who constitute part of the dominant classes, races, and groups often do their part to oppress and violate those in subordinate positions. This is not to say, however, that these women—these "dominant/subordinate Others"—are not oppressed within the realms of the privileged. (For example, under capitalism, the privileged are generally those who are usually Western, white, Christian, middle or upper class, heterosexual, physically able, and male.) Indeed, the imposition of violence upon those who are defined as more subordinate is consistent with the colonized mentality. It is, therefore, the real *contradiction*—within this process—that enables white or privileged women who are in the dominant position in society to be called dominant/subordinate others.

Although most of these women would not consciously perceive themselves as such, this is the reality of their condition. "Dominant" refers to their particular economic, social, sexual, cultural, and racial position, while "subordinate" refers to their status as second-class citizens within not only their own social sphere but also within society as a whole. Furthermore, colonization is both an individual and a collective experience. In it, all women, regardless of race, class, or culture, share a colonized position in different ways, in accordance with their own particular contexts of being subordinate to men. Yet women also belong to different classes, races, and organizations of men as defined by particular contextual relations and constraints and thus suffer oppression differentially.

Furthermore, "collaboration" is not the exclusive domain of the dominant/subordinate woman. One of the foremost characteristics of this contradictory process is that the maintenance of colonization generates the complicity of the colonized in their own oppression. And this complicity is partly owing to the role of the collaborator. Hence, by concentrating only on the differences between themselves and less fortunate women, rather than embracing commonalities and alliances, they are reinforcing and perpetuating their own, and other women's, colonization. Underlying Fanon's well-documented analysis of the complexities embedded in this system is thus the importance of paradox, contradiction, and difference.

> At opportune moments [the colonizer] combines his policy of brutal repression with spectacular gestures of friendship, manoeuvres calculated to sow division, and "psychological action". Here and there he tries with success to revive tribal feuds, using *agents provocateurs* and practicing what might be called counter subversion. (Fanon 1961, 136)

In the following discussion, building on colonization theory, I will show how recent borderland/transformational feminisms contribute to developing a critical and dialectical framework to critique male violence against women and children and family terrorism.

BORDERLAND FEMINISMS

A wide range of feminists have addressed issues like colonization and globalization and have engaged a multiplicity of forms of gender, sex, and racial oppression, in an arena of Borderland feminism. As Susan Stanford Friedman notes, "Border talk is everywhere—literal and figural, material symbolic. . . . In an increasingly globalized and transnational context, feminism has become ever more acutely attuned to the meanings of borders as markers of positionality and situatedness" (Friedman 1998, 3). Drawing on her own experiences as a lesbian Chicana, Gloria Anzaldúa provides us with one of the most poignant, expressive, and eloquent illustrations of the connotation of the borderland metaphor.

> The U.S.-Mexican border *es una herida abierta* where the Third World grates against the first and bleeds. And before a scab forms it hemorrhages again, the lifeblood of two worlds merging to form a third country—a border culture. Borders are set up to define the places that are safe and unsafe, to distinguish *us* from *them*. A border is a dividing line, a narrow strip along a steep edge. A borderland is a vague and undetermined place created by emotional residue of an unnatural boundary. It is in a constant state of transition. The prohibited and forbidden are its inhabitants. *Los atravesados* live here: the squint-eyed, the perverse, the queer, the troublesome, the mongrel, the mulato, the half-breed, the half dead; in short those who cross over, pass over, or go through the confines of the normal. Gringos in the U.S. Southwest consider the inhabitants of the borderlands transgressors, aliens—whether they posses documents or not, whether they're Chicanos, Indians or Blacks. Do not enter, trespassers will be raped, maimed, strangled, gassed, shot. The only "legitimate" inhabitants are those in power, the whites and those who align themselves with whites. Tension grips the inhabitants of the borderlands like a virus. Ambivalence and unrest reside there and death is no stranger. (Anzaldúa 1987, 3–4)

Updating her borderland/Borderland analogy, Anzaldúa explains, "Borderlands with a small b is the actual southwest borderlands or any borderlands between two cultures, but when I use the capital B it's a metaphor for the process of many things: psychological, physical, mental" (Anzaldúa in Keating, 2000, 176). Sandra Harding draws on Anzaldúa's expression to discuss, what she calls a "Borderland epistemolgy," which articulates the complexities involved in relations of colonization being addressed by this kind of Borderland transformative feminism:

> Women, racial/ethnic minorities, the victims of imperialism and colonialism, and the poor are in some respects functionally "strangers" to the dominant cultures and practices that structure their lives. . . . Their needs and desires are not the ones that have found expression in the design and functioning of the dominant institutions. . . . And yet these groups are not completely outside the dominant institutions—they are no longer off in Africa or barefoot and pregnant in the kitchen. They are instead on the margins, the periphery; they are "outsiders within" or on the "borderlands." (1998, 155)

Hence, as she puts it: "Borderlands have emerged as expanding and crowded territories of contemporary social life (159). Further, Gloria Anzaldúa's dialectical description of a Borderland epistemology speaks to multiple dimensions of philosophical and concrete contradictions and paradoxes, which are associated with the ongoing development and shifting nature of transformative critical feminisms.

> Change is constant and unrelenting. It's a source of tension. With no sense of closure or completion, it is overwhelming. The who-we-are is changing. Living in the midst of different vortexes makes it hard for us to make sense of the chaos and put the pieces together. But it is in the cracks between worlds and realities where changes in consciousness can occur. In this shifting place of transitions, we morph, adapt to new cultural realities. As time goes by things start to solidify again and we erect new walls. They stay in place until the next generation kicks holes in them. When the dust settles, who knows what the new structures will look like? (Anzaldúa in Keating 2000, 280)

hooks in turn reminds us that many early Borderland transformative feminists were bisexual and lesbian and their contributions were essential to this kind of revolutionary feminist thought: "Women who were lesbians, of all races and classes, were at the forefront of the radicalization of contemporary feminist resistance to patriarchy in part because this group had by their sexual preference already placed themselves outside the domain of heterosexist privilege and protection, both in the home and in the workplace. No matter their class, they were social outcasts, of the objects of patriarchal abuse and scorn" (hooks 2000a, 102).

Indeed, it is important to note that much of the theoretical and practical work affecting the emerging project of dialectical transformative feminism must be credited to the research and writings of a number of radical feminists of color who have developed significant critiques of the limitations of white reformist feminism. These include the work of Angela Davis, Audre Lorde, bell hooks, Patricia Hill Collins, Valerie Smith, Joy James, and the texts assembled by Gloria Anzaldúa and Cherri Moraga, Lisa Albrecht and Rose M. Brewer, and M. Jacqui Alexander and Chandra Talpade Mohanty. However, these are hardly definitive and only touch on a multiplicity of a wealth of transformative feminist texts. These theorists and many others who call attention to the saliency of race, ethnicity, class, gender, and sexuality provide salient critiques of Eurocentric mainstream, reformist, gynocentric, and vulgar feminisms (which are not, unfortunately, exclusive to white feminists) for failing to make these distinctions. They critique universalism and binary oppositional thought, which essentializes differences with a more contextual and dialectical transdisciplinary approach. These borderland feminists recognize and embrace notions of contradiction and thus the real nature of difference among women, while advancing an insurgent multicultural agenda and transformative critical feminist epistemology.

The best work of borderland/tranformative feminists involves the active incorporation of contextual mediations of real concrete experiences to the development of a critical theoretical perspective. Hill Collins argues that Afrocentric feminist thought involves a multiple focus on gender, race, and class oppression that is rooted in concrete experiences of oppression and struggle. As she explains it:

> Viewing the world through a both/and conceptual lens of the simultaneity of race, class, and gender oppression and of the need for a humanist vision of community creates new possibilities for an empowering Afrocentric feminist knowledge. Many Black feminist intellectuals have long thought about the world in this way because this is the way we experience the world. (1990, 221–22)

Indeed, the radical nature of Borderland Afrocentric feminism is informed by a critical appraisal of the essentialism underlying both racist Eurocentric feminism and sexist Afrocentric philosophy. Hill Collins demonstrates the courage and insight characteristic of those espousing maverick dialectical epistemological viewpoints, while addressing the contradictory nature of Afrocentric thought. Identifying the gender blindness and male bias of much of the work of Afrocentrism hardly excludes its utility for critical liberatory, practical, and theoretical research. Rather the development of a more inclusive feminism that addresses the diversity of difference is necessarily critical of the either-or mentality of Eurocentric knowledge. In fact, an Afrocentric project reframes the dominant vision of the world in that it is located within an African, rather than European, contextual framework.

Valerie Smith, in addition, addresses the contradictory, multifarious nature of black feminism with work theoretically grounded in practical relations particular to African Americans. She writes, "Black feminism, at once imaginative, critical and theoretical, is simultaneously deconstructive and reconstructive, reactive and proactive. Historically it has revealed ways in which the lives and cultural productions of black women have been overlooked or misrepresented within Eurocentric and androcentric discourses" (1990, 271). Smith further explicates the Borderland metaphor in noting, "To borrow Mary Poovey's term, I am drawn to 'border cases,' issues that challenge the binary logic that governs the social and intellectual systems within which we live and work. As Poovey argues, border cases are 'the site of intensive debate . . . because they [threaten] to challenge *the* opposition upon which all other oppositions are claimed to be based' " (Smith 1990, 272).

For Smith, "Black feminists seek not only to dismantle the assumptions of dominant cultures, and to recover and reclaim the lives and texts of black women, but also to develop methods of analysis for interpreting the ways in which race, class, and gender are inscribed in cultural productions" (1990, 271). Smith argues that

> Afro-Americanist and Anglo-American feminists depended historically upon totalizing formulations of race on the one hand, gender on the other. Male authored Afro-Americanist criticism assumed a conception of blackness that concealed its masculinist presuppositions; Anglo-or Euro-centered feminism relied upon a notion

of gender that concealed its presumption of whiteness. It has fallen to feminists whose work explicitly addresses issues of race, class, sexual preference, and nationality to confront the implications of difference within these modes of oppositional discourse. (271)

In her absorbing study of white women and racism, Vron Ware accentuates the connections of racism and white imperialism with the ideology and historical reality of colonization (1992). She notes that these patterns resonate "throughout Europe, North America and wherever whites have colonized non-European peoples," and goes on to describe a number of other behaviors and attitudes that "haunt racist societies" (241). This astute examination, however, does not limit its examination to the most dominant and generally acceptable understanding of colonization as a primarily economic psychosocial conquest of one nation, or group of peoples, by another. It also expands on this insidious, sophisticated, and subordinating complex, intricate, and often contradictory system that adopts the more radical connotations of this process as a multileveled and diverse set of conditions that are embedded in the multifarious dimensions of relations of gender, sexuality, class, age, and ethnicity—as well as race. In this sense, it has an enormous—if often neglected—role in the practices and perceptions of a preponderance of feminisms that overtly or covertly tend toward essentialized proclivities that promote a ubiquitous and unidimensional view of womankind. For, in fact, Ware makes us graphically aware of the contradictory and often dialectical hierarchical conditions inherent within the realities of colonization as it pertains to women in accordance with the real materiality of their positions and experience. It is within this context that the fundamental and revelatory paradoxical realities of colonization become explicit, especially in relation to the situation of the privileged white woman within the contestatory domain of feminist debate. Indeed, this becomes clearer and more visible within her ingenious delineation of the paradoxical intricacies and multidimensional nature of this process.

[T]he dichotomies are seemingly endless, and gender, race and class do not always fit so neatly on one or other side of the dividing line. Civilization, for example, is the other side of the coin from savagery. In some contexts, white women might indeed be associated with the idea that female nature is inherently uncivilized, primitive when compared to men, and lacking self-control. In the context of imperialism or modern racism, the dominant ideology would place white women firmly in the civilized camp, in opposition to non-European women whose lack of social and political rights are to be read as a mark of cultural savagery. *This means that white women can occupy both sides of a binary opposition, which surely accounts for much of the confusion and ambivalence to be found in the ideology of gender relations.* (Ware 1992, 237; emphasis mine)

Hence, as Ware would seem to indicate, the critical assertion associating women's multiple conditions with colonization is by no means an essentialized or universalized notion. It is rather one that is predicated on the dialectical reality of a multiplicity of differences and levels of colonization as well as on the often paradoxical and contradictory reality that many women are often both colonized and colonizer. Indeed, it is within this context that classic analyses of colonization can be applied to situations that appear to be similar to—although, it must be emphasized, can in no way be treated as identical or equal to—ones described within these seminal studies. Jean-Paul Sartre's explication of this "conflictual" status proves particularly enlightening, for situating and understanding the conscious or unconscious role, which distinguishes many privileged white feminists. Drawing on Albert Memmi's (1965) powerful interrogation of colonization, in regard to this "category," Sartre reveals:

> He belongs to one of those native . . . groups that are "more or less privileged in comparison with the colonized masses, but . . . rejected . . . by the colonizing group," which, however, "does not completely discourage" their efforts to integrate themselves into European society. Linked by actual liabilities to the subproletariat, but separated from it by meager privileges, the members of this group live in a constant state of uneasiness. (Sartre 1965, xxi–xxii)

Therefore, the notion of the collaborator necessarily takes into account that its "doubled" role can be both simultaneous or one in which the dominance of one position over the other is contextually mediated by the material conditions of everyday life. An understanding of these kinds of complexities, however, necessitates their location within a critical perspective that rejects the kinds of binary-oppositional thought that are so prevalent within much of the theory and practices of vulgar and pseudofeminisms. And it is this failure to comprehend and situate the seductive and insidious nature of the Western colonialist narrative that blinds many to the ideological bias and restrictiveness of their perspectives and actions. It is in this light that charges of racism (as well as other conscious or unconscious prejudicial biases) against feminists who universalize relations from a privileged perspective can be better understood. Such Borderland feminism also provides a critique of subordinating colonized behaviors and practices, as among the myriad forms of violence and family terrorism that impede and destroy the lives of so many women and children within the global community.

Audre Lorde, in her plea to a group of feminists to transcend the defensiveness that often hinders those of us who share some of the characteristics of the more powerful societal elite, recognizes the conflictual and contestatory nature of examining and acknowledging certain ideological premises that often taint and shape our vision. "Racism and homophobia are real conditions of all our lives in this place and time. I *urge each one of us here to reach down into that deep place of knowledge inside herself and touch that terror and loathing of any difference that lives there. See whose face it wears.* Then the personal as the political can begin to illuminate all our choices" (1984, 113).

The antidefeatism and liberating dimensions of this kind of dialectical translation is empowering in that it does not restrict one's involvement in critical feminisms due to shared elite characteristics and ideological bias, but rather treats recognition of multiple forms of oppression as a necessary step toward a decolonized, inclusive, liberatory approach. Indeed, within this kind of perspective is understood as being contextually mediated. As an example, Sartre describes the contribution of those like Albert Memmi who found themselves in the precarious position that is described as being "neither" or "both" colonizer and colonized.

> He has understood the system so well because he felt it first as his own contradiction. He explains clearly . . . that such rendings of the spirit, plainly introjections of social conflicts, do not dispose the individual to action. But the man who suffers them, if he becomes aware of himself, can enlighten others through self-examination: a "negligible force in the confrontation," he *represents* no one, but since he *is* everyone at once, he will prove to be the best of witnesses. (Sartre 1965, xxii)

But, as Patricia Hill Collins warns us, it would be a mistake to fetishize marginalization, warning how this perspective can be misappropriated and depoliticized. As she explains it:

> For African-American women as a collectivity, redefining marginality as a potential source of strength fostered a powerful oppositional knowledge ([Hill] Collins 1990). Moreover, the work of Black women and other similarly situated groups participated in a much larger project that used the margins as a source of intellectual freedom and strength (see, e.g., Anzaldúa 1987).
>
> Despite these contributions, the continued efficacy of marginality as a space of radical openness remains questionable. Over time, the connections between the center/margin metaphor as a heuristic device and actual core/periphery relations became less clear. While continuing to reference power relations, talk of centers and margins became increasingly distanced from its initial grounding in structural, group-based power relations. (Hill Collins 1998, 128–39)

Hill Collins thus argues that notions of marginality and resistance must be grounded in analyses of the structures of gender, race, sexuality, and class power and avoid loose notions that locate resistance and marginality in whatever subject-position a writer chooses to validate. Moreover, as I argue in the next section, adequately theorizing oppression and resistance requires engaging of the thematics of globalization, a theme that I will suggest is centrally relevant to my focus on violence against women and children.

GLOBALIZATION AND THE OPPRESSION
OF WOMEN AND CHILDREN

In addition to providing tools to critically analyze colonization and violence against women and children, Borderland theory is also important in that it addresses the forms of globalization that currently are structuring more and more domains of everyday life. Zillah Eisenstein argues that the "rearticulation of race/sex/gender borders for the twenty-first century is undermined by the global market even as the boundaries of the fantasmatic 'east' and 'west' are re-encoded (in the 'export' version of feminism" (1996, 109–10). She notes, "We are living through the transition from the bourgeois nation-state to an unknown governance structure of transnational global capital: a nation-state defined by global capital and its racialized, patriarchal, cybermedia-led relations" (Eisenstein 1998, 22).

Within this context, it becomes apparent that many aspects of Anzaldúa's elaboration of living in the Borderlands are apt characterizations of many of the kinds of oppression that typify the everyday lives of those trapped within the prison of family terrorism. Indeed, these kinds of contextual dialectical approaches, which are predicated on and committed to changing real material conditions, are extremely useful for addressing issues such as male violence against women and the abuse of children. It is within this context that situations of family terrorism, focused on in this text, are intended as a shocking reminder of the kinds of practical atrocities that must be confronted within feminist theory and practice.

However, not all feminists have addressed the situation of family and state terrorism on a global scale. Anzaldúa's irate indictment of Borderland violence, however, raises the issue of globalized terror and provides perspectives from which family terrorism on a global scale can be elucidated. Joy James offers a historical, contextual analysis of the dehumanizing and growing disparity between the haves and the have-nots. She identifies the devastating effects of globalization on women and children, in particular:

> Throughout the 1980s, Western underdevelopment and IMF austerity programs worldwide pushed women and children of color deeper in poverty. The Environmental Defense Fund in 1994 cited the World Bank and the debt crisis as largely responsible for income disparities between the richest and poorest nations, which were at a ratio of ten to one in 1948, grew to 30 to one in 1960, and exploded to sixty to one in 1989. . . . According to the UNICEF report, nearly 900 million people, one-sixth of humanity, had sunk deeper into poverty by 1988. These increasing rates of impoverishment, disease, and death occur mostly in Africa and Latin America, where average incomes declined 10 percent to 25 percent in the 1980s, and spending on health and education were reduced 50 percent and 25 percent, respectively. At least half a million young children die each year from debt-induced poverty in these two regions. (James 1996, 229)

On a global level, the issues of family terrorism include economic, political, and cultural violence against oppressed peoples, the shifting nature of alienation, in part precipitated by rising unemployment and expanding poverty rates, and escalating forms of oppression such as slavery and child prostitution. World poverty statistics in the new millennium are indeed shocking:

> Poverty goes beyond lack of income. It encompasses economic, social, and governance dimensions. Economically, the poor are not only deprived of income and resources, but of opportunities. . . . 1.2 billion people are estimated to still live on less than $1 per day, and almost 3 billion on less than $2 per day. 110 million primary school age children are out of school, 60 percent of them girls. 31 million people are infected with HIV/AIDS. And many more live without adequate food, shelter, safe water, and sanitation. (Asian Development Bank 2001, www.adb.org)

Jan Pettman (1996) and others have established, the unpredictable and chaotic transfigurations generated by globalization have had hardly beneficial effects on the state of international womanhood. Pettman, for one, takes great pains to preface her findings on the prevalent effects of globalization on women, by citing the difficulties in generalizing about women's relations with varying states due to obvious lack of information, censorship, and inaccurate reports. Still, it is clear that decolonization, independence, and shifts in many world states—especially within the so-called third or developing world—have not significantly improved the majority of women's status.

> Almost all states have become increasingly centralised and bureaucratized, and increasingly important in women's lives. . . . Almost all states have been concerned to control women's sexuality and fertility, and the status of women often signal priorities in state and nation building. . . . Despite the variety of state projects and women's response to them, we can make some generalisations about women and the state, which appear to be universal. (Pettman 1996, 13)

Furthermore, Pettman notes how state discourse renders women invisible, often refuses to address their problems and the specificities of their oppression, and exploits their labor.[10] Shockingly, the "torture of women and girls persists on a daily basis across the globe. . . . Torture is fed by a global culture which denies equal rights with men, and which legitimises violence against women." Although the perpetuators are sometimes agents of the state and armed groups, *"most often they are members of their own family, community or employers. For many women, their home is a place of terror"* ("Broken Bodies, Shattered Minds: The Torture of Women Worldwide," *Amnesty International News Release*, Mar. 6, 2001, www.amnesty.org, my emphasis).

Kevin Bales (1999) provides cogent explications of the colonization process in his courageous exposé of contemporary slavery as provoked by current multinational globalization. Indeed, one of the most repellent, underreported, yet astounding consequences of this combination of the escalation of population, unequal development under global capitalism, and intensifying poverty is the development of what Bales defines as the "New Slavery." He estimates that there

are more than twenty-seven million slaves in the world today—indeed, some estimates put the figure as high as two hundred million (1999, 9). While he does not
highlight this point, his analyses demonstrate that the majority of these slaves are
women and children. It is worth noting that the reference is not to what is often
euphemistically referred to as slave labor, but actual slavery, where *"a person [is]
held by violence or the threat of violence for economic exploitation"* (Bales 1999, 280).

Bales describes the continuation of master-slave relations that perpetuate the
heritage and evils of colonization in the contemporary era. As an example, he
depicts a girl who is one of the approximately thirty-five thousand young women
who are enslaved as prostitutes in the highly lucrative and burgeoning sex trade
market in Thailand (Bales 1999, 43f)—and which is supported by the U.S. military, UN, IMF, World Bank, Thai government, and multinational corporations.
As Bales points out, only one in twenty of the between half a million and one
million Thai prostitutes is a slave (43). But the wages of those who are not are
hardly lucrative, given that the average working prostitute receives only a small
percentage of the customary $4.00 cost for her services (Rogers, *Ms.*, Oct./Nov.,
1999, 52). Bales's characterization of Siri—a fifteen-year-old debt bondage slave,
who was sold to a brothel in Thailand by her parents when she was fourteen and
is forced to "entertain" an average of fifteen men per night—is an evocative report
of the insidiousness of colonization (1999, 34).

> When I sat with Siri in the brothel in Thailand and looked into the flat deadness of
> her eyes, listened to the hopelessness in her voice, and the destruction of her person-
> ality and her will to escape, I glimpsed the horror of a life captured and destroyed to
> feed the greed of the slaveholder. It is not easy to crush a human mind, but with
> enough brutality, time, and indifference to suffering it can be done. Around the
> world it *is* being done. The slaveholders provide the brutality, the corrupt police and
> governments ensure that slavery is practiced with impunity, and the overarching
> materialism of our global economy justifies a general indifference. (Bales 1999, 246)

Bales goes on to explain the deep-rooted intricacies and incarcerating power
of colonization—which takes place at many different dimensions. In fact, he
compares the problems associated with liberation of slaves with those experienced
by abused children (and many women, I might add). It is within this kind of
dialectical context that the notion of colonization is useful in addressing issues of
violence against women and children. For in addition to slavery, the prostitution
of women and children is growing on a global scale.[11]

Jyota Sangera (1997) argues that prostitution is indeed a central "income generating strategy" for the global economy. Sangera provides a striking analysis of
the industrialization and transnationalization of the sex trade, the ways that the
industry functions in developing countries' economies, and the ways that women
are incorporated into a new sex industry that includes disgusting practices such as:

> savvy and skillful prostitutes massage male egos and bodies with adroit expertise;
> young, aboriginal girls are purveyed as virgins to customers expressing such demands;

women of every colour and ethnicity can be procured via the sex industry; young girls, fresh from the countryside, are trained in hazardous sexual acrobatics such as inserting razor blades, glass bottles and lighted cigarettes into their vaginas in order to entertain; and venues for sexual adventures can be arranged in Brazil, Cuba, Russia, Kenya, Goa, Sri Lanka, Vietnam, Thailand, the Philippines, Taiwan, etc. (1997, 5)

It is also depressing to note the incorporation of children into the sex industry. The ECPAT, an international advocacy organization in Thailand, estimates that one million children are child prostitutes in Asia:

[M]any of the girls are sold into prostitution by their families, and as indentured sexual servants they are forced to work off the debt. Unable to leave or find alternative employment, they often become slaves to the brothel and bar owners. . . . The most vulnerable group are the women and girls working in back-alley brothels who are kept in tiny rooms or displayed like zoo animals with numbered placards. Many of them were sold into "debt bondage" by their poor, rural families who received a lump sum in return. Once they get locked into these brothels the girls must work off their debt, servicing on average from five to twenty clients a day. (*Ms.*, Mar./Apr., 1997, 15–16)

Betty Rogers, in her well-documented and shocking exposé of the slave trade and trafficking of children in Thailand (*Ms.*, Oct./Nov., 1999, 45–53), also provides extensive documentation of this indictment. Indeed, it is so well investigated, yet so underreported, that aspects of her findings are worth quoting at length.

The explosion of the sex trade and the resulting trafficking of girls sold by their families or who sell themselves to survive goes to the heart of what has gone awry with Thailand's economic transformation. The current sex trade is not just an unexpected by-product of modernization. It is the result of a *distinct strategy of development, one that has been supported by the U.S. and Thai militaries, the United Nations, the World Bank, the International Monetary Fund (IMF) and Western donor nations.* (48; emphasis mine)

Rogers further points out that the U.S. military was of crucial importance in helping establish the sex industry in Thailand when "Robert S. McNamara, U.S. secretary of defense, oversaw the signing of a Recreation and Relaxation, or R&R, contract with the Thai government to provide vacation furloughs for soldiers fighting in Vietnam" (48).[12] McNamara returned to Thailand as head of the World Bank in 1971, and the organization encouraged Thailand to develop its tourist trade as a source of foreign exchange to ward off its debts. The result was that the sex industry became a key element of the national economy. Rogers concludes, "Sex workers are now the primary breadwinners for many families: according to the ILO, urban prostitutes transfer U.S. $300 million in net income to rural families annually, a sum that exceeds the budget of many government development programs" (48).

Hence, viewed on a global scale, the majority of the poor and underclassed in the United States (and the world system) are women and children. Both the U.S. Agency for International Development and the Save the Children Organization readily admit to what they refer to as the "sexism" of poverty. According to a UN study:

> Although the gender gap in rates of economic activity is narrowing, the nature of women's and men's participation in the labour force continues to be very different. Women still have to reconcile family responsibilities and market work and they work in different jobs and occupations than men, most often with lower status. Women have always engaged in the less formal types of work, working as unpaid workers in a family business, in the informal sector or in various types of household economic activities. They also continue to receive less pay than men. In manufacturing, for example, in 27 or the 39 countries with data available, women's wages were 20 to 50 per cent less than those of men. However, the limited data suggest that the differential between women's and men's earnings narrowed between 1990 and 1997 in the majority of these countries. ("The World's Women 2000 Overview," United Nations 2000; www.un.org)

The revolting grounds for this cancerous expansion of female poverty, according to the International Fund for Agricultural Development, is due to "the shift to capitalism in many countries that until recently had centrally planned economies" (*New York Times*, May 27, 1997, 1). An International Labor Organization study, conducted in 1996, rationalized this "discrepancy" on "the negative impact of economic reform and transition to market economies has tended to hit women harder than men. . . . The newly free-market economies, for example, have typically concentrated their limited job-training resources on men" (*New York Times*, May 27, 1997, 1).

Moreover, with the ever-shifting nature of state lines and boundaries, immigration has become far more prevalent and a source of scapegoating among those peoples who compose the "haves" of this new global situation. And it is not without regard that many of these new groups of immigrants represent the disenfranchised and marginalized of the world. Most often they are people of color whose "difference" provokes a revitalization of the kinds of "identity politics" and "culture wars" that maintain colonized attitudes and suppress the kinds of real internationalist coalition politics that must be adopted for the preservation and conservation of a humanistically sane planet. And it is hardly surprising to note that:

> Huge numbers of women and girls are forced migrants and refugees—in Bosnia, Angola, Rwanda, Haiti, and other countries. They comprise almost 80 percent of displaced persons in Africa, Asia, and Latin America. Two-thirds of the total refugee

population in Somalia were women. In Bosnia, 80 percent of the 23 million refugees uprooted by the violence were women. (Eisenstein 1998, 140)

As Sangera notes, women are undergoing a feminization of migration in the third world as a result of globalization. In her words:

In the new configuration of forces of the global economy, women have been identified as the new natural resource. Thus, third world women are the new prime export item and come to constitute the new ingredient for national development and international trade. As the new resource, it is their reproductive labour which is in growing demand. As a result, third world women are moving in to constitute the backbone of the service sector at an international plane, engaging primarily in domestic and sex work. In the production of industries, they continue to constitute the bulk of the workforce, making garments, shoes, electronics, etc. for the world market. The demand for third world women as labour is whetted on account of the pressure to intensify capital accumulation—this feminized category of labour is constructed through a sophisticated combination of economic need, racist stereotyping and patriarchal oppression. Consequently, this labour is the most accessible, vulnerable and exploitable for the forces of global capitalism. (1997)

Audre Lorde has adequately captured the Borderland perspective toward difference, while at the same time advocating a position that has become increasingly more urgent, given these times of global upheavals and scapegoating of immigrants—and those who are "other." Indeed, she provides perhaps one of the most impressive accounts of the dialectical and historical contextualization of both the initial necessities for what has been labeled "identity politics" as well as the necessary transformation of this position, into the more dialectical theory and politics that both respect and embrace differences, such as a transformative alliance politics.

Those of us who stand outside the circle of this society's definition of acceptable women; those of us who have been forged in the crucibles of difference—those of us who are poor, who are lesbians who are Black, who are older—know that *survival is not an academic skill*. It is learning how to stand alone, unpopular and sometime reviled, and how to make common cause with those others identified as outside the structures in order to define and seek a world in which we can all flourish. It is learning how to take our differences and make them strengths. (Lorde 1984, 112)

While we should recognize the growing role of the global oppression of women and children, we should avoid collapsing and symmetrizing relations between the colonized and women, thus failing to see the contradictory and conflicted nature of social reality. Laura Donaldson notes the destructive consequences of one-dimensional and decontextualized employment of colonization theory in relation to women:

Further, the woman = colonized, man = colonizer metaphor lacks any awareness of gender—or colonialism, for that matter—as a contested field, an overdeterminded sociopolitical grid whose identity points are often contradictory. Historical colonialism demonstrates the political as well as theoretical necessity of abandoning the idea of women's (and men's) gender identity as fixed and coherent. Instead, it imbues us with a conception of gender as a site of conflicting subjective processes and makes it impossible to ignore the contradictory social positioning of white, middle-class women as both colonized patriarchal objects and colonizing race-privileged subjects. (Donaldson 1992, 6)

Once again the saliency of the interrelationships of contradiction, dialectical both/and epistemology, and the realities of the real concrete material conditions of gender, sexuality, class, and race are emphasized in Donaldson's explanation of misrepresentation of colonization theory. However, it is a mistake to equate this blunder with the majority of feminists and, by association, to promote their demonization as proponents of identity politics and victim feminism, which has been exploited by some vulgar feminists critics.

Indeed, much feminist discourse on family terrorism has been sensationalized and attacked by both antifeminists and the mainstream media and has become the focal point of widespread attacks on feminism that often identify feminism with controversial positions on rape, violence against women, or pornography. On the other hand, many mainstream liberal feminists have concentrated on issues that appear to appeal to an elite or privileged group of women who seem to be out of touch with the realities of material, concrete conditions of the everyday lives of women. As Carol Stabile describes it, mainstream feminist groups including the National Association of Women "invested most of its time, energy, and funding into the ill-fated Equal Rights Amendment campaign. . . . And during the mid-eighties, when cutbacks in health and welfare spending were drastically affecting huge numbers of women, men, and their children, feminists like Catherine MacKinnon and Andrea Dworkin were pursuing antipornography legislation as the solution to violence against women" (1994, 57).

Hence, in conclusion we must discuss issues of feminist practice and the theory and politics needed to address violence against women and children.

FROM THEORY TO PRACTICE: CONTRADICTION, STRUGGLE, AND DECOLONIALIZATION

Audre Lorde's eloquent and incisive words on the complex multidimensional theoretical nature and concrete reality of difference as lived experience powerfully express the seminal importance of this notion within the ever-developing environment of contemporary revolutionary feminist thought. Moreover, her impassioned plea for a dialectical synthesis of difference and "common cause" aptly articulates an important arena of heated debate within feminist theory. Lorde's inspirational words also underlie the faith of borderland feminists in international, multicultural alliances. Rather than rejecting oppositions and disagreements, it is important to agree to accept and often transcend such contradictions. Recognizing that, as Mary Childers and bell hooks so insightfully remind us, not only are "contradictions" *not* unresolvable binary oppositional relations, they point to conflicts that should be resolved, social antagonisms that should be overcome, and problems that should be solved. Dealing with these kinds of conflicts, however, often becomes a frustrating process in that contradictions become reduced and symmetrized into battle-oriented oppositions of ideas and theoretical positions. Such a war of words can, and too often does, perpetuate the maintenance of the colonized divide-and-conquer mentality. Such reduction of struggle to a battle of ideas is frequently apparent in academic journal agonistics, which can, unfortunately, be confusing and have the overall effect of alienating the potential progressives and academic scholars of the future. As Childers and hooks point out:

> We live in a culture that makes it seem as though having contradictions is bad—most of us try to represent ourselves in ways that suggest we are without contradictions. Contradictions are perceived as chaos and not orderly, not rational, everything doesn't follow. Coming out of academe, many of us want to present ourselves as just that: orderly, rational. We also must struggle for a language that allows us to say: we have contradictions and those contradictions do not necessarily make us quote "bad people" or politically unsound people. We have to be willing as women and as feminists and as other groups of people, including men who enter feminist discussion, to work with those contradictions and almost to celebrate their existence because they mean we are in a process of change and transformation. I think it has been very hard to do that. (1990, 70)

One major problem associated with this pivotal conceptualization called "contradiction" is identified by feminist philosopher Sandra Bartky, who links material concrete practices to the concept of contradictions. Bartky also indicates the fundamental role of contradiction in the lives of the borderland peoples who populate global society: "Clearly, any adequate account of the 'contradictions' of late capitalism, that is, of the conflicts, the instabilities, the ways in which some parts of the social whole are out of phase with others, would be a complex and elaborate task. But whatever a complete account of these contradictions would look like, it is essential to understand as concretely as possible how the contradictory factors we are able to identify are lived and suffered by particular people" (Bartky 1990, 13–14).

Indeed, Bartky grasps the crux of the issue of the nature of contradiction and the necessity for readopting and assessing it, especially in regard to the development of a dialectical feminism and addressing the chaos of global change. She also rightly points out that it was "contradiction" that provoked both the new left and the second-wave feminist movement.

What triggered feminist consciousness most immediately, no doubt, were the civil rights movement and the peace and student movements of the sixties; while they had other aims as well, the latter movements may also be read as expressions of protest against the growing bureaucratization, depersonalization, and inhumanity of late capitalist society. Women often found themselves forced to take subordinate positions within these movements; it did not take long for them to see the contradiction between the oppression these movements were fighting in the larger society and their own continuing oppression in the life of these movements themselves. (Bartky 1990, 13)

Bartky contends that "two features of current social reality which, if not sufficient, are at least necessary conditions for the emergence of feminist consciousness. These features constitute, in addition, much of the content of this consciousness. I refer, first, to the existence of what Marxists call 'contradictions' in our society and, second, to the presence, due to these same contradictions, of concrete circumstances which would permit a significant alteration in the status of women" (1990, 12).

Bartky also argues that cognizant awareness of everyday material relations provides the critical and reflexive consciousness that provokes a metacritical feminist outlook. Moreover, she proceeds to explain the multileveled dimensions of this kind of perspective, which are hardly absolute or essentialized, but involve removing the blinders of ideological formulations and myths that have obstructed so much of our vision of the real world. Indeed, this is a task that has become identified with those being described as borderland feminists, who, owing to real material conditions of difference and otherness, are often, but not always, revolutionary women of color. Bartky's lucid delineation of dialectical process helps to bring together the significance of its relationship to the deeper and more complex intricacies of colonization:

The relationship between consciousness and concrete circumstances can best be described as "dialectical." Feminist consciousness is more than a mere reflection of external material conditions, for the transforming and negating perspective which it incorporates first allows these conditions to be revealed *as* the conditions they are. But on the other hand, apprehension of some state of affairs as intolerable, as to-be-transformed, does not, in and of itself, transform it. (Bartky 1990, 15)

Patricia Hill Collins expands on and clarifies the essential renunciation of dualistic thinking that underlies a critical-dialectical feminist perspective (1990 and 1998). She provides insights into the kinds of distinctive knowledge that is to be gained by those who analyze oppression and domination from the perspective of "difference" and "otherness." However, because she is advocating a dialectical "both/and" perspective, she is promoting the alliance politics epistemology encouraged by many borderland feminists. Thus, Hill Collins and other borderland feminists eschew the dualistic, restricted ideologies attributed to some scholars who advocate viewpoints labeled "identity politics" or "epistemic privilege."

Moreover, contrary to antifeminists like Paglia and Hoff Sommers, a wide range of feminists eschew the "victim" mentality, stressing instead agency and struggle, moving from theory to practice. As Anzaldúa puts it:

> We are beginning to realize that we are not wholly at the mercy of circumstances, nor are our lives completely out of our hands. That if we posture as victims we *will* be victims, that hopelessness is suicide, that self-attacks stop us in our tracks. We are slowly moving past the resistance within, leaving behind the defeated images. We have come to realize that we are not alone in our struggles nor separate not autonomous but that we—white black straight queer female male—are connected and interdependent. (Anzaldúa 1981)

Indeed, for decades, feminists have stressed the need to posit women as subjects and agents and not just objects and victims. Gerda Lerner, for example, argued that many earlier feminists eschewed the symmetrized victimology that antifeminists like Paglia, Wolf, Hoff Sommers and others attribute to the contemporary feminist imaginary and imagined feminist cabal they denounce as "gender," "insider," "victim," or whatever other snappy epithet is currently employed. Indeed, Lerner's sharp critique of patriarchy does not impede the underlying understanding, recognition, and commitment shared by many feminists toward the role of agency, empowerment, and consciousness, stressing instead both oppression and struggle with a context that recognizes women's shared and different, collective and individual experiences.

> While women have been victimized by . . . aspects of their long subordination to men, it is a fundamental error to try to conceptualize women primarily as victims. To do so at once obscures what must be assumed as a given of women's historical situation: Women are essential and central to creating society; they are and always have been actors and agents in history. . . . The tension between women's actual historical experience and their exclusion from interpreting that experience I have called "the dialectics of women's history."
>
> The contradiction between women's centrality and active role in society and their marginality in the meaning-giving process of interpretation and explanation has been a dynamic force, causing women to struggle against their condition. When, in that process of struggle, at certain historic moments, the contradictions in their relationship to society and to historical process are brought into the consciousness of women, they are often correctly perceived and named as deprivations that women share. . . . This coming-into-consciousness of women becomes the dialectical force moving them into action to change their condition and to enter a new relationship to male-dominated society. (Lerner 1986, 5)

Thus, it is important to note that appropriately responding to violence against women requires positioning women as agents and not just victims. Even feminists who had employed the term *victim* used it in a far more dialectical/contradictory manner than the fallacious, flattened versions described by antifeminists, the popular media, and some mainstream feminists. As Bart and Moran explain it, "we do not define women as simply victims who have no agency or coping strategies, although the issue is usually presented as either one or the other. Women use agency in coping with our lives, including our exploitation, though women have considerably less power institutional relationships than men. One does not negate the other, although for some feminist theorists the term *victim* is taboo" (1993, xv).

Moreover, contrary to the claims of many critics of feminism, most feminists do not identify colonization and oppression with men alone and construct a Manichaean opposition between men and women. The contradictory and paradoxical nature of colonization demonstrates how white women, for instance, could be colonized by the white male patriarchy in both the domestic and public spheres, yet could at the same time be colonizer in relation to the disenfranchised or people of color and to her own children. Thus, feminist appropriations of colonization theory are neither anti-men per se nor do they posit women alone or exclusively as victims.

Indeed, the hyperbolic depictions of "victim feminism" by antifeminists are not only a symmetrization of dialectical relations and multifarious conditions, they are countered by critical transformative feminisms, which address the complexities of violence against women and children within the contextual frameworks of colonization and globalization. For many of these insurgent feminisms necessarily examine, in Bat-Ami Bar On's words,

> the violence that women partake in—a violence that feminists tend to avoid discussing—whether in the case of child abuse, battering relations, genocide or war. What I wonder about is if and how feminist understandings of violence, understandings shaped so much by the feminist analyses of the rape of women by men, will change when having to grapple seriously with the fact of women's engagements with violence, with women as abusive mothers and partners, women torturers, women guerrilla fighters, women police officers, women terrorists, women combat soldiers, women hunters, or women who [are] training [in] the martial arts and [who] study and teach self-defense." (1996, 4)

Bar On identifies major revisions in epistemological and ideological thoughts and beliefs for the necessary and appropriate inclusion of the reality of different women as collaborators and colonizers, terrorists, torturers, and murders. This project involves recognizing heterogeneity, difference, and contradiction at the same time it analyses shared oppression and seeks practices to overcome violence against women and children. Bar On herself is confident that new emergent forms of critical feminisms, in relation to the multicontextual and often enigmatic dimensions of violence against women and children on national and global scales, will develop and become a legitimate arena of theory and praxis.

Yet I would argue that her hopes have long been realized in the eclectic and diverse dialectical, transformative feminisms that are being constructed by a multiplicity of activists and Borderland feminists on a global scale (which is not to exclude white insurgent critical feminisms who are also contributing to a transformative epistemology).[13] At the same time, however, the pseudofeminist backlash ignores or attacks actual movements and struggles to address violence against women and children and has recently developed a new diversionary tactic to decenter attention from violence against women and children. Ironically, now it is boys rather than women who are being victimized. Hoff Sommers's recent book *The War against Boys* (2000) claims that feminists and the educational and political establishments are privileging girls and ignoring the problems of boys who are the new super-oppressed group in her fantasy. It is thus highly ironic that the concept of "victimization"—previously stigmatized by antifeminists—has been "sanitized" and transposed to attack primarily feminists and women for a bizarre new "crisis"—the victimization of boys. Not only does it present a very universalized depiction of boys, but it participates in the white male backlash against feminism that has been accelerating in the past decade.

The current terrain thus reveals a highly conflicted field of feminist and antifeminist theory and practice concerning patriarchal violence against women and children. Because, as I have argued throughout this study, there are multiple causes of violence, there are accordingly a multiplicity of practices to address the problem. Thus, because the causes of violence against women and children are complex, overdetermined, and multiple, there is no one answer to the question "What is to be done?" We can distinguish between liberal reformist strategies that work within the system and more revolutionary transformative strategies. Kathleen Ferraro points out that within the feminist antibattering movement of the early 1970s, "there were debates between those focused on legal and service reform and those committed to radical transformation of patriarchy. The more radical position stressed the relationship between male-dominated nuclear families and woman battering." However this critical feminist perspective has, unfortunately, "been obliterated from domestic violence discourse. Critique of women's position within the family and the larger culture has been silenced by the rhetoric 'of family values' " (Ferraro 1996, 83–84).

Today, liberal, radical, and transnational feminisms include activist and grassroots projects that involve community-based projects such as the creation of battered women's shelters and support groups and working within the UN and other global organizations for women's rights. A number of transformative feminists today, however, call for a more radical decolonization of women in response to efforts at recolonization within globalization. There are, indeed, many levels to decolonization just are there are different dimensions of colonization and globalization (see the sections above). Gloria Anzaldúa and other Borderland feminists call for development of epistemological and practical strategies to make visible and resist the pathological ideological process of colonization. In regard to the underlying racist and sexist dimensions that characterize not only the organization of (most) societies but also the psychic mentalities of both the colonized and the colonizer, she advances a critical transformative feminist theory and praxis of decolonization. Anzaldúa asserts that to "combat racism and sexism and . . . 'work through' internalized violence, . . . we [must] attempt to decolonize ourselves and to find ways to survive personally, culturally and racially" (1990b, xvii).

Borderland feminist Gloria Yamato provides us with an apt description of the multifarious and insidious consequences and insidious power of the psychic dimensions of colonization on the colonized, in her delineation of "internalized oppression":

> Members of the target group are emotionally, physically, and spiritually battered to the point that they begin to actually believe that their oppression is deserved, is their lot in life, is natural and right, and that it doesn't even exist.
>
> The oppression begins to feel comfortable, familiar enough that when ol' Massa lay down de whip, we gots to pick up and whack ourselves and each other. Like a virus, its hard to beat racism because by the time you come up with a cure it's mutated to a "new cure resistant" form. One shot just won't get it. Racism must be attacked from many angles. (Yamato 1990, 20)

It is this kind of colonized behavior that is often attributed to abused children and especially battered women, who are so often not only physically but also mentally tortured so that their perspective on the world becomes that of the colonizers in regard to themselves. Yamato thus correctly argues that feminists must address the psychically debilitated colonized mentalities that have been systematically ingrained in the "hearts and minds" of women and children being violated, terrorized, injured, maimed, and killed within the constraints of family and global terrorisms (which often interact). Because this process closely resembles the analogies of colonization and internalized oppression, feminists need a theory and practice of decolonization. This practice would ridicule and neutralize the ideological myths of the "willing victim" and the fallacious "victimization" debates that are proving divisive for feminisms in general and perpetuating particular damage and delegitimation on any feminisms committed to studying, intervening in, or recontexualing family and globalized terrorism, poverty, or slavery.

Moreover, as M. Jacqui Alexander and Chandra Talpade Mohanty argue, decolonization must constantly struggle against ever new and insidious forms of recolonization (1997, xxii). Alexander and Mohanty argue that "recolonization" is a response to global crises of capitalism that require new modes of disciplining and controlling subject peoples. In their words:

> Because no variety of feminism—particularly feminism in the Third World—has escaped state intervention, control, discipline, and surveillance; and because the state (particularly the postcolonial state) facilitates the transnational movement of capital within national borders and is, therefore, instrumental in the reconfiguring of global

relationships; and because capitalism and these processes of recolonization structure the contemporary practices of postcolonial and advanced capitalist/colonial states, the state figures centrally in any analytic attempt to grapple with colonial legacies. Thus, a focus on the state seems especially crucial at a time when many of the attempts to manage the global crisis in capitalism are enacted by the state apparatus. [Structural Adjustment Policies (SAP), the most recent unequal realignments among multinational capital, the International Monetary Fund, and the World Bank, are cases in point.] (1997, xxiii)

One example of recolonization discussed above involves the increasing com- modification of women and children in the global labor market, ranging from cheap labor to prostitution to slavery. As Sangera notes, women and children are "new cash crops" in the new global economy whose bodies and labor-power are superexploited. Decolonization, in this context, would thus involve struggles against capitalist and patriarchal global oppression and the liberation of minds and bodies. Decolonization is thus both a theory and practice that involves an epistemological reframing that involves thinking transnationally and seeing femi- nist democracy in global terms (Alexander and Mohanty 1997). In fact, Valentine M. Moghadam in her critical global feminist studies and analyses of "Transna- tional Feminism" reminds us that:

Responses to this state of affairs have come from various sources, including transna- tional feminist networks (TFNs). These are organizations whose membership spans three or more countries, bringing together women of diverse nationalities around a common agenda, typically pertaining to women's human rights or to economic pol- icy issues. In concert with other transnational advocacy networks, TFNs have addressed themselves to the crises and growing inequalities decribed above through research, advocacy, lobbying, and direct action. As advocates for women, they criti- cize the inequalities women face in the spheres of production and reproduction. (Moghadam 2001, 6)

Addressing issues of recolonization by capital and the state requires worldwide alliances and solidarities to struggle against violence against women on a global scale. Alexander and Mohanty suggest that transformative feminists learn from Audre Lorde "the necessity of accountability in envisioning, forming, and main- taining community. For us this means becoming attentive to and accountable for the work that we are called upon to do and scrutinizing the very terms and ways in which we gain self- and community definition. . . . [Yet] we develop these tools in order to better understand and engage with the world, and in order to bring about revolutionary change" (1997, ix–x).

Hence, in addition to local struggles and movements, new global alliances and solidarities have been and continue to be developed. Leading feminist activist and scholar Charlotte Bunch articulates the importance and challenges of coalition politics writing:

For coalitions are one of the most common strategies for creating social change, and the arguments that accompany them are recurring themes in all movements. Discourse about when, where, and how to build coalitions is particularly important when we seek to make change that is inclusive of diverse perspectives. For feminists the ability to create a movement that includes and responds to the diversity of women's lives are crucial. (Bunch 1990, 49).

There are, however, problems with abstract invocations of alliance, especially at a global level. For as Sangera reminds us:

> Just as a class is not a homogenous or universal category and is internally divided along gender lines, gender itself is not a homogenous or universal category. While all women are subjected to some measure of patriarchal prejudice within each class, and this fact may form the basis of gender solidarity among women across classes, yet women are in turn hierarchically located with respect to each other on the basis of class, racial, ethnic and regional background. Thus while a woman from a marginalized cultural community such as the Tamang from Nepal may face patriarchal discrimination just as a white woman from a privileged class in Canada may, the commonality of oppression ends right there, and this commonality too is very fragile. An exploration of the special matrices of power and privilege which defines a Tamang woman's life will reveal that their reality is linked to the woman from Canada not through bonds of similarity but through a hierarchical structure of privilege and oppression with the former unequivocally oppressed in relation to the latter who is categorically privileged. (1997, 3)[14]

Thus, in conclusion I would argue for the need to recognize differences *and* solidarities, to valorize the importance of local struggles *and* global alliances, to examine intersections between the global *and* the local, and to accept contradictions *and* differences among divergent groups and cultures. For those among the more privileged groups, this involves solidarity with a wide range of oppressed groups and support of a multiplicity of struggles and movements. And it requires solidarity that embraces and, when appropriate, negotiates differences. In Eisenstein's transformative vision:

> Many women across the globe are building dialogues that contribute to a public discourse that deploys public-mindedness in the fight against violence, hunger, poverty, the destruction of the environment, and sexual/racial oppression. Some women see transnational capitalist patriarchy and its consumerist culture as the "real" culprit of these evils, while others see different variations of this theme.
>
> In order to build transnational democratic discussions and actions, women will have to deliberate carefully and continually across political, cultural, and economic differences. Such dialogue which both mutes and invites conflict—can build a transnational public of women's and girl's voices that creates the very same liberatory democratic process it imagines. (Eisenstein 1998, 163)

NOTES

1. Alice Echols raises similar concerns about the binary dichotomies implicit in many antiporn positions, which could impede contextual analyses and research into male violence against women: "Many women involved in this struggle . . . recommend some form of censorship to eliminate pornography. While the elimination of violence is crucial, there is reason to be dismayed by the movements' assumption, despite the dearth of solid, confirming evidence, that pornography is a causative factor. And there is reason to be alarmed by its casual attitude toward establishing causality" (1993, 448).

2. Morgan had second thoughts about the use of colonization theory, identifying potential problems associated with use of the metaphor in that "Such comparisons are invidious in terms of human suffering—no scale dare weigh that, and no analysis, political or otherwise, had better 'compare and contrast' that—although such more-oppressed-than-thou approaches are attempted all the time" (1992, 39).

For precisely this reason, the colonial analogy is insufficient to describe women's predicament as universal: we are not only colonized as women per se, but also as members of varied gender, race, class, sexual, and other kinds of populations who have been colonized in a diversity of ways. Consequently, the manner in which colonization is employed both within this text and by many feminists encompasses the multidimensional nature of this pathological process, and in no way treats it as a one-dimensional relation. Indeed, bell hooks accuses those who reduce this expression of "appropriating the horror of the slave experience to enhance their own cause" (1981, 126). In other words "to imply . . . that all women suffer the same oppression simply because we are women, is to lose sight of the many varied tools of patriarchy" (Lorde, cited in Minh-ha 1989, 101).

3. Patricia Hill Collins (1998), for instance, urges this multiperspectival approach and argues against privileging women of color as the most oppressed objects of colonization, pointing out that black women too can be colonizers or collaborators (241ff). She notes how women of color can privilege their own marginality for personal advancement and gain, showing how the conception of marginality can be depoliticized and misappropriated. Hill Collins also stresses the specificity of particular experiences of oppression and the need for alliances between marginalized groups.

4. Hill Collins (1998) clarifies the need for dialectical both/and perspectives that articulate both the differences in types of women's oppression according to determinant of class, race, sexuality, and so on, and the commonalities of oppressed women and need for alliances between women and other oppressed groups.

5. In a later text, hooks goes on to explain her relationship to Freire's writing and politics:

There has never been a moment when reading Freire that I have not remained aware of not only the sexism of the language but the way he (like other progressive Third World political leaders, intellectuals, critical thinkers such as Fanon, Memmi, etc.) constructs a phallocentric paradigm of liberation—wherein freedom and the experience of patriarchal manhood are always linked as though they are one and the same. For me this is always a source of anguish for it represents a blind spot in the vision of men who have profound insight. And yet, I never wish to see a critique of this blind spot overshadow anyone's (and feminists in particular) capacity to learn from the insights. . . . Freire's own model of critical pedagogy invites a critical interrogation of this flaw in the work. (1993b, 148)

6. On the public/private distinction, which is a founding category of bourgeois social and political theory and that relegates women to the family and domestic spaces, Linda J. Nicholson writes: "These categories have played an important role within feminist theory, and I believe rightly so. Many feminist theorists have correctly intuited that these categories point to societal divisions that have been central to the structuring of gender in modern Western society, at least. Some theorists have even argued that a more-general separation, expressed in the opposition between 'domestic' ['private'] and 'public,' has been universally important in organizing gender" (1984, 221). On the distinction, see also Fraser 1989 and Muszynski 1991.

7. McBride was trained in interdisciplinary study of social ethics and specializes in the intersection of religious studies with feminist, psychoanalytic, and legal theory. As I note in chapter 3, he deploys an eloquent and multiperspectival analysis of the social, political, psychological, and economic factors, which takes account of the diversity of causes of wife battering.

8. Valerie Smith also emphasizes the significance of intersectionality as a theoretical concept. The term, according to Smith, first coined by Kimberlie Crenshaw, provides an "underlying premise" of much black feminist thinking. It enables black feminists to "explore what it means to deploy intersectionality as a mode of cultural or textual analysis, what it means to read at the intersections of constructions of race, gender, class and sexuality" (1998, xiv).

9. McBride writes, "Although many heterosexual males may not consider themselves homosexual, they nonetheless enact sublimated or even actual acts of rape through the domination and terrorizing of gay men or those perceived to be gay. In this context the fear of women and what they symbolize doubles back on itself. . . . Homophobes evince a deep anxiety that, because their bodies are the same as gay men, they too might be gay" (1995, 26–27).

10. Pettman goes on to state that:

No state could seriously attempt equality in work, or to pay fairly for women's work, without profound transformation of all social and power relations. The domestication of women means naturalising women's work as a labour of love, and so perpetuates the "double load" and containment of women. Many states exclude women from state rights as private or dependent, or as communal property. Women have great difficulties in becoming citizens. State legislation regarding marriage, divorce, legitimacy of children and status of women, profoundly affects women's rights and their access to resources and choices. . . . Most states still translate women's issues into welfare issues, and contain women as a category or special-need group, rather than analysing the gendered impact of state policies and the impact of gender power on peoples lives. (1996, 14)

Indeed, a 1995 UN report on the economic value of women's work looked at thirty-one countries at various stages of development and concluded that "if you take into account both the uncompensated work women do and the wage discrimination against women, you come up with a figure of $11 trillion" (*New York Times*, Aug. 18, 1995).

11. According to a Congressional Report on "Trafficking in Women and Children: The U.S. and International Response":

The trafficking of people for prostitution and forced labor is one of the fastest growing areas of criminal activity and one that is of increasing concern to the United States and the international community. Although men are also victimized, the overwhelming majority of those trafficked are women and children. An estimated 1 million people are trafficked each year worldwide 50,000 to the United States. Trafficking is now considered the third largest source of profits for organized crime, behind only drugs and guns, generating billions of dollars annually.

Trafficking affects virtually every country in the world. The largest number of victims come from Asia, with over 225,000 victims each year from Southeast Asia and over 150,000 from South Asia. The former Soviet Union is now believed to be the largest new source of trafficking for prostitution and the sex industry, with over 100,000 trafficked each year from that region. An additional 75,000 or more are trafficked from Eastern Europe. Over 100,000 come from Latin America and the Caribbean, and over 50,000 victims from Africa. Most of the victims are sent to Asia, the Middle East, Western Europe and North America.

According to estimates, over 1 million women and children are trafficked each year worldwide for forced labor, domestic servitude, or sexual exploitation. (Francis Miko, "RL30545: Trafficking in Women and Children, The U.S. and International Response," Updated Feb. 14, 2001, Congressional Research Service)

12. Rogers goes on to report:

A general in the Thai air force negotiated the treaty, and his wife ran Thailand's first sex-tour agency, Tommy Tours. The agreement shifted Thailand's long-established local prostitution industry into high gear, "upgrading" the extent and quality of services. The U.S. military invested considerable funds and expertise, making the sex industry more efficient in the process. The various agreements among the U.S. military, entrepreneurs, and the Thai government's involvement in the sex trade, and the resulting job opportunities launched an exodus of rural youth from their home into burgeoning urban centers. Although the U.S did not introduce prostitution to Thailand, it certainly made the sex trade more visible, better organized and more lucrative. (Rogers, *Ms.*, Oct./Nov., 1999)

13. To be sure, many Western feminists' vision is clouded by Eurocentrism and their own privileged and often elite positions that blind them to recognizing the realities of multiplicities of race, ethnicity, sexuality, class, ableness, age, and the diversities of the multidimensional and hierarchical relations of domination that oppress so many less-privileged women and children. Although it is necessary to recognize and attack their unconscious investment and legitimization of white racist ideology, we cannot reject, out of hand, all their ideas and contributions to the development of critical transformative feminisms. Rather, as with other great scholars and thinkers who harbor sexist, racist, homophobic, and classist prejudices, we must both criticize them and translate from them, and hence witness the evolution and transformation of some of their most revelatory theories and practices. Indeed, this process embodies the enlightening and constructive nature of dialectics and contradiction.

14. Jyota Sangera, in her astute and shocking report on globalization and the sex trade

that I cited earlier, condemns the "victim" discourse and urges us to grasp commonalities and differences, arguing:

In a majority of the writings on trafficking and the sex industry the women concerned are presented as victims either of patriarchy, or a crude, undifferentiated capitalism. While recognizing the overwhelming forces of global economics which create common structural patterns which affect and oppress us all as women, this paper strongly argues to transcend the "victim mould" in order to comprehend the various layers of reality defining both trafficking and the sex industry. We need to identify and comprehend the myriad of distinctions and differences as well as the similarities defining various regions and social groups to which women belong. Above all we need to recognise that even when oppressed by external factors women consistently reject the "victim mould" and find negotiating spaces to assert their agency and dignity. (1997)

Bibliography

Abu-Lughod. 1989. "On the Remaking of History: How to Reinvent the Past." In *Remaking History: Dia Art Foundation: Discussions in Contemporary Culture*, no. 4. Edited by Barbara Kruger and Phil Mariani, 111–30. Seattle, Wash.: Bay Press.

Adams, Carol J. 1993. " 'I Just Raped My Wife! What Are You Going to Do about It, Pastor?': The Church and Sexual Violence." In *Transforming Rape Culture*. Edited by Barbara Kruger and Phil Mariani, 58–86. Minneapolis, Minn.: Milkweed Editions.

Albrecht, Lisa, and Rose M. Brewer, editors. 1990. *Bridges of Power: Women's Multicultural Alliances*. Philadelphia: New Society Publishers.

Alcoff, Linda, and Elizabeth Potter. 1993. "Introduction: When Feminisms Intersect Epistemology." In *Feminist Epistemologies*. Edited by Linda Alcoff and Elizabeth Potter, 1–14. New York: Routledge.

Aldrich, Nelson W., Jr. 1995. "How to Avoid Date Rape." In *Debating Sexual Correctness: Pornography, Sexual Harassment, Date Rape, and the Politics of Sexual Equality* [1994]. Edited by Adele M. Stan, 175–89. New York: Delta.

Alexander, M. Jacqui, and Chandra Talpade Mohanty. 1997. *Feminist Genealogies, Colonial Legacies, Democratic Futures*. New York: Routledge.

Alexander, Nikol G., and Drucilla Cornell. 1997. "Dismissed or Banished? A Testament to the Reasonableness of the Simpson Jury." In *Birth of a Nation'hood: Gaze, Script, and Spectacle in the O. J. Simpson Case*. Edited by Toni Morrison and Claudia Brodsky Lacour, 57–96. New York: Pantheon.

Alternative Views. 1993. "Appalled at Paglia." With Camille Paglia, Ann Cvetovitch, Irene Kacandes, Douglas Kellner, and Frank Morrow. Public Access Television, Austin, Texas.

Altman, Dennis. 1982. *The Homosexualization of America*. Boston: Beacon.

Amnesty International. 2001. "Broken Bodies, Shattered Minds—The Torture of Women Worldwide." *Amnesty International News Release*, March 6, www.amnesty.org.

Anzaldúa, Gloria. 1981. "Foreword to the Second Edition." In *This Bridge Called My Back: Writings By Radical Women of Color*. Edited by Cherríe Moraga and Gloria Anzaldúa. New York: Kitchen Table: Women of Color Press.

———. 1987. *Borderlands: La Frontera: The New Mestiza*. San Francisco: Aunt Lute.

———. 1990a. "En rapport, In Opposition: Cobrando cuentas a las nuestras." In *Making Face, Making Soul: Creative and Critical Perspectives of Women of Color*. Edited by Gloria Anzaldua, 142–48. San Francisco: Aunt Lute.

———. 1990b. "Introduction: Haciendo caras, una entrada." In *Making Face, Making*

Soul: Creative and Critical Perspectives by Women of Color. Edited by Gloria Anzaldua, xv–xxviii. San Francisco: Aunt Lute.

Armstrong, Louise. 1995. *Of "Sluts" and "Bastards." A Feminist Decodes the Child Welfare Debate*. Monroe, Maine: Common Courage.

Bahar, Saba. 1996. "Human Rights Are Women's Rights: Amnesty International and the Family." *Hypatia* 11, no. 1 (Winter): 105–34.

Bailey, Cathryn. 1997. "Making Waves and Drawing Lines: The Politics of Defining the Vicissitudes of Feminism" *Hypatia* 12, no. 3 (Summer): 17–28.

Bales, Kevin. 1999. *Disposable People: New Slavery in the Global Economy*. Berkeley: University of California Press.

Bar On, Bat-Ami. 1993. "Marginality and Epistemic Privilege." In *Feminist Epistemologies*. Edited by Linda Alcoff and Elizabeth Potter, 83–100. New York: Routledge.

———. 1994. "Introduction." In *Modern Engendering: Critical Feminist Readings in Modern Philosophy*. Edited by Bat-Ami Bar On, xi–xviii. Albany: State University of New York Press.

———. 1996. "Introduction." *Hypatia* 11, no. 4 (Fall): 1–4.

Barkan, Elazer. 1993. "Fin de Siecle Cultural Studies." *Tikkun* 8, no. 4: 49–51, 92–93.

Barker, Isabelle V. 2000. "Editing Pornography." In *Feminism and Pornography*. Edited by Drucilla Cornell, 643–52. Oxford: Oxford University Press.

Barker, Victoria. 1997. "Definition and the Question of 'Woman.'" *Hypatia* 12, no. 2 (Spring): 185–215.

Barreca, Regina. 1991. *They Used to Call Me Snow White . . . But I Drifted: Women's Strategic Use of Humor*. New York: Penguin.

Barrett, Michele. 1988. *Women's Oppression Today: The Marxist/Feminist Encounter: Revised Edition*. London: Verso.

Barry, Kathleen. 1996. "Deconstructing Deconstructionism (or, Whatever Happened to Feminist Studies?)" In *Radically Speaking: Feminism Reclaimed*. Edited by Diane Bell and Renate Klein, 188–92. North Melbourne, Australia: Spinifex.

Bart, Pauline B., and Eileen Geil Moran. 1993. "Preface." In *Violence against Women: The Bloody Footprints*. Edited by Pauline B. Bart and Eileen Geil Moran, xiii–xvi. Newbury Park, Calif.: Sage.

Bartky, Sandra. 1990. *Femininity and Domination: Studies in the Phenomenology of Oppression*. New York: Routledge.

Bateson, Gregory. 1972. *Steps to an Ecology of Mind*. New York: Ballantine.

———. 1976. "Foreword." In *Double-Bind: The Foundation of the Communicational Approach to the Family*. Edited by C. Sluzki and D. Ransom, xi–xvi. New York: Grune and Stratton.

———. 1979. *Mind and Nature: A Necessary Unity*. New York: Bantam Books.

Baumgardner, Jennifer, and Amy Richards. 2000. *Manifesta: Young Women, Feminism, and the Future*. New York: Farrar, Straus and Giroux.

Bell, Diane, and Renate Klein, editors. 1996. *Radically Speaking: Feminism Reclaimed*. North Melbourne, Australia: Spinifex.

Bellafante, Ginia. 1998. "Feminism: It's All about Me!" *Time*. June 29: 54–60.

Benhabib, Seyla, and Drucilla Cornell. 1987. "Introduction." In *Feminism as Critique: On the Politics of Gender*. Edited by Seyla Benhabib and Drucilla Cornell, 1–9. Minneapolis: University of Minnesota Press.

Berger, Peter, and Thomas Luckmann. 1967. *The Social Construction of Reality: A Treatise in the Sociology of Knowledge.* New York: Anchor.

Best, Steven, and Douglas Kellner. 1991. *Postmodern Theory: Critical Interrogations.* New York: Guilford.

Bickford, Susan. 1997. "Anti-Anti-Identity Politics: Feminism, Democracy, and the Complexities of Citizenship." *Hypatia* 12, no. 4 (Fall): 111–31.

Black Women's Liberation Group, Mount Vernon, New York. 1970. *Sisterhood Is Power-ful: An Anthology of Writings from the Women's Liberation Movement.* Edited by R. Morgan, 404–6. New York: Vintage.

Bloch, Maurice. 1990. "New Foreword." In *Prospero and Caliban: The Psychology of Colonization.* Edited by Octave Mannoni, v–xx. Ann Arbor: University of Michigan Press.

Boggs, Carl. 1995. "Revolution Interrupted: Who Stole the Politics from Feminism?" *LA Village View.* May 26–June 1: 8.

Bottomore, Tom, editor. 1983. *A Dictionary of Marxist Thought.* Tom, L. Harris, V. G. Kiernan, R. Miliband, editorial board. Cambridge: Harvard University Press.

Brenner, Johanna. 1993. "The Best of Times, The Worst of Times: U.S. Feminism Today." In *New Left Review,* no. 200 (Jul./Aug.): 101–59.

Brooks, Ann. 1997. *Postfeminisms: Feminism, Cultural Theory, and Cultural Forms.* London: Routledge.

Brownmiller, Susan. 1975. *Against Our Will: Men, Women and Rape.* New York: Banton.

———. 1989. *Waverly Place.* Canada: Signet.

Brush, Lisa D. 1993. "Violent Acts and Injurious Outcomes in Married Couples: Methodological Issues in the National Survey of Families and Households." In *Violence against Women: The Bloody Footprints.* Edited by Pauline B. Bart and Eileen Geil Moran, 240–51. Newbury Park, Calif.: Sage.

Buchwald, Emilie, Pamela Fletcher, and Martha Roth, editors. 1993. *Transforming Rape Culture.* Minneapolis, Minn.: Milkweed.

Bulkin, E., M. Bruce Pratt, and B. Smith. 1984. *Yours in Struggle: Three Feminist Perspectives on Anti-Semitism and Racism.* Ithaca, N.Y.: Firebrand.

Bunch, Charlotte. 1990. "Making Common Cause: Diversity and Coalitions," In *Bridges of Power: Women's Multicultural Alliances.* Edited by Lisa Albrecht and Rose M. Brewer, 49–56. Philadelphia: New Society Publishers.

———. 1991. "Recognizing Women's Rights as Human Rights." *Response* 13, no. 4: 13–16.

Bunch, Charlotte, and Susana Fried. 1996. "Beijing '95: Moving Women's Human Rights from Margin to Center" *Signs* 22, no. 1 (Fall): 200–204.

Butler, Alice. 1998. "Domestic Violence: Data, Programs, and Funding." *CRS Report for Congress.* The Library of Congress: Congressional Research Service, Dec. 14.

Cameron, Elspeth. 1992. "WOMAN-THINK '92." *Chatelaine.* Sept.: 89–91.

Caputi, Jane. 1993. "The Sexual Politics of Murder." In *Violence against Women: The Bloody Footprints.* Edited by Pauline B. Bart and Eileen Geil Moran, 5–25. Newbury Park, Calif.: Sage.

Carpenter, Mary Wilson. 1996. "Female Grotesques in Academia: Ageism, Antifeminism, and Feminists on the Faculty." *Antifeminism in the Academy.* Edited by V. Clark, S. N. Garner, M. Higonnet, and K. H. Katrak, 141–65. New York: Routledge.

Caute, David. 1970. *Fanon.* London: Fonatana.

———, editor. 1967. *The Essential Writings of Karl Marx..* London: Panther.

Chambers, Veronica. 1995. "Betrayal Feminism." In *Listen Up: Voices from the Next Feminist Generation.* Edited by Barbara Findlen, 21–28. Seattle, Wash.: Seal.

Chancer, Lynn S. 1998. *Reconcilable Differences: Confronting Beauty, Pornography, and the Future of Feminism.* Berkeley: University of California Press.

Chesler, Phyllis. 1994. *Patriarchy: Notes of an Expert Witness.* Monroe, Maine: Common Courage.

Childers, Mary, and bell hooks. 1990. "A Conversation about Race and Class." In *Conflicts in Feminism.* Edited by Marianne Hirsch and Evelyn Fox Keller, 60–81. New York: Routledge.

Chin, Paula. 1992. "Street Fighting Woman." *People.* April 20: 125–27.

Chisholm, Dianne. 1993. "Violence against Violence against Women." In *The Last Sex: Feminism and Outlaw Bodies.* Edited by A. Kroker and M. Kroker, 28–66. New York: St. Martin's.

Christensen, Kimberly. 1997. " 'With Whom Do You Believe Your Lot Is Cast?' White Feminists and Racism." *Signs: Journal of Women in Culture and Society* 22, no. 3 (Spring): 617–48.

Christian, Barbara. 1996. "The Race for Theory." In *Radically Speaking: Feminism Reclaimed.* Edited by Diane Bell and Renate Klein, 311–20. North Melbourne, Australia: Spinifex.

Clark, V., S. Nelson Garner, M. Higonnet, and K. Katrak, editors. 1996. *Antifeminism in the Academy.* New York: Routledge.

Colletti, Lucio. 1975. "Marxism and the Dialectic." *New Left Review,* no. 93 (Sept.–Oct.): 3–30.

Coney, Sandra. 1996. "The Last Post for Feminism." In *Radically Speaking: Feminism Reclaimed.* Edited by Diane Bell and Renate Klein, 275–76. North Melbourne, Australia: Spinifex.

Connolly, William E. 1992. *Identity/Difference: Democratic Negotiations of Political Paradox.* Ithaca, N.Y.: Cornell University Press.

Creed, Barbara. 1993. "From Here to Modernity: Feminism and Postmodernism." In *A Postmodern Reader.* Edited by Joseph Natoli and Linda Hutcheon, 398–418. Albany: State University of New York Press.

Crenshaw, Kimberle Williams. 1997. "Color-Blind Dreams and Racial Nightmares: Reconfiguring Racism in the Post-Civil Rights Era." In *Birth of a Nation'hood: Gaze, Script, and Spectacle in the O. J. Simpson Case.* Edited by Toni Morrison and Claudia Brodsky Lacour, 97–168. New York: Pantheon.

Cuomo, Chris J. 1996. "War Is Not Just an Event: Reflections on the Significance of Everyday Violence." *Hypatia* 11, no. 4 (Fall): 30–45.

Daly, Mary. 1978. *Gyn/Ecology: The Metaethics of Radical Feminism.* Boston: Beacon.

Das Gupta, Tania. 1991. "Introduction and Overview." In *Race, Class, Gender: Bonds and Barriers.* Edited by Jesse Vorst et al. Winnipeg: Society for Socialist Studies.

Davis, Angela Y. 1981. *Women, Race, and Class.* New York: Vintage Books.

———. 1985. *Violence against Women and the Ongoing Challenge to Racism.* Albany, N.Y.: Kitchen Table: Women of Color Press.

———. 1996. "Foreword." In Joy James, *Resisting State Violence,* vii–viii. Minneapolis: University of Minnesota Press.

Davis, Angela Y., and other political prisoners. 1971. *If They Come in the Morning.* New York: Signet.

Davis, Mary Alice. 1998. "Feminists. Journalists. Feminist Journalists. These Are Some Dark Days, but We'll All Survive." *Austin American-Statesman,* July 19.

De Lauretis, Teresa. 1994. "The Essence of Triangle or, Taking the Risk of Essentialism Seriously: Feminist Theory in Italy, the U.S., and Britain." In *The Essential Difference.* Edited by Naomi Schor and Elizabeth Weed, 1–39. Bloomington: Indiana University Press.

Denfield, Rene. 1995. *The New Victorians: A Young Woman's Challenge to the Old Feminist Order.* New York: Warner.

Devitt, Tiffany. 1992. "Media Circus at Palm Beach Rape Trial." *EXTRA!: Special Issue,* 9–10, 24.

Devitt, Tiffany, and Jennifer Downey. 1992. "Battered Women Take a Beating from the Press." *EXTRA!: Special Issue,* 14–16.

Diamond, Sara. 1995. "Patriot Games." *The Progressive* 59, no. 9 (September): 26–28.

Dickason, Anne. 1976. "Anatomy and Destiny: The Role of Biology in Plato's Views of Women." In *Women and Philosophy: Toward a Theory of Liberation.* Edited by Carol C. Gould and Marx W. Wartopsky, 45–53. New York: Perigree.

Dobash, R. Emerson, and Russell Dobash. 1979. *Violence Against Wives: A Case Against Patriarchy.* New York: Free Press.

Donaldson, Laura E. 1992. *Decolonizing Feminisms: Race, Gender, and Empire-Building.* Chapel Hill: The University of North Carolina Press.

Douglas, John, and Mark Olshanker. 1995. *Mind Hunter: Inside the FBI'S Elite Serial Crime Unit.* New York: Pocket Atar.

Douglas, Susan J. 1994. *Where the Girls Are: Growing up Female with the Mass Media.* New York: Times Books.

Dowd, Maureen. 1996. "Liberties: Daddy in Chief." *New York Times,* June 2, E15.

Dowd Hall, Jacquelyn. 1983. "The Mind That Burns in Each Body." In *Powers of Desire: The Politics of Sexuality.* Edited by Ann Snitow, Christine Stansell, and Sharon Thompson, 328–47. New York: New Monthly Review.

Dowling, Colette. 1981. *The Cinderella Complex: Women's Hidden Fear of Independence.* New York: Summit Books.

Draper, Patricia. 1975. "!Kung Women: Contrasts in Sexual Egalitarianism Foraging and Sedentary Contexts." In *Toward an Anthropology of Women.* Edited by Rayna R. Reiter, 77–83. New York: Monthly Review.

duCille, Ann. 1997. "The Unbearable Darkness of Being: 'Fresh' Thoughts on Race, Sex, and the Simpsons." In *Birth of a Nation'hood: Gaze, Script, and Spectacle in the O. J. Simpson Case.* Edited by Toni Morrison and Claudia Brodsky Lacour, 293–338. New York: Pantheon.

Duggan, Lisa, and Nan D. Hunter. 1995. *Sex Wars: Sexual Dissent and Political Culture.* New York: Routledge.

Dworkin, Andrea. 1993. "Living in Terror, Pain: Being a Battered Wife." In *Violence against Women: The Bloody Footprints* [1989]. Edited by Pauline B. Bart and Eileen Geil Moran, 237–39. Newbury Park, Calif.: Sage.

Easlea, Brian. 1973. *Liberation and the Aims of Science: An Essay on Obstacles to the Building of a Beautiful World.* London: Suffolk University Press.

Ebert, Teresa L. 1992. "Ludic Feminism, the Body, Performance, and Labor: Bringing *Materialism* Back into Feminist Cultural Studies." *Cultural Critique,* no. 23 (Winter): 5–50.

———. 1996. *Ludic Feminism and After: Postmodernism, Desire, and Labor in Late Capitalism.* Ann Arbor: University of Michigan Press.

Echols, Alice. 1983. "The New Feminism of Yin and Yang." In *Powers of Desire: The*

Politics of Sexuality. Edited by A. Snitow, C. Stansell, and S. Thompson, 439–59. New York: Monthly Review.

Ehrenreich, Barbara. 1983. *The Hearts of Men: American Dreams and the Flight from Commitment*. New York: Anchor.

———. 2001. *Nickel and Dimed: On (Not) Getting By in America*. New York: Metropolitan Books.

Eichler, Margrit. 1985. "And the Work Never Ends: Feminist Contributions." *Canadian Review of Sociology and Anthropology* 22, no. 5: 619–44.

Eisenstein, Zillah. 1981. *The Radical Future of Liberal Feminism*. London: Longman.

———. 1996. *Hatreds: Racialized and Sexualized Conflicts in the 21st Century*. New York: Routledge.

———. 1998. *Global Obscenities: Patriarchy, Capitalism, and the Lure of Cyberfantasy*. New York: New York University Press.

———, editor. 1979. *Capitalist Patriarchy and the Case for Socialist Feminism*. New York: Monthly Review.

Elshtain, Jean Bethke. 1987. *Women and War*. New York: Basic.

Enloe, Cynthia. 1990. *Banana Beaches & Bases: Making Feminist Sense of International Politics*. Berkeley: University of California Press.

———. 1993. *The Morning After: Sexual Politics and the End of the Cold War*. Berkeley: University of California Press.

———. 2000. *Maneuvers: The International Politics of Militarizing Women's Lives*. Berkeley: University of California Press.

Etienne, Mona, and Eleanor Leacock. 1980. "Introduction." In *Women and Colonization: Anthropological Perspectives*. Edited by Mona Etienne and Eleanor Leacock, 1–23. New York: Praeger.

Faludi, Susan. 1991. *Backlash: The Undeclared War against American Women*. New York: Crown.

———. 1993. "Whose Hype?" *Newsweek*. Oct. 25: 61.

———. 1995. "I'm Not a Feminist But I Play One on TV." *Ms.* Mar./Apr.: 31–39.

———. 1996a. "Statistically Challenged." *The Nation*. April 15: 10.

———. 1996b. "Who's Calling Whom Elitist?" *The Nation*. January 8/15: 25–28.

Fanon, Frantz. 1968. *The Wretched of the Earth* [1961]. Translated by C. Farrington. New York: Grove.

Farganis, Sondra. 1994. *Situating Feminism: From Thought to Action*. Newbury Park, Calif.: Sage.

Ferguson, M., K. Katrak, and V. Miner. 1996. "Feminism and Antifeminism: From Civil Rights to Culture Wars." In *Antifeminism in the Academy*. Edited by V. Clark, S. Nelson Garner, M. Higonnet, K. Katrak, 35–66. New York: Routledge.

Fernandez, Sandy M. 1996. "Faux Feminists." *Utne Reader*. Jul.–Aug.: 9–10.

Ferraro, Kathleen J. 1996. "The Dance of Dependency: A Genealogy of Domestic Violence." *Hypatia* 11, no. 4 (Fall): 77–91.

Findlen, Barbara, editor. 1995. *Listen Up: Voices from the Next Feminist Generation*. Seattle: Seal.

Findley, Heather. 2000. "Paglia 101." *Girlfriend's Magazine: Lesbian Culture, Politics, and Entertainment*. September, www.salon.com.

Fine, Michelle. 1993. "The Politics of Research and Activism: Violence against Women."

In *Violence against Women: The Bloody Footprints*. Edited by Pauline B. Bart and Eileen Geil Moran, 278–89. Newbury Park, Calif.: Sage.

Fiorenza, Elisabeth S. 1996. "Ties That Bind: Domestic Violence against Women." In *Women Resisting Violence: Spirituality for Life*. Edited by M. J. Mananzan, M. A. Oduyoye, E. Tamez, J. S. Clarkson, M. C. Grey, and L. M. Russell, 39–55. New York: Orbis.

Fiske, John. 1994. *Media Matters: Everyday Culture and Political Change*. Minneapolis: University of Minnesota Press.

Flax, Jane. 1986. "Women Do Theory." In *Women and Values: Readings in Recent Feminist Philosophy*. Edited by Marilyn Pearsall, 1–7. Sacramento, Calif.: Wadsworth.

Foreman, Ann. 1977. *Femininity as Alienation: Women and the Family in Marxism and Psychoanalysis*. London: Pluto.

Fowlkes, Diane L. 1997. "Moving from Feminist Identity Politics to Coalition Politics through a Feminist Materialist Standpoint of Intersubjectivity in Gloria Anzaldua's *Borderlands/La Frontera: The New Mestiza*." *Hypatia* 12, no. 2 (Spring): 105–24.

Fraser, Nancy. 1989. *Unruly Practices: Power, Discourse, and Gender in Contemporary Social Theory*. Minneapolis: University of Minnesota Press.

French, Marilyn. 1992. *The War against Women*. New York: Ballantine.

Friedan, Betty. 1963. *The Feminine Mystique*. New York: Dell.

Friedman, Marilyn, and Jan Narveson. 1995. *Political Correctness: For and Against*. Lanham, Md.: Rowman & Littlefield.

Friedman, Susan Stanford. 1998. *Mappings: Feminism and the Cultural Geographies of Encounter*. Princeton, N.J.: Princeton University Press.

Friend, Tad. 1994. "Yes; Feminist Women Who Like Sex." *Esquire* 121, no. 2 (February): 48–52.

Freire, Paulo. 1972. *Pedagogy of the Oppressed*. New York: Herder and Herder.

Fuss, Diana. 1994. "Reading Like a Feminist." In *The Essential Difference*. Edited by Naomi Schor and Elizabeth Weed, 98–115. Bloomington: Indiana University Press.

Gallop, Jane. 1997. *Feminist Accused of Sexual Harassment*. Durham, N.C.: Duke University Press.

Gillespie, Marcia Ann. 1996. "The Posse Rides Again." In *Radically Speaking: Feminism Reclaimed*. Edited by Diane Bell and Renate Klein, 141–42. North Melbourne, Australia: Spinifex.

Ginsberg, Elaine, and Sara Lennox. 1996. "Antifeminism in Scholarship and Publishing." In *Antifeminism in the Academy*. Edited by V. Clark, S. Nelson Garner, M. Higonnet, and K. Katrak, 169–99. New York: Routledge.

Giroux, Henry. 1994. "Living Dangerously: Identity Politics and the New Cultural Racism." In *Between Borders: Pedagogy and the Politics of Cultural Studies*. Edited by Henry Giroux and Peter McLaren, 29–55. New York: Routledge.

———. 1996. "Black, Bruised, and Read All Over." *Taboo: The Journal of Culture and Education* II (Fall): 3–24.

Gitlin, Todd. 1995. *The Twilight of Common Dreams: Why America Is Wracked by Culture Wars*. New York: Metropolitan.

Goldberg, Michelle. 2001. "Feminism for Sale." AlterNet.org, Jan. 8, www.alternet.org.

Golden, Kristen. 1994. "The Not-So-Fine Print." *Ms.* Sep./Oct.: 39.

Gordon, Linda. 1988. *Heroes of Their Own Lives: The Politics and History of Family Violence—Boston 1880–1960*. New York: Viking.

Gould, Carol. 1984. "Private Rights and Public Virtues: Women, the Family, and Democracy." In *Beyond Domination: New Perspectives on Women and Philosophy*. Edited by Carol Gould, 3–18. Totowa, N.J.: Rowman & Allanheld.

———. 1976. "The Woman Question: Philosophy of Liberation and the Liberation of Philosophy." In *Women and Philosophy: Toward a Theory of Liberation*. Edited by Carol C. Gould and Marx W. Wartopsky, 5–44. New York: Perigree.

Gould, Carol C., and Marx W. Wartovsky, editors. 1976. *Women and Philosophy: Toward a Theory of Liberation*. New York: Perigree.

Goulet, Denis. 1973. "Introduction." In *Education: The Practice of Freedom*. Edited by Paulo Freire. London: Writers and Readers Publishing Cooperative.

Greenberg, David, F. 1988. *The Construction of Homosexuality*. Chicago: The University of Chicago Press.

Grosz, Elizabeth. 1994. "Sexual Difference and the Problem of Essentialism." In *The Essential Difference*. Edited by Naomi Schor and Elizabeth Weed, 82–97. Bloomington: Indiana University Press.

Guy-Sheftall, Beverly, and Kimberly Wallace Sanders. 1996. "Educating Black Women Students for the Multicultural Future." *Signs* 22, no. 1 (Fall): 210–13.

Haag, Pamela. 1996. " 'Putting Your Body on the Line': The Question of Violence, Victims, and the Legacies of Second-Wave Feminism." *Differences: A Journal of Feminist Cultural Studies* 8, no. 2: 23–67.

Haggerty, Rebecca. 1994. "Feminism as a Cudgel." *Z Magazine*. April: 9–11.

Hall, Calvin, S. 1954. *A Primer of Freudian Psychology: Freud's Great Discoveries on Human Behavior*. New York: Mentor.

Hampshire, Stuart, editor. 1956. *The 17th Century Philosophers: The Age of Reason*. New York: New American Library.

Hannah-Moffat, Kelly. 1995. "To Charge or Not to Charge: Front Line Officers' Perceptions of Mandatory Charge Policies." In *Wife Assault and the Canadian Justice System: Issues and Policies*. Edited by M. Valverde, L. Macleod, and K. Johnson, 36–61. Toronto: Centre of Criminology, University of Toronto.

Haraway, Donna. 1988. "Reading Buchi Emecheta: Contests for Women's Experience in Women's Studies." *Inscriptions* nos. 3 and 4: 107–24.

Harding, Sandra. 1984. "Is Gender a Variable in Conceptions of Rationality? A Survey of Issues." In *Beyond Domination: New Perspectives on Women and Philosophy*. Edited by Carol Gould, 43–63. Totowa, N.J.: Rowman & Allanheld.

———. 1986. *The Science Question in Feminism*. Ithaca, N.Y.: Cornell University Press.

———. 1993. "Rethinking Standpoint Epistemology: 'What Is Strong Objectivity?' " In *Feminist Epistemologies*. Edited by Linda Alcoff and Elizabeth Potter, 49–82. New York: Routledge.

———. 1998. *Is Science Multicultural? Postcolonialisms, Feminisms, and Epistemologies*. Bloomington: Indiana University Press.

Harding, Sandra, and Uma Narayan. 1998. "Border Crossings: Multicultural and Postcolonial Feminist Challenges to Philosophy (Part II)." *Hypatia* (Summer): 1–5.

Harstock, Nancy. 1986. "Feminist Theory and the Development of Revolutionary Strategy." In *Women and Values: Readings in Recent Feminist Philosophy*. Edited by Marilyn Pearsall, 8–18. Belmont, Calif.: Wadsworth.

Heberle, Rene. 1996. "Deconstructive Strategies and the Movement against Sexual Violence." *Hypatia* 11, no. 4 (Fall): 63–76.

Heywood, Leslie, and Jennifer Drake, editors. 1997. *Third Wave Agenda: Being Feminist, Doing Feminism.* Minneapolis: University of Minnesota Press.

Higginbotham, A. Leon Jr., Francois Aderson Bellegarde, and Linda Y. Yueh. 1997. "The O. J. Simpson Trial: Who Was Improperly 'Playing the Race Card?' " In *Birth of a Nation'hood: Gaze, Script, and Spectacle in the O. J. Simpson Case.* Edited by Toni Morrison and Claudia Brodsky Lacour, 31–56. New York: Pantheon.

Higgins, Kathleen Marie. 1993. "Review of *Sexual Personae: Art and Decadence from Nefertiti to Emily Dickinson.*" *Philosophy and Literature,* 369–70.

Hill Collins, Patricia. 1990. *Black Feminist Thought.* Boston: Unwin Hyman.

———. 1993. "The Sexual Politics of Black Womanhood." In *Violence against Women: The Bloody Footprints.* Edited by Pauline B. Bart and Eileen Geil Moran, 85–104. Newbury Park, Calif.: Sage.

———. 1998a. *Fighting Words: Black Women and the Search for Justice.* Minneapolis: University of Minnesota Press.

———. 1998b. "It's All in the Family: Intersections and Gender, Race, and Nation." *Hypatia* (Summer): 62–63.

Hirshman, Linda. 1994. "Making Safety a Civil Right." *Ms.* Sept./Oct.: 44–47.

Hoageland, Lisa Maria. 1994. "Fear of Feminism." *Ms.* Nov./Dec.: 18–21.

Hoagland, Sarah Lucia. 1986. " 'Femininity,' Resistance, and Sabotage." In *Women and Values: Readings in Recent Feminist Philosophy.* Edited by Marilyn Pearsall, 78–86. Sacramento, Calif.: Wadsworth.

Hoff Sommers, Christina. 1994. *Who Stole Feminism? How Women Have Betrayed Women.* New York: Simon and Schuster.

———. 2000. *The War against Boys: How Misguided Feminism Is Harming Our Young Men.* New York: Simon and Schuster.

Hoffman, Abbie. 1989. "Reflections on Student Activism." In *The Best of Abbie Hoffman* [1988]. 412–21. New York: Four Walls Eight Windows.

hooks, bell. 1981. *Ain't I A Woman: Black Women and Feminism.* Boston: South End Press.

———. 1984. *Feminist Theory: From Margin to Center.* Boston: South End Press.

———. 1988. *Talking Back: Thinking Feminist. Thinking Black.* Toronto: Between the Lines.

———. 1990. *Yearning: Race, Gender, and Cultural Politics.* Boston: South End Press.

———. 1992. *Black Looks: Race and Representation.* Toronto: Between the Lines.

———. 1993a. "bell hooks Speaking about Paulo Freire—The Man and His Work." In *Paulo Freire: A Critical Encounter.* Edited by Peter McLaren and Peter Leonard, 146–54. New York: Routledge.

———. 1993b. *Sisters of the Yam: Black Women and Self-Recovery.* Toronto: Between the Lines.

———. 1994a. *Outlaw Culture: Resisting Representations.* New York: Routledge.

———. 1994b. *Teaching to Transgress: Education as the Practice of Freedom.* New York: Routledge.

———. 1995. *Killing Rage: Ending Racism.* New York: Henry Holt.

———. 1996. "Passionate Pedagogy: Erotic Student/Faculty Relationships." *Z Magazine.* March: 45–51.

———. 2000a. *Where We Stand: Class Matters.* New York: Routledge.

———. 2000b. *Feminism Is for Everybody: Passionate Politics.* Cambridge, Mass.: South End Press.

hooks, bell, and Cornel West. 1991. *Breaking Bread: Insurgent Black Intellectual Life.* Toronto: Between the Lines.

Huff, Darrell. 1954. *How to Lie with Statistics.* New York: W. W. Norton.

Humm, Maggie, editor. 1992. *Modern Feminisms: Political Literary Cultural.* New York: Columbia University Press.

Hutcheon, Linda. 1989. "The Post-Modern Ex-Centric: The Center That Will Not Hold." In *Feminism and Institutions.* Edited by Linda Kauffman, 141–65. Oxford: Basil Blackwell.

Iley, Chrissey. 1994. "Camille Paglia: The Mouth That Roars." *The Globe and Mail.* Jan. 22: D5.

Inness, Sherrie A, editor. 1998. *Millennium Girls: Today's Girls Around the World.* Lanham, Md.: Rowman & Littlefield.

Islan, David and Letellier, Patrick. 1991. *Men Who Beat the Men Who Love Them: Battered Gay Men and Domestic Violence.* New York: Harrington Park Press.

Ivans, Molly. 1991. "I Am the Cosmos." *Mother Jones.* Sept./Oct.: 8–9.

Jacoby, Russell. 1995. "Marginal Returns: The Trouble with Post-Colonial Theory." *Lingua Franca.* Sept./Oct.: 30–37.

Jaggar, Alison. 1984. "Human Biology in Feminist Theory: Sexual Equality Reconsidered." In *Beyond Domination: New Perspectives on Women and Philosophy.* Edited by Carol Gould, 21–42. Totowa, N.J.: Rowman & Allanheld.

Jakobsen, Janet R. 1995. "Agency and Alliance in Public Discourses about Sexualities." *Hypatia* 10, no. 1 (Winter): 133–54.

James, Joy. 1996. *Resisting State Violence.* Minneapolis: University of Minnesota Press.

Janack, Marianne. 1997. "Standpoint Epistemology without the 'Standpoint'?: An Examination of Epistemic Privilege and Epistemic Authority." *Hypatia* 12, no. 2 (Spring): 125–39.

Jones, Ann. 1990. "Family Matters." In *The Sexual Liberals and the Attack on Feminism.* Edited by Dorchen Leidholdt and Janice G. Raymond, 61–66. New York: Pergamon.

———. 1994a. *Next Time She'll Be Dead: Battering and How to Stop It.* Boston: Beacon Press.

———. 1994b. (interviewed by Gloria Jacobs). "Where Do We Go from Here?" *Ms.* Sept./Oct.: 56–63.

———. 1996. *Women Who Kill.* Boston: Beacon.

Kamen, Paula. 1991. *Feminist Fatale: Voices from the "Twentysomething" Generation Explore the Future of the "Women's Movement."* New York: Donald I. Fine.

Kaminer, Wendy. 1993. "Feminism's Identity Crisis." *The Atlantic Monthly.* October: 51–68.

———. 1995. "Feminism's Third Wave: What Do Young Women Want?" *The New York Times Book Review.* June 4: 3, 22–23.

———. 1996. *True Love Waits: Essays and Criticisms.* Reading, Mass.: Addison-Wesley.

Keating, AnaLouise. 2000. *Gloria E. Anzaldua: Interviews.* New York: Routledge.

Kellner, Douglas. 2001. *Grand Theft 2000: Media Spectacle and a Stolen Election.* Lanham, Md.: Rowman & Littlefield.

Kelly, Deidre. 1994. "Reign of Rhetoric." *Globe and Mail.* Nov. 7.

Kinsley, Michael. 1994. "An American Tragedy." *Sporting News.* June 27: 10–12.

Kurz, Demie. 1993. "Social Science Perspectives on Wife Abuse: Current Debates and

Future Directions." In *Violence against Women: The Bloody Footprints*. Edited by Pauline B. Bart and Eileen Geil Moran, 252–69. Newbury Park, Calif.: Sage.

Labi, Nadya. 1998. "Girl Power." *Time*. June 29: 60–62.

Lakoff, Robin Tolmach. 2000. *The Language War*. Berkeley: University of California Press.

Landsberg, Michele. 1998. "Stop the Post Mortem, Feminism Lives On." *The Toronto Star*. July 5.

LaRocque, Emma D. 1995. "Violence in the Aboriginal Communities." In *Wife Assault and the Canadian Justice System: Issues and Policies*. Edited by M. Valverde, L. Macleod, and K. Johnson, 104–22. Toronto: Centre of Criminology, University of Toronto.

Lather, Patti. 1991. *Getting Smart: Feminist Research and Pedagogy with/in the Postmodern*. New York: Routledge.

Lerner, Gerda. 1986. *The Creation of Patriarchy*. New York: Oxford University Press.

Levine, Judith. 1992. *My Enemy, My Love: Women, Men, and the Dilemmas of Gender*. New York: Anchor.

Levine, Mark, and Daniel Greenberg, editors. 1970. *The Tales of Hoffman: Edited from the Official Transcript*. New York: Bantam.

Lord, M. G. 1997. "Pornutopia: How Feminist Scholars Learned to Love Dirty Pictures." *Lingua Franca: The Review of Academic Life* 7, no. 4 (Apr./May): 40–48.

Lorde, Audre. 1984. *Sister Outsider*. Freedom, Calif.: The Crossing Press.

Lugones, Maria C., and Elizabeth V. Spelman. 1986. "Have We Got a Theory for You! Feminist Theory, Cultural Imperialism, and the Demand for 'The Woman's Voice.'" In *Women and Values: Readings in Recent Feminist Philosophy*. Edited by Marilyn Pearsall, 19–31. Sacramento, Calif.: Wadsworth.

Macedo, Donald. 1992. "Foreword." In *The Social Mind: Language, Ideology, and Social Practice*. Edited by James Paul Gee, vii–xiv. New York: Bergin & Garvey.

Maglin, Nan Bauer, and Donna Perry, editors. 1996. *"Bad Girls/Good Girls": Women, Sex, and Power in the Nineties*. New Brunswick, N.J.: Rutgers University Press.

Males, Mike A. 1996. *The Scapegoat Generation: America's War on Adolescents*. Monroe, Maine: Common Courage.

Mama, Amina. 1997. "Heroes and Villians: Conceptualizing Colonial and Contemporary Violence against Women in Africa." In *Feminist Genealogies, Colonial Legacies, and Democratic Futures*. Edited by M. Jacqui Alexander and Chandra Talpade Mohanty, 46–62. New York: Routledge.

Mannoni, Octave. 1990. *Prospero and Calibran: The Psychology of Colonization*. Ann Arbor: The University of Michigan Press.

Marks, John. 1979. *The Search for the "Manchurian Candidate": The CIA and Mind Control*. New York: Times Books.

Martin, Patricia Yancey, and Robert A. Hummer. 1993. "Fraternities and Rape on Campus." In *Violence against Women: The Bloody Footprints*. Edited by Pauline B. Bart and Eileen Geil Moran, 114–31. Newbury Park, Calif.: Sage.

Matalin, Mary. 1993. "Stop Whining!" *Newsweek*. October 25: 62.

Mathews, Nancy A. 1993. "Surmounting a Legacy: The Expansion of Racial Diversity in a Local Anti-Rape Movement." In *Violence against Women: The Bloody Footprints*. Edited by Pauline B. Bart and Eileen Geil Moran, 177–200. Newbury Park, Calif.: Sage.

McBride, James. 1995. *War, Battering, and Other Sports: The Gulf Between American Men and Women.* Atlantic Highlands, N.J.: Humanities Press.

McRobbie, Angela. 1994. *PostModernism and Popular Culture.* London: Routledge.

Memmi, Albert. 1965. *The Colonizer and the Colonized.* Boston: Beacon.

Meyers, Marian. 1997. *News Coverage of Violence against Women: Engendering Blame.* London: Sage.

Minh-ha, Trinh T. 1989. *Woman, Native, Other: Writing Postcoloniality and Feminism.* Bloomington: Indiana University Press.

Modleski, Tania. 1991. *Feminism without Women: Culture and Criticism in a "Postfeminist" Age.* New York: Routledge.

Moghadam, Valentine. 2001. "For Gender Justice and Economic Justice: Transnational Feminism and Global Inequalities," Annual Meetings of the International Studies Association, Chicago, Feb.

Mohanty, Chandra Talpade. 1994. "Under Western Eyes: Feminist Scholarship and Colonial Discourses." In *Colonial Discourse and Post-Colonial Theory: A Reader* [1988]. Edited by Patrick Williams and Laura Chrisman. New York: Columbia University Press.

Moore, Cathy. 1999. *Ceasefire!: Why Women and Men Must Join Forces to Achieve True Equality.* New York: Free Press.

Moore, Henrietta. 1994. *A Passion for Difference: Essays in Anthropology and Gender.* Bloomington: Indiana University Press.

Moraga, Cherrie, and Gloria Anzaldua, editors. 1981. *This Bridge Called My Back: Writings By Radical Women of Color.* New York: Kitchen Table: Women of Color Press.

Morgan, Robin. 1984. *Sisterhood Is Global: The International Women's Anthology.* New York: Anchor.

———. 1992. *The Word of a Woman: Feminist Dispatches 1968–1992.* New York: W. W. Norton.

———, editor. 1970. *Sisterhood Is Powerful: An Anthology of Writings from the Women's Liberation Movement.* New York: Vintage.

Murphy-Milano, Susan. 1996. *Defending Our Lives: Getting Away from Domestic Violence and Staying Safe.* New York: Anchor.

Muszynski, Alicja. 1991. "What Is Patriarchy?" In *Race, Class, Gender: Bonds and Barriers.* Edited by Jesse Vorst et al., 64–87. Toronto: Garamond.

Narayan, Uma. 1995. " 'Male-Order' Brides: Immigrant Women, Domestic Violence, and Immigration Law," *Hypatia* 10, no. 1 (Winter): 104–19.

———. 1997. *Dislocating Cultures: Identities, Traditions, and Third-World Feminism.* New York and London: Routledge.

Newman, Amy. 1994. "Hegel's Theoretical Violence." In *Modern Engendering: Critical Feminist Readings in Modern Western Philosophy.* Edited by Bat-Ami Bar On, 155–66. Albany: State University of New York Press.

Nicholson, Linda J. 1984. "Feminist Theory: The Private and the Public." In *Beyond Domination: New Perspectives on Women and Philosophy.* Edited by Carol Gould, 221–30. Totowa, N.J.: Rowman & Allanheld.

Nietzsche, Friedrich. 1967. *The Birth of Tragedy and the Case of Wagner.* Translated by Walter Kaufmann. New York: Vintage.

O'Brien, Mary. 1981. *The Politics of Reproduction.* Boston: Routledge & Kegan Paul.

O'Neill, William L. 1975. *Coming Apart: An Informal History of America in the 1960's.* New York: Quadrangle.

O'Sullivan, Chris. 1993. "Fraternities and the Rape Culture." In *Transforming Rape Culture*. Edited by E. Buchwald, P. Fletcher, and M. Roth, 23–30. Minneapolis, Minn.: Milkweed Editions.

O'Sullivan, Chris, T. J. Hartley, D. Saunders, and J. Fiske. 1983. *Key Concepts in Communication*. London: Methuen.

Omolade, Barbara. 1983. "Hearts of Darkness." In *Powers of Desire: The Politics of Sexuality*. Edited by Ann Snitow, Christine Stansell, and Sharon Thompson, 350–67. New York: Monthly Review.

———. 1986. "Black Women and Feminism." In *Women and Values: Readings in Recent Feminist Philosophy*. Edited by Marilyn Pearsall, 139–46. Sacramento, Calif.: Wadsworth.

Orr, Catherine M. 1997. "Charting the Currents of the Third Wave." *Hypatia* 12, no. 3 (Summer): 29–45.

Paglia, Camille. 1991. *Sexual Personae: Art and Decadence from Nefertiti to Emily Dickinson*. New York: Vintage.

———. 1992. *Sex, Art, and American Culture: Essays*. New York: Vintage.

———. 1993. "Interviewed by Stewart Brand." *Wired, Premiere Issue*. 53–57, 107.

———. 1994. *Vamps and Tramps: New Essays*. New York: Vintage.

———. 1995a. "Interview." *Playboy*. May.

———. 1995b. "Rape and the Modern Sex War." In *Debating Sexual Correctness: Pornography, Sexual Harassment, Date Rape, and the Politics of Sexual Equality*. Edited by Adele M. Stan, 21–25. New York: Delta.

———. 1998. "Book Search: *Sexual Personae: Art and Decadence from Nefertiti to Emily Dickinson*." barnes&noble.com.

Paglia, Camille, and Neil Postman. 1991. "She Wants Her TV! He Wants His Book!" *Harpers Magazine*. March: 44–55.

Partnow, Elaine, editor. 1992. *The New Quotable Woman*. New York: Meridian.

Pearsall, Marilyn, editor. 1986. *Women and Values: Readings in Recent Feminist Philosophy*. Belmont, Calif.: Wadsworth.

Peck, Abe. 1985. *Uncovering the Sixties: The Life and Times of the Underground Press*. New York: Pantheon.

Pettman, Jan Jindy. 1996. *Worlding Women: A Feminist International Politics*. London: Routledge.

Phelps, Timothy M., and Helen Winternitz. 1992. *Capital Games: Clarence Thomas, Anita Hill, and the Story of a Supreme Court Nomination*. New York: Hyperion.

Poelzer, Irene. 1991. "Metis Women and the Economy of Northern Saskatchewan." In *Race, Class, Gender: Bonds and Barriers*. Edited by Jessie Vorst et al., 195–211. Winnipeg: Society for Socialist Studies.

Pollitt, Katha. 1994. *Reasonable Creatures: Essays on Women and Feminism*. New York: Vintage.

———. 1995. "Not Just Bad Sex." In *Debating Sexual Correctness: Pornography, Sexual Harassment, Date Rape, and the Politics of Sexual Equality* [1993]. Edited by Adele M. Stan, 162–71. New York: Delta.

———. 1996. "What Did You Do in the Gender Wars?" In *"Bad Girls/Good Girls": Women, Sex, and Power in the Nineties*. Edited by Nan Bauer Maglin and Donna Perry, 6–8. New Brunswick, N.J.: Rutgers University Press.

————. 2001. *Subject to Debate: Sense and Dissents on Women, Politics, and Culture.* New York: The Modern Library.

Quindlen, Anna. 1996. "And Now, Babe Feminism." In *"Bad Girls/Good Girls": Women, Sex, and Power in the Nineties.* Edited by Nan Bauer Maglin and Donna Perry, 3–5. New Brunswick, N.J.: Rutgers University Press.

Rapping, Elayne. 1994. *Media-tions: Forays into the Culture and Gender Wars.* Boston: South End Press.

————. 1996. "None of My Best Friends: The Media's Unfortunate 'Victim/Power' Debate." In *"Bad Girls/Good Girls": Women, Sex, and Power in the Nineties.* Edited by Nan Bauer Maglin and Donna Perry, 265–74. New Brunswick, N.J.: Rutgers University Press.

Raymond, Janice G. 1990. "Sexual and Reproductive Liberalism." In *The Sexual Liberals and the Attack on Feminism.* Edited by Dorchen Leidholdt and Janice G. Raymond, 103–11. New York: Pergamon.

————. 1996. "Connecting Reproductive and Sexual Liberalism." In *Radically Speaking: Feminism Reclaimed.* Edited by Diane Bell and Renate Klein, 231–46. North Melbourne, Australia: Spinifex.

Reed, Adolph, Jr. 1997. "Token Equality." *The Progressive.* Feb.: 18–19.

Reiter, Rayna. 1975. "Introduction." In *Toward an Anthropology of Women.* Edited by Rayna R. Reiter, ix–xxv. New York: Monthly Review.

Robinson, Victoria, and Diane Richardson. 1996. "Repackaging Women and Feminism." In *Radically Speaking: Feminism Reclaimed.* Edited by Diane Bell and Renate Klein, 179–87. North Melbourne, Australia: Spinifex.

Roiphe, Katie. 1993. *The Morning After: Sex, Fear, and Feminism on Campus.* New York: Little Brown.

————. 1995. "Date Rape's Other Victim." In *Debating Sexual Correctness: Pornography, Sexual Harassment, Date Rape, and the Politics of Sexual Equality* [1993]. Edited by Adele M. Stan, 149–61. New York: Delta.

Rosten, Leo. 1968. *The Joys of Yiddish.* New York: Pocket Books.

Rowbotham, Sheila. 1974. *Women, Resistance, and Revolution: A History of Women and Revolution in the Modern World.* New York: Vintage Books.

————. 1991. *The Past Is Before Us: Feminism in Action since the 1960s.* Boston: Beacon.

————. 1992. *Women in Movement: Feminism and Social Action.* New York: Routledge.

Rowland, Robyn, and Renate Klein. 1996. "Radical Feminism: History, Politics, Action." In *Radically Speaking: Feminism Reclaimed.* Edited by Diane Bell and Renate Klein, 9–36. North Melbourne, Australia: Spinifex.

Ryan, William. 1992. "Blaming the Victim." In *Race, Class, and Gender in the United States: An Integrated Study.* Edited by Paula S. Rothenberg, 364–97. New York: St. Martin's.

Sandoval, Chela. 1990. "Feminism and Racism: Report on the 1981 National Women's Studies Association Conference." In *Making Face, Making Soul: Creative and Critical Perspectives of Women of Color.* Edited by Gloria Anzuldua, 55–71. San Francisco: Aunt Lute.

Sangera, Jyoti. 1997. "In the Belly of the Beast: Sex Trade, Prostitution, and Globalization." Discussion Paper For South Asia Regional Consultation on Prostitution, Feb. 17–18, Bangkok, Thailand.

Sartre, Jean-Paul. 1948. *Anti-Semite and Jew.* New York: Schoken.
------. 1965. "Introduction." In *The Colonizer and the Colonized.* Albert Memmi, xxi–xxix. Boston: Beacon.
------. 1968. "Preface." In *The Wretched of the Earth.* Edited by Frantz Fanon, 7–31. New York: Grove Press.
Savran, David. 1996. "The Sadomasochist in the Closet: White Masculinity and the Culture of Victimization." *Differences: A Journal of Feminist Cultural Studies* 8, no. 2: 127–52.
Schechter, Susan (interviewed by Mary Suh). 1989. "Understanding Battered Women." *Ms.* Apr.: 62–63.
Schor, Naomi. 1994a. "The Essentialism Which Is Not One: Coming to Grips with Irigaray." In *The Essential Difference.* Edited by Naomi Schor and Elizabeth Weed, 40–62. Bloomington: Indiana University Press.
------. 1994b. "Introduction." In *The Essential Difference.* Edited by Naomi Schor and Elizabeth Weed, vii–xix. Bloomington: Indiana University Press.
Schneir, Miriam, editor. 1994. *Feminism: The Essential Historical Writings.* New York: Vintage.
Segal, Lynne. 1999. *Why Feminism?* New York: Columbia University Press.
Sekyi-Otu, Ato. 1996. *Fanon's Dialectic of Experience.* Cambridge: Harvard University Press.
Shah, Sonia. 1996. "Book Review: *To Be Real: Telling the Truth and Changing the Face of Feminism.*" *Z Magazine.* June: 55–59.
Shalit, Wendy. 1999. *A Return to Modesty: Discovering the Lost Virtue.* New York: Free Press.
Sheffield, Carole. 1992. "Hate-Violence." In *Race, Class, and Gender in the United States: An Integrated Study.* Edited by Paula S. Rothenberg, 388–97. New York: St. Martin's.
------. 1995. "Hate-Violence." In *Race, Class, and Gender in the United States: An Integrated Study* (Third Edition). Edited by Paula S. Rothenberg, 432–41. New York: St. Martin's.
Showalter, Elaine. 2001. *Inventing Herself: Claiming a Feminist Intellectual Heritage.* New York: Scribner.
Sidel, Ruth. 1992. *Women and Children Last: The Plight of Poor Women in Affluent America.* New York: Penguin.
------. 1996. *Keeping Women and Children Last: America's War on the Poor.* New York: Penguin.
Siegel, Deborah L. 1997a. "Reading between the Waves: Feminist Historiography in a 'Postfeminist' Moment." In *Third Wave Agenda: Being Feminist, Doing Feminism.* Edited by Leslie Heywood and Jennifer Drake, 55–82. Minneapolis: University of Minnesota Press.
------. 1997b. "The Legacy of the Personal: Generating Theory in Feminism's Third Wave." *Hypatia* 12, no. 3 (Summer): 46–75.
Sisken, Alison. 2001. "Violence Against Women Act: History, Federal Funding, and Reauthorizing Legislation." *CRS Report for Congress,* Feb. 23. The Library of Congress: Congressional Research Services.
Smith, Barbara, editor. 1983. *Home Girls: A Black Feminist Anthology.* New York: Kitchen Table: Women of Color Press.

Smith, Beverly. 1982. "Black Women's Health: Notes for a Course." In *All the Women Are White, All the Blacks Are Men, But Some of Us Are Brave: Black Women's Studies*. Edited by G. Hull, P. Bell Scott, and B. Smith. New York: The Feminist Press.

Smith, Dorothy. 1987. *The Everyday World as Problematic: A Feminist Sociology*. Toronto: University of Toronto Press.

Smith, Joan. 1989. *Misogynies: Reflections on Myths and Malice*. New York: Fawcett Columbine.

Smith, Marcia. 1997. "When Violence Strikes Home." *The Nation*. June 30: 23–24.

Smith, Sidonie, and Julia Watson, editors. 1992. *De/Colonizing the Subject: The Politics of Gender in Women's Autobiography*. Minneapolis: University of Minnesota Press.

Smith, Valerie. 1990. "Split Affinities: The Case of Interracial Rape." In *Conflicts in Feminism*. Edited by Marianne Hirsch and Evelyn Fox Keller, 271–87. New York: Routledge.

———. 1998. *Not Just Race, Not Just Gender: Black Feminist Readings*. New York: Routledge.

Smolowe, Jill. 1994. "When Violence Hits Home." *Time*. July 4: 18–25.

Smythe, Aibhe. 1996. "A (Political) Postcard." In *Radically Speaking: Feminism Reclaimed*. Edited by Diane Bell and Renate Klein, 169–78. North Melbourne, Australia: Spinifex.

Sorisio, Carolyn. 1997. "A Tale of Two Feminisms: Power and Victimization in Contemporary Feminist Debate." In *Third Wave Agenda: Being Feminist, Doing Feminism*. Edited by Leslie Heywood and Jennifer Drake, 134–49. Minneapolis: University of Minnesota Press.

Soto-Aquino. 1999. "Elder Abuse: Incidence and Prevention." *CRS Report for Congress*, Dec. 10. Library of Congress: Congressional Research Service.

Sparks, Holloway. 1997. "Dissident Citizenship: Democratic Theory, Political Courage, and Activist Women." *Hypatia* 12, no. 4 (Fall): 74–110.

Spender, Dale. 1982. *Women of Ideas*. London: Ark Paperbacks.

Spivak, Gayatri Chakravorty, with Ellen Rooney. 1994. "In a Word. *Interview.*" In *The Essential Difference*. Edited by Naomi Schor and Elizabeth Weed, 151–84. Bloomington: Indiana University Press.

Stabile, Carol A. 1994. "Feminism without Guarantees: The Misalliances and Missed Alliances of Postmodernist Social Theory." *Rethinking Marxism* 7, no. 1 (Spring): 48–61.

Stan, Adele M., editor. 1995. *Debating Sexual Correctness: Pornography, Sexual Harassment, Date Rape, and the Politics of Sexual Equality*. New York: Delta.

Stark, Kio. 1994. "I'm O.K., You're O.K." *The Nation*. Jan. 31: 137–40.

Steeves, H. Leslie. 1987. "Feminist Theories and Media Studies." *Critical Studies in Mass Communication* 8, no. 2 (June): 95–131.

Stein, Nan. 1993. "No Laughing Matter: Sexual Harassment in K-12 Schools." In *Transforming Rape Culture*. Edited by E. Buchwald, P. Fletcher, and M. Roth, 310–31. Minneapolis, Minn.: Milkweed Editions.

Steinberg, Shirley R., and Joe L. Kincheloe. 1997. "Introduction: No More Secrets—Kinderculture, Information Saturation, and the Postmodern Childhood." In *Kinder-Culture: The Corporate Construction of Childhood*. Edited by Shirley R. Steinberg and Joe L. Kincheloe, 1–30. Boulder, Colo.: Westview.

Steinem, Gloria. 1983. *Outrageous Acts and Everyday Rebellions*. New York: Plume, New American Library.

———. 1995. "Interviewed by Faith Popcorn." *Interview*. June.

Stephenson, June. 1995. *Men Are Not Cost-Effective* (Revised Edition). New York: Harper Perennial.

St. John, Yanick, and Joe Feagin. 1997. "Racial Masques: Black Women and Subtle Gendered Feminism." In *Subtle Sexism: Current Practice and Prospects for Change*. Edited by Nijole B. Benokraitis, 179–200. London: Sage Publications.

Straus, Murray. 1997. "An Interview." In *Family Violence Across the Lifespan: An Introduction*. Edited by Ola Barnett, Cindy Miller-Perrin, and Robin Perrin, 41–42. Thousand Oaks:, Calif.: Sage.

Summers, Ann. 1975. *Damned Whores and God's Police: The Colonization of Women in Australia*. Harmondsworth, Middlesex: Penguin.

———. 1989. "The Hedda Conundrum." *Ms.* Apr.: 54.

"Survivors: Best Books in the '90s." *Linguafranca: The Review of Academic Life*. Oct.: 14.

Tanenbaum, Leora. 1994. "Fear of Feminism," *In These Times*. Nov. 28: 36–38.

Tanehaus, Sam. 1999. "Damsels in Distress." *Vanity Fair*. November: 142–48.

Taylor, John Russell. 1978. *Hitch: The Life and Times of Alfred Hitchcock*. New York: Berkley.

Teodori, Massimo, editor. 1969. *The New Left: A Documentary History*. Indianapolis: Bobbs-Merrill.

Tjaden, Patricia, and Nancy Thoennes. 1988. "Prevalence, Incidence, and Consequences of Violence Against Women: Findings From the National Violence Against Women Survey." National Institute of Justice Centers for Disease Control and Prevention, November.

———. 2000. "Extent, Nature, and Consequences of Partner Violence: Findings From the National Violence Against Women Survey, NIJCDC." Washington, D.C.: U.S. Department of Justice, Office of Justice Programs, July.

Todd, Janet, editor. 1977. *A Wollstonecraft Anthology*. New York: Columbia University Press.

Tong, Rosemarie. 1998. *Feminist Thought: A More Comprehensive Introduction*. Boulder, Colo.: Westview.

Traitler-Espiritu, Reinhild. 1996. "Violence against Women's Bodies." In *Women Resisting Violence: Spirituality for Life*. Edited by M. J. Mananzan, M. A. Oduyoye, E. Tamez, J. S. Clarkson, M. C. Grey, and L. M. Russell, 66–79. New York: Orbis.

United Nations Population Fund (UNFPA). 2000. *Live Together, Worlds Apart: Men and Women in a Time of Change—The State of World Population* (videotape).

Valverde, Mariana, Linda MacLeod, and Kirsten Johnson. 1995. "Introduction." In *Wife Assault and the Canadian Criminal Justice System: Issues and Policies*. Edited by M. Valverde, L. MacLeod, and K. Johnson. Toronto: Centre of Criminology, University of Toronto Press, 1–9.

Walker, Alice. 1982. *The Color Purple*. New York: Pocket Books.

Walker, Lenore E. 1989. *Terrifying Love: Why Battered Women Kill and How Society Responds*. New York: Harper & Row.

Wallace, Michele. 1990. *Invisibility Blues: From Pop to Theory*. London: Verso.

Wallach Scott, Joan. 1997. "Comment on Hawkesworth's 'Confounding Gender.' " *Signs: Journal of Women in Culture and Society* 22, no. 3 (Spring): 697–706.

Wallerstein, Immanuel. 1990. "Culture as the Ideological Battleground of the Modern World-System." In *Global Culture: Nationalism, Globalization and Modernity*. Edited by Mike Featherstone, 31–55. London: Sage.

———. 1994. "The Agonies of Liberalism: What Hope Progress." *New Left Review*, no. 204 (Mar./Apr.): 3–17.

Ware, Vron. 1992. *Beyond the Pale: White Women, Racism, and History*. London: Verso.

Watkins, Susan Alice, Marisa Rueda, and Marta Rodriguez. 1992. *Feminism for Beginners*. Cambridge: Icon.

Watson, Julia, and Sidonie Smith. 1992. "Introduction: De/Colonization and the Politics of Discourse in Women's Autobiographical Practices." In *De/Colonizing the Subject: The Politics of Gender in Women's Autobiography*. Edited by Sidonie Smith and Julia Watson, xi–xxxi. Minneapolis: University of Minnesota Press.

Watzlawick, Paul. 1976. *How Real Is Real? Confusion, Disinformation, Communication*. New York: Vintage.

West, Cornel. 1984. "The Paradox of the Afro-American Rebellion." In *The 60's without Apology*. Edited by S. Sayres, A. Stephanson, S. Aronowitz, and F. Jameson, 44–58. Minneapolis: University of Minnesota Press.

———. 1993. "Black Culture and Postmodernism." In *A Postmodern Reader*. Edited by Joseph Natoli and Linda Hutcheon, 390–97. Albany: State University of New York Press.

———. 1994. *Race Matters*. New York: Vintage.

Wilden, Anthony. 1980. *The Imaginary Canadian: An Examination for Discovery*. Vancouver: Pulp Press.

———. 1987. *The Rules Are No Game: The Strategy of Communication*. London: Routledge and Kegan Paul.

Wilder, Carol. 1978. "The Palo Alto Group: Difficulties and Directions of the 'Interactional View' for Interpersonal Communication Research." Paper presented at the Annual Meeting of the International Communication Association, Chicago, Illinois, April.

Willett, Cynthia. 1994. "Hegel, Antigone, and the Possibility of a Woman's Dialectic." In *Modern Engendering: Critical Feminist Readings in Modern Western Philosophy* [1987]. Edited by Bat-Ami Bar On, 167–81. Albany: State University of New York Press.

Williams, Patricia. 1996. "Talking about Race, Talking about Gender, Talking about How We Talk." In *Antifeminism in the Academy*. Edited by V. Clark, S. Nelson Garner, M. Higonnet, and K. Katrak, 69–94. New York: Routledge.

———. 1997. "American Kabuki." In *Birth of a Nation'hood: Gaze, Script, and Spectacle in the O. J. Simpson Case*. Edited by Toni Morrison and Claudia Brodsky Lacour, 273–92. New York: Pantheon.

Willis, Ellen. 1984. "Radical Feminism and Feminist Radicalism." In *The 60's without Apology*. Edited by S. Sayres, A. Stephanson, S. Aronowitz, and F. Jameson, 91–118. Minneapolis: University of Minnesota Press.

———. 1993a. "Feminism, Moralism, and Pornography." In *Powers of Desire: The Politics of Sexuality* [1979], 460–67. New York: Monthly Review.

———. 1993b. "Notes on Cam P." *Dissent*. (Spring): 251–54.

———. 1996. "Villains and Victims: 'Sexual Correctness' and the Repression of Feminism." In *"Bad Girls/Good Girls": Women, Sex, and Power in the Nineties*. Edited by Nan Bauer Maglin and Donna Perry, 44–53. New Brunswick, N.J.: Rutgers University Press.

Wolf, Naomi. 1993. *Fire with Fire: The New Female Power and How It Will Change the 21st Century*. New York: Random House.

———. 1995. "Are You a Bad Girl?" In *Debating Sexual Correctness: Pornography, Sexual Harassment, Date Rape, and the Politics of Sexual Equality* [1991]. Edited by Adele M. Stan, 212–17. New York: Delta.

Wolff, Robert Paul. 1976. "There's Nobody Here But Us Persons." In *Women and Philosophy: Toward a Theory of Liberation*. Edited by Carol C. Gould and Marx W. Wartopsky, 128–44. New York: Perigree.

Wollstonecraft, Mary. 1977. "A Vindication of the Rights of Women." In *A Wollstonecraft Anthology* [1792]. Edited by Janet Todd, 84–114. New York: Columbia University Press.

Yamato, Gloria. 1990. "Something about the Subject Makes It Hard to Name." In *Making Face, Making Soul: Creative and Critical Perspectives by Women of Color*. Edited by Gloria Anzaldua, 20–24. San Francisco: Aunt Lute.

Yelin, Louise. 1993. "Recuperating Radical Feminism." *Social Text* no. 35 (Summer): 113–20.

Young, Cathy. 1999. "Introduction." "Excerpt" from *Ceasefire!: Why Women and Men Must Join Forces to Achieve True Equality* (www.amazon.com).

Yuen Quan, Kit. 1990. "The Girl Who Wouldn't Sing." In *Making Face, Making Soul: Creative and Critical Perspectives of Women of Color*. Edited by Gloria Anzaldúa, 212–20. San Francisco: Aunt Lute.

Zaretsky, Eli. 1973. *Capitalism, the Family, and Personal Life*. New York: Harper Colophon.

———. 1995. "The Birth of Identity Politics in the 1960's: Psychoanalysis and the Public/ Private Division." In *Global Modernities*. Edited by Mike Featherstone, Scott Lash, and Roland Robertson, 244–59. London: Sage.

Zia, Helen. 1996. "How Now?" *Ms.* Jul./Aug.: 49–57.

Index

abuse, 85, 111–12, 117, 128; addressing, 139, 171, 195–202; of children, 4–5, 131n10, 133–34, 134, 180; of elders, 4, 134–35; escalated by false feminism, 96–97; and poverty, 1–2, 133, 143–44, 158, 162; social agencies' unwillingness to intervene, 139; of spouses, 3, 133, 153, 156. *See also* family terrorism; violence

abused women: myths about, 138–48, 152–53; as scapegoats, 106, 125–28, 152, 155; shelters for, 41n12, 150–51, 199; social safeguards for, 149–52

abusers, 1, 131n11, 133–34; males exonerated by the media, 145; prosecution of, 151, 153–56; victims studied rather than perpetrators, 106, 125–28

academic feminism, 62

Academy of Family Physicians, 163n1

AFDC (Aid to Families with Dependent Children), 161, 164n6

African American feminism, 79, 183–84

Against Our Will (Brownmiller), 99

Against Sadomasochism, 63

aggression, 53–54

Aid to Families with Dependent Children (AFDC), 161, 164n6

Aldrich, Nelson W., Jr., 98

Alexander, M. Jacqui, 200–201

Alexander, Nikol G., 140

Allen, Michael, 131n12

alliances, 202

Alred, Gloria, 156

American Academy of Family Physicians, 139, 146

American Bar Association, 151

American Dream as a myth, 161

American Enterprise Institute, 73, 82n11

American Medical Association (AMA), 95–96, 145

Amnesty International, *Children's Report for the 2000 Campaign to Stamp Out Torture*, 134

antifeminist feminism. *See* false feminism

anti-intellectualism, 31–33, 73, 88

Anzaldúa, Gloria, 18, 182, 188–89, 197, 199

Apollonian vs. Dionysian, 52

assault, 4–5, 95–96, 147–49; laws against, 153–54, 156

atheoretical faux feminism, 32–33

attitudes: toward males, 86–88; toward women and children, 31, 152–54

Backlash (Faludi), 34, 78–79

backlash against feminism, 38, 39n4, 78–79; by false feminists, 5, 8, 17–21, 34–35

bad feminism, 65

"bad girl" feminism, 23

bad vs. good, 57, 93

Bales, Kevin, 1–2, 190–91

Barker, Isabelle V., 36–38

Bar On, Bar-Ami, 198

Barreca, Regina, 90; *They Used to Call Me Snow White . . . But I Drifted*, 89

227

globalization, 1–2, 200–201, 205n14; and oppression, 188–95; and poverty, 190
Goldberg, Michelle, 33–34
Golden, Kristen, 163n1
golems, 121
good vs. bad, 57, 93
Gordon, Linda, 6–7, 85, 101, 124, 136, 139; *Heroes of Their Own Lives,* 107
Gore, Al, 54, 81n7
Goulet, Denis, 172
Gray White, Debra, 141
gun advocacy, 55–56

Harding, Sandra, 168, 182
Helmreich, William B., 137
Herbert, Bob, 163n2
Herman, Judith Lewis, 137
Heroes of Their Own Lives (Gordon), 107
Heywood, Leslie, 38, 40n6
hierarchical gendered divisions, 176
Higgins, Kathleen, 80n4
Hill, Anita, 3, 10n4, 28
Hill Collins, Patricia, 142, 179, 184, 186–87, 196, 203nn3–4
Himmelfarb, Gertrude, 64
Hirshman, Linda, 102
History of Women's Suffrage (Stanton, Anthony, and Gage), 76
Hoffman, Abbie, 75
Hoff Sommers, Christina, 22–23, 31, 41n10, 41n12, 72–73, 151; errors and misrepresentations, 76–78, 99–102, 108–9, 163n1; *The War against Boys,* 15, 82n11, 86, 199–200; *Who Stole Feminism,* 26, 43, 72, 101, 129n5, 129n3
Holtzworth-Munroe, Amy, 131n11
homophobia, 186
homosexuality, 80nn1–2, 180
hooks, bell, 79, 140, 159–60, 173, 195–96, 203n2; on bisexual and lesbian women, 183; definition of feminism, 40n9; on false feminism, 25, 43, 45–46, 55, 72, 99; on family terrorism, 135–37; on mass-marketed false feminism, 33, 37; misrepresentations of black women, 141–42; misrepresentations of femi-

nism, 16, 67, 87; on patriarchal violence, 177, 203n5
House Un-American Committee, 75
How to Lie with Statistics (Huff), 85, 109
Huff, Darrell, *How to Lie with Statistics,* 85, 109
husband battering: myths, 104–5; syndrome, 111–12

identity politics, 194
immigration, 193
"I'm Not a Feminist But I Play One On TV" (Faludi), 22
income disparities, 1–2, 160–62, 189
Independent Women's Forum (IWF), 28–31, 82n11, 151, 163n1
index, defined, 179
individualism, 20, 34, 71
individual men vs. the collective male, 87
inequality, 162
infirmary feminists, 92
insider feminists, 31–32
International Fund for Agricultural Development, 192
International Labor Organization, 192
International Women's Forum, 31
interpersonal relations and ineffectiveness of scientific methods, 106, 109
intersectionality, 179, 204n8
intimate partner violence, 133, 135–36
Invasion of the Body Snatchers, 22
issues, 57, 62
IWF (Independent Women's Forum), 28–31

Jacobson, Neil S., 131n11
Jacoby, Susan, 77
James, Joy, 3, 6, 175, 189
John M. Olin Foundation, 73
Joint Commission on Accreditation of Healthcare Organizations (JCAHO), 145
Jones, Ann, 79, 125–28, 132n14, 149–52, 157; on Nussbaum and Steinberg, 114, 116, 118–20, 122–23; on research on violence, 103–4, 107–9, 111; on vio-

About the Author

Rhonda Hammer is a research scholar at the UCLA Center for the Study of Women and teaches in women's studies and communication at UCLA. She is the author of many articles in feminism and cultural studies and co-author of *Rethinking Media Literacy: A Critical Pedagogy of Representation.*